PRAISE FOR *MARKETING WITH STRATEGIC EMPATHY*

'Claire has an innate talent for discovering the actual motivation and truth behind consumer responses. Her command of the insights tools and methodologies in this book, coupled with an adaptable style and intuitive sense for how to employ those tools helps her arrive at the big "AHA" moment more quickly and more frequently than any other insights professional I have worked with.'
Mic Zavarella, Senior Director, Marketing, PepsiCo

'This book is a refreshing antidote to the over-reliance on "big data" in today's consumer insights world. Claire has graciously shared her excellent techniques for discovering truly actionable insights. Consumer research textbooks typically have given short shrift to qualitative research methods; this book doesn't do this and is a great resource for students and practitioners alike.'
Nicki Shovar, Instructor, Marketing Research Methods, UC Berkeley Extension; former Director of Consumer Research, Ubisoft

'This is a well-written book that combines evidence, practical examples and case studies, enabling the reader to gain insight into some of the inner drivers and subconscious motives behind decision making. Even non-profits exist in a dynamic world with lots of competition for resources and leaders need to be able to put themselves into the shoes of the people they want to influence and serve. As a leader of a global mental health non-profit advocacy organization, the issues, concepts and ideas presented in *Marketing with Strategic Empathy* resonate profoundly with what I have observed and experienced – there is much to learn from this book and applying the concepts will enrich non-profit leaders and their organizations.'
Professor Gabriel Ivbijaro, President, World Federation for Mental Health; Chair, World Dignity Project

'Claire is one of the most insightful people in the insights business. *Marketing with Strategic Empathy* avoids the typical abstract pontificating and gives us real, tangible, she-was-there examples of how insights can lead to richer consumer connections. Her book helps clients and creative people alike understand the mysteries of consumer (human) behaviour.'
John Robertson, Simpler&Simpler strategic branding and ad agency

'Marketers often rely on competitive analysis and traditional needs-based research to develop their strategies, but rarely truly understand what is driving the customer's decision making. Claire's methodologies go many layers deeper into the customer's mindset and provide brands future insight to develop products their customers will not just want, but *desire*.'
Mark Dipko, Automotive Strategy Expert

'This is a brilliant guide for anyone in the position of understanding consumers and shoppers. Claire does a beautiful job of weaving together academic theory with sheer wisdom that only comes from deep field experience. I'm personally equipping everyone in our team with this book.'
Chris Tjaden, Director of Strategy and Insights, 10 Red Design

Marketing with Strategic Empathy

Inspiring strategy with deeper consumer insight

Claire Brooks

KoganPage

First published in Great Britain and the United States in 2016 by Kogan Page Limited

2nd Floor, 45 Gee Street	1518 Walnut Street, Suite 900	4737/23 Ansari Road
London EC1V 3RS	Philadelphia PA 19102	Daryaganj
United Kingdom	USA	New Delhi 110002
www.koganpage.com		India

© Claire Brooks, 2016

The right of Claire Brooks to be identified as the author of this work has been asserted by her in accordance with the Copyright, Designs and Patents Act 1988.

Strategic Empathy ® is a registered trademark belonging to Claire Brooks.

ISBN   978 0 7494 7754 7
E-ISBN   978 0 7494 7755 4

British Library Cataloguing-in-Publication Data

A CIP record for this book is available from the British Library.

Library of Congress Cataloging-in-Publication Data

Names: Brooks, Claire, author.
Title: Marketing with strategic empathy : inspiring strategy with deeper
   consumer insight / Claire Brooks.
Description: 1st Edition. | Philadelphia : Kogan Page, 2016. | Includes
   bibliographical references and index.
Identifiers: LCCN 2016022405 (print) | LCCN 2016029777 (ebook) | ISBN
   9780749477547 (paperback) | ISBN 9780749477554 (eISBN) |
Subjects: LCSH: Marketing--Management. | Consumer behavior. | Organizational
   change. | BISAC. BUSINESS & ECONOMICS / Marketing / Research. | PSYCHOLOGY
   / Industrial & Organizational Psychology. | BUSINESS & ECONOMICS /
   Consumer Behavior.
Classification: LCC HF5415.13 .B736 2016 (print) | LCC HF5415.13 (ebook) |
   DDC 658.8/02–dc 3
LC record available at https://lccn.loc.gov/2016022405

Typeset by Graphicraft Limited, Hong Kong
Print production managed by Jellyfish
Printed and bound by CPI Group (UK) Ltd, Croydon, CR0 4YY

CONTENTS

07   The Strategic Empathy Process Phase Two: Activate insights into strategy   157

08   The Strategic Empathy Process Phase Three: Inspire – communicate strategic learning   179

Additional resources to support this text can be downloaded at:
www.modelpeopleinc.com/strategic-empathy

LIST OF CASE STUDIES AND DETAILED EXAMPLES

Note: The following list describes the strategic application and product category of case studies and detailed examples used in-text, with page numbers for reference (and is not a list of on-page headings).

Chapter 7

Chapter 8

Chapter 9

LIST OF FIGURES
AND TABLES

Figures

Tables

ABOUT THE AUTHOR

Claire Brooks is the President of ModelPeople Inc, a global brand insights and strategy consulting business with offices in the US and UK. She lived in Africa and India as a child and was educated in languages and social sciences at Cambridge University. Before joining ModelPeople in 2004, she was a marketing line manager and agency strategic planner for 16 years and also designed and led core and elective MBA marketing courses at Durham University Business School.

PREFACE

This is a book about how global corporations, in practice, use deep insights to develop effective marketing strategies in a VUCA world. Using over 50 case studies from my strategy consulting practice, it takes the reader into the world of the Fortune 500 managers who use Strategic Empathy® skills and techniques to develop winning new strategies for famous brands.

I wrote the book because I've concluded that traditional theory and current best practice of marketing strategy formation are out of sync. The world is moving too fast for traditional models of strategy planning and market research. The emphasis in Fortune 500 brand marketing corporations is flexible marketing strategy formation which involves a wide group of stakeholders across functions and from outside agencies.

The challenge facing organizations today is how to equip managers, employees and other stakeholders with skills and tools for this new paradigm. The idea of Strategic Empathy® was developed in my consulting practice. At its core is the idea that empathy with consumers, customers or service users can be learned as a form of 'muscle memory' which facilitates flexible strategy formation and activation. This book explains how managers in both for-profit and not-for-profit organizations can use Strategic Empathy® processes and tools to learn, activate and communicate deep insights and strategies for success, not only with consumers and customers but with all the organization's stakeholders.

The book is theoretically grounded throughout, and takes a multidisciplinary approach to understanding how consumers think, feel and behave – consciously and non-consciously – with perspectives from sociology, anthropology, biology, psychology, behavioural economics and neuroscience. The emphasis is on how to use proven Strategic Empathy® tools, techniques and case studies developed over the last 12 years in my insights and strategy consulting practice, ModelPeople Inc (which have been anonymized to protect client confidentiality).

My perspective has been formed after 30 years as a marketing line manager, business school professor and strategy consultant and coach. I hope the book will give practical and useful new skills, tools and ideas to insights, marketing, strategy and planning managers in both for-profit and non-profit organizations and in creative agencies. I think my marketing MBA students would have found this book helpful, so I also hope it will give Masters-level students in these disciplines comprehensive insight into real-world marketing strategy formation, as well as useful tools for their own academic research.

ACKNOWLEDGEMENTS

For the staff, associates and clients of ModelPeople Inc, and for my former students, with gratitude.

With special thanks to Andrew Long for editing and proofing. Many thanks also for the contributions and encouragement of Clare Grace, Jeff Myers, Mark Paris, Andrea Sharp and Nicki Shovar; and to the team at Kogan Page, especially Jenny Volich, Charlotte Owen and Philippa Fiszzon.

LIST OF ABBREVIATIONS

BOGO (or BOGOF): Buy-one-get-one-free; a type of sales promotion.

CMC: Computer-mediated communities. For example, brand communities (eg branded fan pages on Facebook or brand sponsored forums like Dell World) or independent user communities (like Mumsnet for parents).

CSR: Corporate social responsibility. The new business purpose: creating value for customers and society as a whole.

DMA: Designated market area: a group of counties in the United States that are covered by a specific group of television stations. The term was coined by Nielsen Media Research, and they control the trademark on it. There are 210 DMAs in the United States. The top three primary DMAs in 2015–16 are New York, Los Angeles, Chicago. Secondary DMAs are smaller markets.

IDI: In-depth interview, a semi-structured conversation between researcher and participant.

LGBT: An acronym used in demographics, standing for lesbian, gay, bisexual and transgender.

MROC: Market research online communities. A managed community of brand consumers who are retained for a period of time and paid to undertake specific research tasks.

OTC: Over-the-counter medications; those which can be purchased without a prescription.

P&L: Profit and loss account. Reflects brand net profitability.

RTB: 'Reason-to-believe', eg a brand benefit or claim. An element in the reshaped brand positioning model in Chapter 3.

SBU: Strategic business unit.

SKU: Stock-keeping unit, eg Heinz Tomato Sauce. Heinz Organic Tomato Sauce is a separate SKU.

VUCA: Acronym for disruptive change: volatility, uncertainty, complexity, ambiguity.

Why marketing strategists need empathy

01

CHAPTER 1 OBJECTIVES

1 Explore how marketing strategy is formed in both planned and emergent modes.

2 Contrast Strategic Planning and Strategic Learning approaches to marketing strategy formation.

3 Explore how collective Strategic Learning contributes to successful marketing strategy formation.

4 Define Strategic Empathy and why empathy as well as data is required for successful marketing strategy formation.

Introduction: the case for Strategic Empathy®

How could an experienced retail executive develop and implement a marketing strategy that led to such a catastrophic slump in store sales and share price, that he was dubbed one of the most unsuccessful CEOs of the decade by the BBC (Finkelstein, 2014)? Ron Johnson, CEO of US department store chain JC Penney, who formerly ran the hugely successful Apple Stores for a decade, was ousted in 2013 after 17 months in the job. In an extraordinary ad, run on the store's Facebook page in 2013 after CEO Ron Johnson went,

JC Penney apologized for not listening to its customers, but took credit for *learning* from its mistakes:

> It's no secret, recently JC Penney changed. Some changes you liked and some you didn't, but what matters with mistakes is what we learn. We learned a very simple thing: to listen to you, to hear what you need, to make your life more beautiful. Come back to JC Penney. We heard you.

However, JC Penney did not *need* to learn from such huge mistakes. The company's Insights Department had already learned enough about its core customers to suggest that Johnson's new marketing strategy would fail (ModelPeople, 2008–10).

JC Penney's customers are middle-income mothers, who take pride in managing the household budget and providing well for their families. In the US, moms are responsible for $1.6 trillion of household spending (*The Economist*, 2015) and influence many decisions made by other family members. Not a consumer group to risk upsetting. The Penney's mom was loyal to the store brand because of its heritage for quality and value in kids' clothes, stylish home furnishings and men's and women's apparel. Historically, the strategy had been to bring her into the store regularly via frequent sales events. Once (and not until) the rest of the family was provided for, she looked forward to treating *herself* to a new outfit on Penney's women's apparel floor. 'I spend money on my kids, they are still growing,' explained 49-year-old Cindy, a Dallas pre-school teachers' aide and mom to a 12-year-old son and an 11-year-old daughter. 'It's all about the kids. I can wait. I will only buy for a wedding, maybe or if I have a coupon from Penney's.'

Value for money, in the mind of the Penney's shopper was not linked only to quality and sticker price but to her own assessment of whether she 'needed' the item. 'Need' is elastic for a family budget-juggling mom, and this is where sales events come in, because they tempt her into the store and give her permission to spend money on herself as well as the rest of the family. This shopper would select several items for herself and then wrestle with a certain amount of guilt as to whether she could justify the purchase. An event price tipped the balance. 'I got the new dress half-price, it was value for money' means 'I could justify spending money on me instead of another family member' to the JC Penney shopper. Johnson seems to have believed that everyday low pricing (EDLP), rather than event pricing, would retrain customers to stop expecting price cuts but he underestimated the underlying emotional importance of coupons for women who had chosen to define their role as providing for the family first, in that particular life-stage; a very different target customer from Apple's self-focused Millennials.

Academic Noel Tichy (2014) additionally attributes Johnson's failure to cultural mistakes. Johnson built a cult of leadership around himself and his close team, jetting in from California for team meetings and missing the opportunity to absorb the learning and experience of the JC Penney team in Texas. He brought in ex-Apple veterans who also failed to communicate with and learn from their new colleagues. Johnson was finally forced to admit in early 2013 (after the extent of loyal customer defection was revealed):

> I thought people were just tired of coupons and all this stuff. The reality is all of the couponing we did, there were a certain part of the customers that loved that. They gravitated to stores that competed that way. So our core customer, I think, was much more dependent and enjoyed coupons more than I understood.
>
> Brady, 2013

What's striking about this grudging admission is that, even after all the fallout from Johnson's failed marketing strategy, it still shows a lack of deeper understanding of Penney's core customer on his part. Johnson never took the time to learn about his customers' lives; their dreams, aspirations and motivations for shopping at his stores; to imagine how they *think* and *feel*. He never observed *how* and *why* they behave the way they do. He assumed he could change his customers' behaviour with marketing strategy borrowed from Apple. He never developed *empathy* with his new customers. And now, even two years after Johnson's departure, many of them have not returned to the store which once enjoyed their loyalty, despite the reintroduction of coupons. 'I used to go to Penney's every week', said Liz, an internal auditor in Philadelphia. 'But when they stopped doing the coupons, I went to Kohl's [Penney's main competitor] instead' (ModelPeople, 2015).

What is empathy?

Researchers (eg Decety and Lamm, 2006) agree that empathy has two components:

1 A *cognitive* capacity to *take the subjective perspective of another person*.

2 An *affective* ('emotional') response to another person which can involve *sharing that person's emotional state*.

The affective component is the automatic ability to detect the affective state of another and is commonly observed among social groups of animals (de Waal, 2006). Social neuroscience research indicates that similar neural circuits are active when we experience emotions ourselves, and when we see others expressing emotions: we understand others' emotions or pain in the same way we experience our own. By contrast, perspective-taking is thought to be a more recent evolution and relies on effortful cognitive processing to gain deep understanding of another's experiences, beliefs, aspirations and motivations. In other words, **we need to have conscious awareness, knowledge and understanding about how someone else thinks, feels and behaves to have empathy** with their situation. It is not simply a case of 'feeling sorry' for another individual: empathy is based on cognitive understanding and not just affective response. It is this definition of empathy, as cognitive understanding, which we will use going forward.

Now, let's look at how marketing strategy is developed – in theory and in practice – and explore the need for empathy in that process.

How do organizations *really* develop marketing strategy?

Traditionally in commercial organizations, marketing strategy is developed annually in a formal process. This process identifies viable strategic positions in specific markets, describes for each the target customers or consumers and the products or brands which deliver superior value to them, and outlines tactical strategies for each touchpoint between the organization's consumers and brands (such as pricing, sales channel and promotional strategies). A marketing strategy encompasses longer-range (eg five-year) planning as well as annual tactical plans and budgets. The components of a marketing strategy are discussed in more detail in Chapter 3.

Responsibility for developing marketing strategy is typically centred in the marketing department. Alternatively, the marketing function may be tactically focused on communications (advertising, digital assets, promotions, packaging) and strategy may be the responsibility of a centralized strategy department, reporting to the CEO (in the case of JC Penney under Ron Johnson). Product or brand innovation is often the responsibility of yet another function (typically reporting in to strategy or marketing), which is tasked with developing innovation streams to feed future product launches. In addition to the functions directly responsible for developing marketing strategy, specialist input is also sought: for example, from sales, finance or

R&D. In particular, insights and information about the organization's markets, consumers or customers and brands is sought from the insights (or market research) department to support decision-making. Whatever organizational structure is in place, it's typically the case that there is a complex network of people with different functional perspectives and accountabilities – and very likely with different ways of working – involved in developing marketing strategy (see Figure 1.1).

Figure 1.1 Functional inputs to marketing strategy

SOURCE: ModelPeople Inc

Building consensus around the direction of marketing strategy with such a complex network of inputs is one of the challenges that we will address in this chapter, and in Chapters 4–8 we will explain how to do this in practice, and explain helpful methods and tools.

In theory, the annual marketing strategy development process is an efficient way to identify marketing opportunities and allocate company resources efficiently, so that the marketing team knows how to prioritize and manage resources. Yet if you ask marketing personnel how strategy is actually implemented, the answer may reflect that implemented strategy bore little relation to planned strategy! Changes in the consumer or competitive environment, new technologies or even government regulations frequently dictate rapid changes to a planned and approved marketing strategy. Some theorists argue that, in the 21st century we are living in a period of disruptive innovation (see box below) and intense volatility, uncertainty, complexity and ambiguity. There's even an acronym for it: VUCA. Therefore, an *adaptive approach* to strategy formation, based on heightened readiness to learn, experiment and scale up changes to strategy is required.

Disruptive innovation theory

In particular, an adaptive approach to marketing strategy may be required in response to potentially disruptive new technologies and business models. Since Clay Christensen (Bower and Christensen, 1995) first developed his theory of disruption 20 years ago, much attention has been paid to how new market entrants with disruptive innovations have been able to threaten existing market leaders. Christensen noted that incumbent market leaders can fail, *even if they have listened to customers and invested in building distinct capabilities to meet customer needs*. They failed because they focused on sustaining innovation along an existing trajectory to meet the needs of existing customers in more demanding market segments. Meanwhile smaller, scrappier competitors have targeted poorly served segments, especially low-end customers with disruptive innovations or very low-cost models, instead of competing head-to-head with incumbents. For example, Xiaomi (ModelPeople GlobalCultureBlog®, 2015) in China began by offering low-cost smartphones and consumer electronics and is now stealing aspiring young consumers from Apple with higher-end models.

Christensen's theory has come under fire recently as analysis shows that disruptors also pick off the premium customers that incumbents do want by understanding their pain points and activating a superior marketing offering. Uber has picked off affluent taxi-cab users who were tired of shabby cabs and rude drivers. Netflix picked off the movie enthusiasts who were fed up with Blockbuster's late fees and mainstream selection. Apple's iPhone was significantly more expensive than other smartphones but spoke to an on-the-go, design-conscious target market for whom laptops, even Macs, were burdensome. Rather than disproving the need for understanding how consumers think, feel and behave, other academics have now concluded that there is no substitute for 'spadework' in understanding customer needs, doing the strategic analysis and making the tough calls about market targeting and product offering (King and Baatartogtokh, 2015).

The tendency for strategy to evolve rather that to adhere to a formal plan has been recognized for many years: for example, Quinn (1980) described this type of strategy evolution as 'logical incrementalism'. In his book, Quinn explored how, in reality, strategy evolves as internal decisions and external events coalesce to create a consensus for action among top management. 'Planning' did not describe how the executives whom Quinn interviewed formulated strategy as much as a series of incremental steps with internal logic, hence the term 'incrementalism'.

Since Quinn first wrote about strategic incrementalism, many experts (eg Reeves *et al*, 2010) have argued that marketing strategy is often not, in practice, centrally planned and controlled by the marketing or strategy departments, or even the CEO. The work of Henry Mintzberg and McGill University's Faculty of Management in particular has demonstrated that the strategic planning processes carried out by many commercial organizations ignore the frequent reality that strategy formation is not a deliberate, planned approach but is *emergent*: ie a pattern of consistent behaviour which is influenced by the actions of managers, employees and other stakeholders (Mintzberg, 2007). People at many different levels in the organization can, and should, become strategists. The organization's strategists are not just those with *strategy, marketing* or *consumer insights* in their job description; strategists can be product designers, R&D scientists, salespeople or even stakeholders outside the organization itself, such as retail buyers, suppliers or advertising agency executives. If strategy formation is in reality emergent, transformational changes to marketing strategy can result from small initiatives taken by multiple different people. Equipping the multiple, cross-functional strategists within a single organization to be transformational change agents is a challenge that we will explore in this book, and in Chapters 4–9 we will explore useful methods and tools for doing so.

Strategic learning vs strategic planning

Mintzberg *et al* (2009) list 10 schools of thought relating to strategy formation, of which, they note, only three are prescriptive in nature: that is, they describe how strategy *should* be formed. The remaining seven schools are descriptive in nature, describing how strategy *actually is* formed. Under the Learning School approach, strategy formation is a process of ***strategic learning*** – identifying and acting on emergent patterns across the touchpoints between the organization's brands and its customers or consumers. This approach is contrasted with a more formal approach to strategy formation, ***strategic planning*** – which emphasizes deliberate forward planning of strategic positions in specific marketplaces (Figure 1.2).

Figure 1.2 Approaches to strategy formation

Strategic Planning	Strategic Learning
Forward-looking approach	Emergent approach
Identifies specific market positions and implementation	Strategy shifts based on organizational learning

SOURCE: ModelPeople Inc

Strategic learning is not academic and cannot be passive; learning must be related to observed patterns across relevant consumer touchpoints (for example, consumer behaviour, retail sales, advertising or promotional effectiveness) and must inspire strategic action. *Learning is not strategic unless it inspires action.* Strategic learning can inspire an 'ad hoc' response to a pattern of activity that has proven successful, which subsequently creates a 'de facto' shift in strategy. For example, an individual salesperson may champion pilot development of a new frozen dessert for a specific retail account based on competitive sales data, and the product may subsequently be rolled out and become a best-selling brand SKU (stock-keeping unit) with a dedicated production facility. Or strategic learning can be championed by management under broad direction set by leadership or by the marketing strategy itself. For example, a cross-functional group may be tasked with defining how an automotive manufacturer can serve Millennial car buyers better (ModelPeople, 2014).

Academic research emphasizes the importance of going outside the organization and challenging norms to inspire strategic learning. Lampel (1998) notes that searching outside for knowledge is a practice of successful 'Learning Organizations', which deliver superior performance compared with organizations which merely adapt to a changing environment. Hamel (1998) lists several preconditions for successful strategy emergence:

- **Bringing new voices in,** especially young people, newcomers and those in the organization who are not typically involved in developing marketing strategy.
- **Creating new conversations and perspectives** that cut across old ways of looking at the organization's markets, customer needs and products. For example, my automotive design clients routinely bring in experts in

other fields (fashion, interiors, technology) to discuss how they approach design.

- **Unleashing new passions** and a sense of discovery and giving individuals a chance to invest emotionally in developing a firm's future. For example, internal focus groups, bulletin boards and co-creation sessions are often held with staff (including new voices) to give input to strategy.

- **New experiments**: launching small, low-risk experiments in the market to build real-world learning. This has become the standard go-to-market for technology firms.

Marketing strategy formation is *both* planned and emergent

Theory and experience, including my own, suggests that in practice, the process of developing marketing strategy successfully encompasses both planned and emergent approaches. The academic literature suggests that a key role of leadership is not only to plan deliberate marketing strategy as a strategic and operational framework but also to manage the process of strategic learning whereby new strategies can emerge. It follows that a key role of strategy and insights specialists is to conceptualize and implement the process of nurturing strategic learning in support of the CEO. Chapters 4–8 of this book will describe a process for nurturing strategic learning, which realizes the preconditions for strategy emergence and organizational learning suggested above.

MINI CASE STUDY   Strategic learning: fashion

The pace of innovation, combined with disruptive technology innovation, is encouraging companies to adopt a strategic learning approach to nurture emergent marketing strategy. My client, a global fashion brand holding company, had seen a continuing decline in product sales in its biggest SBU (strategic business unit) (ModelPeople, 2015). The marketing and insights team had reviewed existing developed hypotheses as to why, including: substitution with other types of (lower-priced) garment; changes in dress code at work; and fashion cycles. They also had internal data by marketing channel, which indicated that the department store national chains (like JC Penney) and mass chains (like Walmart), historically the largest channels, were showing an above average decline. Therefore, we also wanted to look at changes in purchasing behaviour, particularly given the level of disruption occurring in retail with the growth of online shopping and discount stores like TJ Maxx.

The company had a separate innovation function looking at product and marketing strategy five-plus years out, but sensibly wanted to equip its line managers to address emergent business challenges in marketing strategy, on a much shorter time frame. Therefore, the insights department made a significant investment in designing a Strategic Learning Journey for over 20 of its line managers in product design, merchandising and marketing, from VP down to entry-level managers (who were not typically involved in strategy development). ModelPeople ran a series of immersive research sessions with their target consumer segments in key markets over a four-month period, including four-hour ethnographic interviews and Creative Workshops (see Chapters 5 and 6 for how to do this). The purpose of the ethnographic interviews was to understand the social, cultural and fashion environment in which women were deciding what to wear for different occasions, and how this might be changing. We also ran ethnographic interviews with fashion-oriented trendsetters who were not their core customers to get an idea of how leading-edge fashion consumers might be influencing the market. This effort culminated in several internal Activation Workshops, in which line managers built observations into insights and innovation platforms which were used to develop ideas for marketing strategy over the next one to three years. The consensus among line managers was that their Strategic Learning Journey had been great in terms of the opportunity to gain individual learning, but also, perhaps more importantly, to share ideas with colleagues as to what the immediate future priorities should be.

Organizational learning starts with individual learning

Strategic learning starts, de facto, with the individual, but it cannot remain individualized. Turning individual learning into collective organizational learning is critical to the process of developing marketing strategy. Nonaka (2007) states that successful companies are those that consistently create new knowledge, disseminate it throughout the organization and then activate this new knowledge into new products. (I would add that activation encompasses other dimensions of marketing strategy, as well as new products.) However, Nonaka emphasizes that creating new learning is not just a matter of processing objective facts but of tapping the tacit knowledge of employees and making it available for testing and use by the company as a whole. Tacit knowledge is not objective but comprises highly subjective insights, intuitions and hunches, which may be rooted in experience formed on the job or in personal beliefs and mental models, but which may form the basis for completely new approaches to creating value for customers. Nonaka cites the example of a software developer working on the design for a new bread machine, who developed the idea for a new type of kneading action by observing a master baker kneading dough with his hands. Similarly, the designers for a jeans marketing corporation (ModelPeople, 2015) gained inspiration for a new 'Comfort' waistband with hidden stretch by observing first-hand the fit difficulties which plus-size women have with conventional denim waist bands. For a trendy, size 4 designer, the obvious fit solution was an elastic waistband. However, talking with plus-size women about their reluctance to wear elastic waistbands which cue 'old' or 'fat', the opposite of the youthful, sexy image they wish to project when wearing denim, led to the development of a new approach with hidden stretch and the appearance of a regular denim waist.

Crossan, Lane and White (1999) have suggested a framework which migrates learning from the individual to the group level and then to the organizational level. At the *Intuiting* and *Interpreting* stages, individuals articulate and share tacit learning (experiences and metaphors) within their work group. *Integrating* is the process by which the group arrives at shared understanding relative to a strategic issue. *Institutionalizing* learning by embedding it into the organization's strategy and processes is the final stage in developing collective learning. Collective strategic learning is a precondition for the successful formation of marketing strategy under the Learning School approach.

There is one exception to the rule that collective strategic learning is the precondition for successful strategy emergence. The Entrepreneurial School of strategy formation (Mintzberg *et al*, 2009) emphasizes emergent strategy based on the intuition, insight and experience of the organization's leader. Effectively, the organization has only one strategist, the founder or CEO. While this model has proven highly successful in the case of companies such as Richard Branson's Virgin and the late Steve Jobs' Apple, dependence on one person's learning can also lead to strategic mistakes. For example,

Ron Johnson's entrepreneurial-style approach to strategy formation was developed under Steve Jobs. The consequences of Johnson's entrepreneurial myopia and ignorance of JC Penney's collective 'strategic learning' about their customers are evident in the case study with which this chapter opened. Despite the potential pitfalls, the business world has perhaps been overly focused on individual learning and strategic vision, having developed an envious fascination with entrepreneurs who have created companies based on their own personal vision which have achieved higher market capitalizations than traditional Fortune 500 companies. Some corporations have encouraged individuals to think like entrepreneurs, so as to enable the organization to seize emergent strategic opportunities faster than might traditionally be possible within a large corporation. In other types of organization, strategies grow organically among individuals in many different places and may emerge as dominant strategies simply because they are adopted by the organization collectively.

Strategic learning based on empathy

We have seen that strategic learning requires an organization to identify emergent patterns across the many touchpoints that it has with its customers, consumers or users. Learning can occur anywhere in the day-to-day operations of a business, and it can also be a response to consumer or customer data. The potential to derive learning and insight from such data is now greater than it has ever been, with exponential increases in computing power and increased penetration of data collection devices such as mobile phones and retail scanners, which enable predictive analysis of large data sets, known as 'big data'. Integrating and managing 'big' data streams, and mining them for insight into consumer behaviour which can inspire marketing strategy has become a major strategic focus for many commercial organizations, which is currently in the early stages of realization but promises to offer exciting new opportunities for strategic learning.

Big data can tell us quite a bit about who our consumers or customers are and some aspects of how they behave, and can help us make predictions about future behaviour so as to guide marketing strategy formation. However, big data does not tell us *why* consumers or customers behave the way they do. Nor does it give us textured insight into the situations and circumstances of their behaviour: it does not tell us *how*. Without understanding *why?* and *how?* we only have half the picture.

We may be able to make strategic decisions based on big data. For example, we might decide to pursue a retail strategy of merchandising toothbrushes next to toothpaste, because store data shows a strong correlation between these two types of purchase. Big data may also tell us that whitening toothpastes are the fastest growing SKU, suggesting we pursue an innovation strategy of developing a superior whitening toothpaste. However, big data doesn't actually give us the big picture. It doesn't help us understand, for example, *why* shoppers choose specific products and what their whitening *goals* and *unmet functional and emotional needs* (both stated and latent or subconscious) are. Understanding *why* is essential to developing winning marketing strategies or selecting spaces in which to innovate. It doesn't allow us to hear the stories consumers tell about whitening brand *experiences* so we can design and communicate a better experience. It doesn't allow us to observe *how* consumers use specific whitening product forms and the difficulties they may face, so we don't get to understand the requirements for the industrial *design* of whitening devices or the *sensory dimensions* of whitening consumables such as taste or texture so we can improve *usability*. It doesn't help us understand *context*: the *cultural environment* which makes white teeth aspirational and the *semiotics* which help us understand the cultural dimensions of aspiration; the *retail environment* in which the shopper makes a purchase decision; or *the home environment* where the consumer uses the product. All of these considerations may impact marketing strategy including market selection, product positioning and design and communications.

Quantitative research (which we can define as numerical data derived from a sample population using structured and coded questions) helps us to fill in some of these learning gaps. We can commission quantitative research to tell us about consumer perceptions of whitening products, positive and negative, and we can query or interpolate unmet needs. Advances in text analytics can give us rich insight from uncoded data (derived from open-ended questions), so we can learn more about whitening experiences, unmet needs and dislikes regarding design, usability or sensory aspects. We can commission an Implicit Association Test (Bridger, 2015) to indicate the extent to which our toothpaste brand carries whitening associations compared with competitor brands and help us decide whether our brand can readily be extended into the whitening space. We can put shoppers in eye-tracking glasses to help us observe how they choose whitening products in the store context. And so on. However, much quantitative research creates an over-simplified paradigm for understanding how consumers think and feel in the broader context of their lives. That's because, like big data, quantitative research creates a brand-defined (or retail-defined) context for learning, rather than a *consumer-defined context* which reflects the reality of the consumer or customer's lives and the role the company's products and brands play in their lives. The danger of a brand-defined context for marketing and innovation strategy is that it can encourage an arrogantly inflated view of the role our products and brands play or could play in consumers' lives. If Ron Johnson, instead of comparing (big data) promotional sales percentages with Apple Stores', had met some of his customers and understood the context of his brand within their lives, how middle-income moms thought and felt about shopping for themselves within the broader context of first meeting the needs of their families, then he may have understood why promotional events were so necessary to marketing strategy.

Big data and quantitative research simplify the measurement of marketing KPIs (key performance indicators) which is critical to measuring the effectiveness of marketing strategy. However, they do not give us the unfiltered insights which help us *imagine how* our consumers and customers *think and feel*. We cannot hear the emotional language middle-income moms use to describe their lives, personal goals and efforts to provide for everyone in the family. We cannot observe the context in which she thinks about shopping for herself and what tempts her to buy. Most quantitative data cannot help us *imagine*. It cannot easily spark the personal and subjective hunches, insights and intuitions; the metaphors, stories and mental constructs which Nonaka (2007) and Crossan *et al* (1999) regard as key to inspiring tacit knowledge as a basis for developing organizational learning. Quantitative data *alone* cannot help us develop *empathy* with consumers and customers within the broader context of their lives, which, we will argue, is a precondition for success in marketing strategy.

Strategic Empathy

I have argued that developing empathy with consumers and customers is critical for developing the breakthrough insights that are needed for transformational strategic change. Successful competitive marketing strategy must be grounded in *empathy* as well as data. Let's be clear, empathy is not a soft skill. When empathy-based strategic learning is activated in marketing strategy, it has been proven to be a powerful driver of organizational success in both for-profit and not-for-profit organizations. My company, ModelPeople Inc, calls the activation of empathy-based organizational learning into marketing strategy, *Strategic Empathy®*. Anyone with involvement in marketing strategy formation (ie the multiple 'strategists' to be found at every level of a learning organization!) needs Strategic Empathy skills and practical know-how.

We have seen that for individual 'strategists', strategic learning can happen on the job, but turning individual learning into collective organizational learning is critical to the process of *institutionalizing* it across the organization, that is embedding it in marketing strategy and processes. In many commercial organizations, a *cross-functional team-based* approach ensures the development of collective learning that harnesses multiple perspectives, which Lampel (1998) regards as essential in a learning organization. Such teams need a coordinated approach to developing empathy with how customers think, feel and behave, and *integrating* individual learning into group learning by agreeing on what the key insights are, and how to address them (activate them) in marketing strategy. This team-based approach to learning and strategy activation is what we call the *Strategic Empathy Process*. The Strategic Empathy Process starts with a conscious approach to learning which must be shared by the team as a basis for strategy formation. We call the conscious design of a team-based learning approach a *Strategic Learning Journey*, because the learning is designed to result in insights which can be activated into strategy: ie action results from the learning. Leaders of teams tasked with strategy formation, whether in for-profit or not-for-profit organizations, must develop the skills to curate Strategic Learning Journeys and to encourage collaboration between team members, who may be from different functions or even organizational outsiders.

A Strategic Learning Journey leverages all available forms of data and insight to support learning, but at its core is *immersive, experiential learning* which develops a deep understanding about our consumers or customers and the way our brands fit into their lives: what we can call the *who?*, *why?* and *how?* Chapters 4–9 of this book describe the Strategic Empathy® Process: a leadership tool, with which marketing, strategy and insights specialists can develop Strategic Empathy among teams of cross-functional 'strategists', as a basis for marketing strategy formation. We will show how to design and implement a Strategic Learning Journey and how to ensure individual learning is integrated by the group and activated into strategic objectives and plans. We illustrate the process with case studies derived from 11 years' practical application with global Fortune 500 corporations and not-for-profit organizations.

CASE STUDY   A tech Strategic Learning Journey

Figure 1.3 Installing a router

SOURCE: ModelPeople Inc, 2006

Diane crawled out from underneath her desk with a red face. 'I can't figure this out', she confessed with an embarrassed grimace. She had been trying to install a new router which the Insight team had just watched her purchase in a big-box electronics store. The purchase process itself had been tortuous. Diane was computer-savvy and had tried to do a little online research before she went shopping but was confused about what the different router standards meant in practice. Packaging descriptions were confusing and time after time our researchers watched as sales associates gave conflicting information.

We (ModelPeople, 2007–8) were doing a series of projects for a home networking products marketer, acquired by a highly successful B2B networking corporation, to take advantage of the growth in consumer broadband and home networking devices. The brand had built about a 40 per cent market share in routers (the devices needed to direct an internet signal from the modem to networked devices in the home or small office). Their products had previously been purchased mainly by 'geeks' or by office managers with good technical know-how, who loved the highly functional product design, but did not require intuitive usability. Now however, with the spread of home Wi-Fi, the goal of the company's new Consumer Products Division was to target consumers without this specialized knowledge, and a cross-functional team of insights, marketing and engineering specialists had been formed to spearhead this effort.

Companies with a strong engineering or technical culture can find it difficult to have empathy with ordinary consumers because employees with a high degree of technical skill can have limited patience with people who don't. The Insights Director wanted to inspire marketing, product design and innovation strategy by creating transformational empathy with the average consumer. Our brief was to communicate the in-home design context for routers in both the US and Europe, in order to inform the design brief. We were also asked to explore and document the difficulties which consumers experienced in purchasing and installing the company's products.

First we ran Creative Workshops: co-creation groups in which consumers provided design context for defining a new industrial design voice. Participants took photos of their home routers in the context of their living spaces and discussed what worked about the company's router design relative to interior décor, and where it fell short compared with competitive designs. They also gave feedback on new industrial design concepts developed by the company's design and engineering team. In another phase of research, we accompanied US and UK consumers, who were within a few weeks of purchasing a new router, to the store to shop and then home to install the product they'd purchased. Figure 1.3 shows Mark, the interviewer, and the cameraman Jeff observing Diane. Professional video was taken of each step in the process. Major electronics retailers in the UK and the US had given us permission to film in-store because they were keen to understand how to simplify the purchase process and improve point-of-sale (POS) display to better communicate technical differences. We discovered some key insights, not least that shoppers entered the store having done some basic online research but generally ignorant of what they needed to buy for their specific home situation. Shelf layout and POS needed to help the shopper select the best standard for their home environment and (in the UK) telecoms provider. Staff training was required. And most of all, consumers needed help with the installation process.

Video out-takes of shopper after shopper struggling to find the right product and install it was first shared with the core group of marketing and engineering personnel who worked it into the new product and packaging design briefs. It also resulted in the launch of a new product, the Valet router, designed to facilitate installation with a new interface that leads the consumer step-by-step through what was a frustrating and difficult process. The product was an immediate success: *PC Magazine* (2010) was only one of the reviewers who described the Valet as having 'unprecedented ease of set-up'. The process led by the Insights Director can truly be described as strategic learning, in that it inspired action: in this case, radical changes in product and packaging design and store merchandising.

Chapter 1 summary

1   The uncertainty of an organization's environment means that, typically, marketing strategy formation is both planned and emergent, ie strategy evolves based on organizational learning. Strategists can exist at many levels of the organization and transformational strategic change can be initiated at many levels of the organization.

2   Under the Learning School, strategy formation can be considered as a process of ***strategic learning*** – identifying emergent patterns across the touchpoints between the organization's brands and its consumers (product, promotion etc) and activating learning into strategy.

3   Strategic learning taps multiple sources of data but especially the subjective insight of employees (and the fresh insight of external stakeholders). Learning must be focused on creating empathy with consumers and customers as a basis for marketing strategy formation. Shared empathy-based learning which is activated into strategy is called ***Strategic Empathy®***.

4   Successful companies are those that consistently implement strategic learning in marketing strategy. The role of a leader, therefore, is to enable and manage the process of strategic learning. The Strategic Empathy® Process is a leadership tool for empathy-based strategic learning and marketing strategy formation.

References

Bower, J and Christensen, C (1995) Disruptive Technologies: Catching the wave, *Harvard Business Review*, January–February

Brady, D (2013) Ron Johnson acknowledges JC Penney isn't Apple, *Bloomberg Business*, 29 January

Bridger, D (2015) *Decoding the Irrational Consumer*, pp 109–11, Kogan Page, London – provides an overview of the IAT

Crossan, M, Lane, H and White, R (1999) An organizational learning framework: from intuition to institution, *Academy of Management Review*, vol 24, 3, July

Decety, J and Lamm, C (2006) Human empathy through the lens of social neuroscience, *The Scientific World Journal*, 6, pp 1146–63

The Economist (2015) 11–18 October

Finkelstein, S (2014) *The Worst CEOs of 2013*, BBC Capital, 2 November

Hamel, G (1998) Strategy innovation and the quest for value, *Sloan Management Review*, vol 39, 44 (Winter), pp 7–14

King, A and Baatartogtokh, B (2015) How useful is the theory of disruptive innovation?, *MIT Sloan Management Review*, 15 September

Lampel, J (1998) Towards the learning organization, in Mintzberg, H, Ahlstrand, B and Lampel, J (2009) *Strategy Safari*, p 215, Prentice Hall, London

Mintzberg, H (2007) *Tracking Strategies: Towards a general theory*, Oxford University Press, Oxford

Mintzberg, H, Ahlstrand, B and Lampel, J (2009) *Strategy Safari*, pp 5, 228, Prentice Hall, London

ModelPeople Inc (2007–8) Immersive research for a global networking corporation

ModelPeople Inc (2008–10, 2015) Immersive research conducted for JC Penney over 2008–9. Quotes from shopper research conducted October 2015

ModelPeople Inc (2014) Case study for a global automotive manufacturer

ModelPeople GlobalCultureBlog® (2015) Beijing entry, November

ModelPeople Inc (2015) Immersive research for a global fashion brand company

Nonaka, I (2007) The Knowledge Creating Company, *Harvard Business Review*, July–August

PC Magazine online (2010), March [last reviewed February 2016]

Quinn, J (1980) *Strategies for Change: Logical incrementalism*, Irwin, Toronto

Reeves, M, Deimler, M, Morieux, Y and Nicol, R (2010) *Adaptive Advantage*, BCH White paper, October

Tichy, N (2014) *Succession: Mastering the make-or-break process of leadership transition*, Penguin Random House, New York; adapted excerpt for inclusion in *Fortune* (2014) JC Penney and the Terrible Costs of Hiring an Outside CEO

Waal, F de (2006) *Primates and Philosophers: How morality evolved*, Princeton University Press, Princeton NJ

Strategic learning frameworks

02

Needs, emotions, culture and decision-making

We seldom realize, for example, that our most private thoughts and emotions are not actually our own. For we think in terms of languages and images which we did not invent, but which were given to us by our society.

ALAN WATTS (PHILOSOPHER, 1915–73), 1969

CHAPTER 2 OBJECTIVES

1 Identify four theoretical frameworks for multi-disciplinary strategic learning, the goal of which is developing empathy with consumers and customers as a basis for marketing strategy formation: ie Strategic Empathy.

2 Give an overview of key concepts within each framework: needs, goals and values; emotions; culture and decision-making.

3 Highlight future perspectives which will add significantly to these frameworks of understanding.

Introduction

Josh showed me a picture of an overweight couple. 'Why does the world hate America?' he asked. 'They only see fat American tourists! We have too much of everything, including food. We need to stop consuming.'

During a Creative Workshop about changing meal habits among young adult trendsetters (aged 18–24), I had asked the group to select image metaphors to represent 'breakfast'. The workshop had taken an interesting turn. The date was 25 September 2001, two weeks after the terrorist attacks in Manhattan. We had considered cancelling the project, but concluded that Chicago was far enough away from the epicentre of the attacks and the subject was hardly related. We were wrong. The Sears Tower in Chicago, at that time the nation's tallest skyscraper, had concrete barricades out front and workers on higher floors were receiving counselling to help with post-traumatic emotions and overwhelming physical symptoms such as uncontrollable trembling and nausea. The city was afraid, and for these thoughtful, intelligent young adults, strong emotions had provoked cultural introspection. US culture – popularly rooted in the deprivation, toil and gain of frontier history – values optimism, hard work and the reward of material abundance. Now (to Josh at least) the idea of abundance seemed to provoke anger, sadness and aversion. At that unique point in time, *what did it mean to be American? How did it feel* to be American?

Over the following few years, these themes arose again and again in research with young adults (although the context was less highly charged than in the weeks following 9/11). There appeared to be a new cultural zeitgeist influencing consumers' perceived functional needs, emotional responses and purchase decision-making. For example, in an automotive design study some three years later, we spoke with young adult trendsetters about their 'less is more' design aesthetic. For them 'less is more' was both an emotional and a cultural concept. Emotionally, they rejected the excessive size and ornamentation of the giant SUVs popular at that time (nor could they justify it from a needs perspective); culturally, they felt a new mood of restraint, in common with Josh, just after 9/11.

What is culture and how does it affect consumer behaviour? To what extent are emotions influenced by socio-cultural norms and values (as Watts (1969) suggests)? Are emotions the property of the brain or the body? How does context affect emotional response? These questions are crucial for marketing strategy teams trying to understand consumer behaviour. The emerging field of affective sciences takes a multi-disciplinary approach to these questions, bringing together researchers in psychology, philosophy, economics, sociology, anthropology and neuroscience. However, Klaus Scherer, Director of the Swiss Center for Affective Sciences, believes it will be a major challenge to integrate research from these different perspectives (Scherer, 2009). This challenge also faces consumer insights professionals on a day-to-day basis. The goal of this chapter is to give an overview of four theoretical frameworks which offer a solid foundation for multi-disciplinary strategic learning which will help insights and marketing professionals develop empathy with consumers and customers as a basis for marketing strategy formation.

Framework One: emotions

'What is an emotion?' This is the title of an early paper by William James (1884), who went on to conclude that an emotion is a bodily feeling: we do not tremble because we feel afraid; we feel afraid because we tremble. One of the problems in presenting theoretical frameworks for emotions is the lack of consensus on a definition of emotion. From a neuroscience perspective, emotion is purely a function of the brain. The brain regions which process emotions are also responsible for the interaction between emotion, memory, attention and learning (we will discuss the implications of this for the Strategic Empathy Process in Chapter 8). Other researchers differentiate between types of emotion: for example, primary or 'basic' emotions which are universal adaptive mechanisms elicited automatically with no cognitive processing and designed to promote life-preserving action (building on James' theory); and secondary/tertiary or 'complex' emotions which involve cognitive appraisal and are linked to social and cultural norms. In this section, we will look at useful frameworks for considering emotions as they relate to consumer behaviour. We will also consider how consumer needs relate to emotions.

The basic emotions thesis

The basic emotions thesis identifies seven primary, universal human emotions: anger, happiness, sadness, surprise, disgust, contempt and fear (although academics disagree on the number and type of emotions). Emotions are termed 'basic' because they are held (Tomkins, 1962) to have evolved through natural selection to motivate self-preserving behaviours (such as self-defence) in universal, 'basic' human situations (such as danger or aggression). The basic emotions framework regards emotion as a primitive hangover from our reptilian origins, taking part in subcortical brain structures; while thinking and reasoning is 'cortical' or of a higher order. This suggests that some causes of emotion (even some emotions) are not accessible to conscious awareness. Emotions also arise in goal pursuit, and these emotions are situationally adapted: for example, a perceived opportunity creates excitement; a perceived threat creates anxiety. Emotions are also influenced by progress towards a goal: whether it is fast, for example, resulting in pride and confidence; or slow, resulting in frustration (Nesse, 2004). Evolution explains why humans appear to be 'primed' to feel and behave in a certain way; for example, to feel fear of snakes and to prepare to fight in response to a physical attack. When emotions are aroused they recruit other physiological and cognitive reactions and processes which allow for a coordinated response to an environmental stimulus. For example, anger produces physiological changes such as vasodilation which increases blood flow to the muscles in preparation for fighting. Ekman (1972) argued that 'basic emotions' provoke physiological responses in the form of facial expressions, which are recognizable across cultures, both pre-literate and literate. Other researchers have shown that the same facial expressions have been observed in non-human primates and blind people, suggesting a biological basis for 'emotional' facial expressions. This theory has given rise to some consumer research methods which use facial imagery representing the universal emotions to assess non-verbally a consumer's emotional responses, for example, to an ad campaign. Ekman's work also led to the development of the facial action coding system (FACS), which is used in many everyday spheres (such as airport security screening) to identify emotion based on individual variations in muscle movement in the face.

The basic emotions framework has several areas of weakness, not least that researchers don't agree on the number and types of basic emotions. Moreover, neuroscientists disagree as to whether each basic emotion shows a distinct pattern of neural response. For example, Panskepp (1998) has proposed that basic emotions (in humans and animals) are characterized by a series of neural systems. These systems activate relevant sensory and behavioural processes which have evolved through natural selection: for example, care, which triggers nurturing behaviours; and panic, which is associated with separation in social animals. Nesse (2009) concludes that 'an evolutionary perspective offers a foundation for describing and categorizing emotions in terms of the processes that shaped them'.

Appraisal theories

More recent research moves away from the idea that emotions are basic and universal and suggests that they have evolved biologically and socially to become both complex and culturally influenced. In Klaus Scherer's component process model (CPM), emotion is conceptualized as an emergent, dynamic process based on an individual's appraisal of 'stimulus events' which prepare the body for action. Events can be external, such as a thunderstorm, a social experience or an ad playing on TV. Or they can be internal, such as a physiological change or a memory. According to Scherer (2005), this process involves a 'massive mobilization of forces' including unconscious physiological responses, conscious appraisals and embodied subjective feelings (qualia). Appraisals ('stimulus evaluation checks') involve relevance checks. Relevance checks evaluate stimulus events based on their familiarity, intrinsic pleasantness (do they deliver pleasure or pain – two emotions which Scherer believes are fundamental to all emotions) and the individual's goals or needs. Appraisal is influenced by input from cognitive and motivation mechanisms such as attention, memory, motivation, reasoning and the self-concept. These mechanisms provide stored information (for example, attitudes or preferences about a brand) and evaluation criteria (eg the significance of the stimulus event to my self-concept; my beliefs and values). Appraisals are held (Grandjean *et al*, 2008) to occur at different levels of processing of which the first two levels are non-conscious: sensory-motor (someone threatens us and we take avoidance action) and schematic, which provokes routine action based on familiarity (I always buy the same brand of toothpaste). Only the third level is conscious and effortful. Scherer (2005) suggests there are, not few basic emotions, but an infinite number of emotional episodes, which explains why two individuals may react very differently to stimulus based on the complexity of inputs in each case. Scherer's work distinguishes between utilitarian emotions (such as fear, joy or desire) which prepare the body for action which has consequences for our well-being or survival, and aesthetic emotion (eg in response to art or music), which do not.

Scherer's work makes intuitive sense to marketers because it reflects the complex inputs to the intrinsic appraisals of an emotion episode, such as brand attitudes, preferences and self-concept. Managing these inputs in marketing strategy is discussed further in Chapter 3. His work also encompasses the idea of non-conscious emotional processing, which is critical to understanding how marketing stimulus works, as we will describe later in this chapter. However, Scherer (2005) himself recognized the impossibility of measuring an infinite number of emotions and all of the physiological and subjective outputs involved, and has suggested that there are repetitions called 'modal families' of emotion, which research participants are able to self-report (anger, hostility, contempt, disgust, shame, boredom, sadness, anxiety, surprise, interest, hope, relief, satisfaction, happiness, elation, pride).

Scherer (2005) notes that emotional experiences are described in subjective, culture-specific semantic terms and categories. Similarly, other counter-arguments against the pan-cultural nature of basic emotions have come from anthropologists who argue that both context and culture affect the expression, interpretation and categorization of emotion. For example, Schweder (2001) discusses the observations of anthropologists that different cultures express grief in different ways, such as through public displays of grief, by withdrawing from public life or by exhibiting bodily aches. He concludes that it is likely that 'there may well be culture-specific emotions'; that is 'emotionalized packages' of needs, wants, beliefs and values that play an important part in the life of a specific culture. Linguists have also pointed out that there are wide differences in the semantic expression and meaning of emotional experiences in different cultures (Wierzbicka, 1999). Emotions may also be 'contagious', as when individuals look to other people in a specific social situation to determine what emotion to display: in a crowd situation for example, or on social media (Hatfield *et al*, 1993).

Emotions and memory

Emotion dials up our ability to remember things, which makes evolutionary sense if life-threatening events are to be avoided or pleasurable events replicated. Emotional stimuli capture attention more readily during encoding of an event into memory because they make us pay more attention to the event (Heuer and Reisberg, 1990). We also process the event at a deeper (semantic) level because we are looking for meaning in emotions. Once encoded, emotional events are consolidated over time which leads to longer-term memory retention. This is important for marketing strategy because it means that we remember brand experiences or brand stimuli better if they are associated with positive emotions; and if these positive associations are consistently reinforced, we remember them better and for longer (provided that the specific association with the brand is clearly reinforced, which is where memorable brand symbols such as logos, colours, packaging design etc come in). For example, in a project which I conducted to redesign packaging for a soda brand, we conducted Deep Visualizations with brand loyalists and discovered that the shape of the bottle was extremely important in recalling pleasurable emotional experiences of the brand which had occurred some 20–30 years prior!

LeDoux (1993) initially developed the concept of the 'emotional memory' and identified the importance of the amygdala in remembering something emotionally arousing. There are two types of emotional memory: explicit memories, which are accessible to consciousness and declarative (that is, they can be consciously recalled and described); and implicit memories which are non-conscious and non-declarative (inferred by a change in behaviour or physiology: for example, someone may avoid a particular brand because of a prior bad experience without being able to articulate why, or their heart rate may increase when they think about the brand). Research has shown that we remember emotional memories more vividly and with greater narrative detail, even with awareness of accompanying physiological changes (sweating, feeling sick). There are two types of memory retrieval: *recollection* (the conscious recall of events and facts) and *familiarity* (the sense of having seen stimulus before). Emotional memories are associated with conscious recollection (Ochsner, 2000). In Chapter 6 we discuss the use of a technique called Deep Visualization, which promotes the vivid and detailed recollection of emotional brand memories from long-term memory retention.

Implicit memory retrieval promotes familiarity, the sense that emotional stimulus has been seen before. Priming experiments have demonstrated that even stimulus which is not consciously processed can influence behaviour: for example, Zajonc (1968) exposed images of shapes to participants for the duration of a millisecond, too fast for people to say what they had seen. Subsequently, however, when shown images at speeds where they could consciously process them they showed preference for the images subliminally presented, even though the participants claimed no conscious familiarity. Priming stimuli in a marketing context are emotional brand ideas to which the consumer has been exposed (ie brand positioning and marketing mix). The influence of the 'emotional memory' on consumer behaviour underlines the importance of understanding the consumer's emotional associations with a brand, and reinforcing positive associations, when developing brand positioning and implementing the marketing mix. In Chapter 3 we will explore models for doing this. In Chapters 5 and 6 we discuss methods and tools for gaining deep insights into positive and negative emotional associations. In addition, familiarity operates faster than recollection and, since the brain is lazy, it relies on heuristics or short cuts to retrieve non-conscious memories. This has implications for brand decision-making which we will discuss further below (see Framework Four: decision-making).

Framework Two: needs, goals and values

Marketing strategists spend a great deal of time thinking about consumer 'needs'. On a very simple theoretical level, *needs* are internal sources of motivation, which influence the *goals* which an individual seeks to approach (or avoid). Needs are often elicited by deprivation: if we are deprived of food, we seek food. Early researchers (eg Murray, 1938) pointed to a combination of biological needs (such as hunger) and psychological needs (such as affiliation, recognition). Most famously (though his theory lacked evidence), Maslow (1964) posited that human needs, which are universal – not culture-specific – can be organized in a hierarchy. Humans first seek to satisfy biological needs such as hunger and safety; then psychological needs – love, belonging and self-esteem; and finally self-actualization needs which relate to the individual's personal potential and purpose in life. A more recent study (Tay and Diener, 2010) has shown that, while there are indeed 'universal' needs, they do not need to be fulfilled in hierarchical order, as Maslow suggested, to deliver well-being. This may explain why even people whose basic needs are imperfectly met can derive a degree of well-being if their psychological, social and respect needs are met. The same study indicates that personal well-being is also influenced by the well-being of others in society: the better-off may develop empathy with the less well-off; and actually feel worse themselves, as a result.

Needs also drive emotions. In the last section, we discussed two major theories of emotion, both of which posit that emotion involves evaluation (instinctive or cognitive) of individual goals, and also motivates the individual to act. Some researchers believe that any goal can relate to any emotion. By contrast, evolutionary theorists argue that some emotions always involve specific goals: for example, guilt is always related to moral values. In marketing strategy, needs and related emotions are typically assessed in a hierarchy which includes:

- functional needs: what the consumer wants the brand to do relative to a problem which he or she faces (eg get clothes clean);
- emotional needs: how the consumer wants to feel relative to the problem or brand (eg pride in a job well done; sensory fulfilment from a pleasant detergent scent);

- self-expressive needs: how the consumer wants to look by using the brand (eg looking groomed and attractive when wearing clean clothes; looking savvy by choosing a value brand which works just as well as a premium brand);
- self-actualizing needs: how the brand might help the consumer fulfil personal potential and values.

In Chapter 3 we will discuss how brand benefits are evaluated relative to consumer needs in this hierarchy, and how they are organized in articulating brand positioning strategy.

Values also influence personal and societal goals and therefore emotions. Think, for example, about 'greed is good', an idea which once elicited admiration and now, post-global recession, elicits disgust and anger. It is essential for the marketing strategy team to develop deep understanding of consumer values relative to culture and social norms on their learning journey, because cultural values are a potential point of brand leverage, but also a potential source of damage. For example, US TV chef Paula Deen built up a huge empire based on the values of traditional Southern comfort food and hospitality, but was fired by The Food Network in 2013 when she admitted to making racial slurs. Brands often publish a statement of values to ensure that they are consistently implemented, especially service brands where many people are involved in executing the brand on a daily basis (and therefore developing emergent brand strategy on a daily basis).

Framework Three: culture

Culture is hot. In 2014 Merriam-Webster announced that 'culture' was their word of the year – looked up more times than any other word. Yet (as we saw with emotions) there is no consensus on how to define culture. As philosopher Alan Watts asserted, in the quote which opened this chapter, culture is important to how humans think and feel: we have seen that theoretical frameworks for human emotions and needs acknowledge the influence of cultural beliefs and norms. Moreover, as we will see in Framework Four, consumer behaviour is influenced – both directly and indirectly – by culture and by socio-cultural context. In this section we will explore theoretical frameworks for understanding what culture is and why it is important in understanding how consumers think, feel and behave.

What is culture?

Malinowksi (1884–1942) rejected the idea of evolutionary theorists (such as Sir James Frazer, author of *The Golden Bough*) that human culture progresses from savagery to civilization – from magic to scientific thought. For him, each individual culture was an integral system whose components (including artefacts, goods, ideas, habits, values and skills) are related to each other and to physical surroundings. The function of any aspect of culture, he posited, is to fulfil individual biological, psychological and social needs. Malinowski (1922) emphasized synchrony or the study of the ethnographic present, in contrast to Franz Boas (1920), who emphasized a culture's past history as being what uniquely defined it.

If Malinowski placed emphasis on individual needs, Emile Durkheim, working some 30 years earlier, saw culture as being a separate entity from individuals. In his view, the ideals of liberal individualism current at that time, which saw the purpose of society as satisfying individual needs, were mistaken (Giddens, 1978). Every individual is born into a culture or society which already exists and which shapes his or her development; collective ideas, beliefs, values and symbols ('*représentations collectives*') do not arise from individual states of consciousness but from society as a whole and have one function, which is enhancing the solidarity of the group (Durkheim, 1898). For example, mourning is not an expression of individual grief but a duty imposed by the social group, which draws the group together and expresses permanence in the face of loss. Societal institutions (such as religion) perform the function of expressing the 'collective ideas which give [a society] its unity and its individuality' (Durkheim, 1912).

Lévi-Strauss (1908–2009) applied the principles of linguistics, and linguistic concepts, to human culture, searching for 'deep structures underlying the surface features' (Chandler, 2007) of human culture. His approach became known as structural anthropology. In linguistics theory, language depends on 'codes' or conventions for communication (Jakobson, 1960). These codes are understood by the social group, but they cannot articulate them (unless trained in linguistics). Equally, culture and social behaviour is structured by underlying codes, which are known to the social group and which are usually not consciously articulated (Lévi-Strauss, 1964). For example, underlying codes structure 'masculine' or 'feminine' behaviour and perceptions within culture. Lévi-Strauss (1945) also emphasized 'the concept of system': units of meaning (whether linguistic or cultural) are understood not independently, but in relation to one another, within a system. For example, we understand a sentence based on the relationship between the units of meaning; in the same way we need to look at units of meaning within social systems (we can look at kinship for example, or religion). Finally, Lévi-Strauss (1958) proposed that, just as the role of linguistics is to look for 'general laws', so the role of anthropology is to look for 'universal' human thought processes, which are common across cultures. The primary way in which human thought processes structure meaning is through binary opposites (such as male–female, for example) but the expression of the universal depends on cultural context (as with expressions of masculinity and femininity, for example). In summary, Lévi-Strauss's structural view of culture can be seen as a dialectic concept: a system of collective symbolic communication, which dynamically produces meaning according to underlying codes or conventions. The role of the anthropologist is to understand the underlying codes (for which there is empirical evidence, even if human beings probably cannot consciously explain them) and systems of meaning.

How are these ideas helpful for marketing strategy? For marketing and insights professionals, 'culture' is a framework for understanding: a lens through which we can understand how consumers think, feel and behave collectively, for the purposes of marketing strategy. Brands, product categories (like fashion) and modes of brand communication (like advertising, packaging or retail environment) are systems of meaning. Codes represent territory for distinctive brand positioning and execution which builds brands that are resonant with cultural meaning. Marketing strategists must study culture.

The study of culture

The study of culture involves contrasting perspectives from several fields. Durkheim (1895) defined the study of culture from the sociological perspective of understanding social systems and social consciousness, which arises from 'the conditions in which the social group in its totality is placed'. Lévi-Strauss viewed the study of culture from a structural anthropological perspective: deducing underlying structures of human meaning-making. This book will take the perspective of socio-cultural anthropology, defined by the American Anthropological Association (2016) as a discipline which 'examines social patterns and practices across human cultures', and we will define 'human culture' as: shared beliefs, values, behaviours, symbols of meaning and domains of organization (social, historical, physical world, material world, artistic world etc). The two principal fields of study into human culture are ethnography and semiotics:

- **Ethnography** is the fieldwork-based study and recording of human behaviour in the context of where people live: their socio-cultural systems and everyday practices. Malinowski (1922) was the first to emphasize the importance of an emic or 'insider' approach to ethnography through fieldwork: first-hand observation of individuals in culture at the present time '... to grasp the native's point of view... to become part of his world'. Geertz (1973) described ethnography as 'thick-description', with the aim of drawing 'large conclusions from small but very densely-textured facts... about the role of culture in the construction of collective life'. Geertz acknowledges that his is a semiotic concept of culture (building on the theories of Lévi-Strauss), meaning the analysis of culture (through ethnography) must concern itself with the interpretation of meaning. However, Geertz also warned against losing touch with social context and needs: ie the 'political and economic constraints and biological and physical necessities on which culture rests'. In Chapters 5 and 6 we will discuss in detail how to conduct ethnographic research. Additionally, the internet has enabled socio-cultural systems in the form of sub-cultures to flourish – sometimes wholly – online (Gueorguieva, 2012), which has led to new ways of studying culture: 'netnography' and online ethnography which are also explored in Chapter 5.

- **Semiotics**, which has its roots in linguistics theory, is a huge field of study. Eco (1976) defined semiotics as 'concerned with everything that can be taken as a sign', including objects, customs, the written word, photographic or film images, television, music etc. For de Saussure (1983) semiotics (which he called 'semiology') studies the role of signs in social life. De Saussure distinguished between systems of conventions (*la langue*) which are independent of individual usage (*la parole*). If we apply this distinction to culture, we can make the distinction between underlying codes or systems of conventions which structure meaning; and individual messages in usage. As such, studying signs (semiotics) allows researchers to infer the underlying codes which structure consumer attitudes and behaviour. By identifying codes and messages, semiotics gives marketers a framework within which to manage brand symbols (which are themselves forms of signs) accordingly, through marketing mix elements such as packaging, advertising and retail experience (which are themselves systems of conventions). We explain how to do this in detail in the next chapter and in Chapter 6 we discuss Metaphor Elicitation and Deep Visualization as research tools for understanding codes and brand symbols.

Semiotics theory includes the idea of 'performance' (Mertz, 2007): the relationship between signs and the context in which they appear. Just as speakers adapt language to different communication contexts, so consumers adapt or switch between cultural codes in different contexts, depending on personal goals. For example, in a study for pasta sauce, we found that women switched between 'family' and 'seduction' codes depending on the context of the meal and their own desires at that time! Each of these cultural codes has specific signs: an inter-generational family group around the table; or Chianti and candlelight! Goffman (1959) also points to the way that people use signs to convey personal image, adapting the signs depending on the context. In the same way, consumers adopt different codes depending on what they perceive to be the context; choosing different brands or different styles of clothing, depending on which self-image they wish to project.

Context is also important when it comes to self-identity. In semiotics, deixis is a reference in a sentence that relies on context for correct interpretation. According to Benveniste (1971):

> 'I' is a reality of discourse (context)... 'I' signifies the person who is uttering the present instance of the discourse containing 'I'.

In ethnography, it's important to understand who 'I' is within context. For example, 'I' (the author) am a mother in relation to my child and a spouse in relation to my husband. 'I' am English and also American. Consumers shift self-identity, to reflect different contexts, and they may symbolically consume different products accordingly. 'I' serve mince pies to my family at Christmas and hot dogs to my friends on 4 July.

Lévi-Strauss proposed that cultural codes could be analysed through binary opposites, and we can adapt Greimas' (1984) linguistics-based semiotic square (see Figure 2.1) to help us do this. The semiotic square is helpful for marketing strategy because it can be used to map alignments of ideas and areas of cultural contradiction to help in identifying potential new brand positioning spaces (more on this in Chapter 3).

MINI CASE STUDY   Dora the Explorer

In a study for a global toy manufacturer, we (ModelPeople, 2008) were asked to develop brand positioning for a fantasy play brand of anthropomorphic ponies. The brand was facing very strong competition among its pre-school girl target audience from 'Dora the Explorer'. 'Dora' was an American girl of Mexican heritage who embarked on quests to identifiably real places around the world accompanied by a talking monkey called Boots. We asked mothers to write letters to their daughters, telling them about their dreams for their future and how play related to that, and discovered that Dora occupied a space of cultural contradictions which addressed a mother's ambitions for her daughter as she got ready to start elementary school. If we explain this in terms of the semiotic square, we can see that (for a mother) the binary opposites were 'child's world' and 'adult world' (which her daughter was about to enter). The (closed) child's world is characterized by fantasy characters and scenarios while the (open) adult world is characterized by goals, tasks and real places. In the child's world, mom is the primary relationship, whereas important new, independent relationships form in the adult world. Dora occupied a space between these worlds: a space which blended real/fantasy worlds and cultures. Dora herself was multicultural and also a clever blend of gender stereotypes (clearly a little girl, yet she wears short pants and is feisty, active and determined); she goes out to explore the (open) adult world but with the help of a fantasy friend. Importantly also, while the client's brand was a physical toy, Dora explored on TV and in video games, contemporary (and 'masculine', in the case of video games) media genres to which girls aspired. Dora represents the dream mothers have for their girls' future as they get ready to enter the adult world. Our client faced the choice of keeping their brand in the child's world or finding ways to evolve it to occupy a more blended space and appeal to older girls.

Figure 2.1 Semiotic square: girl's toy category

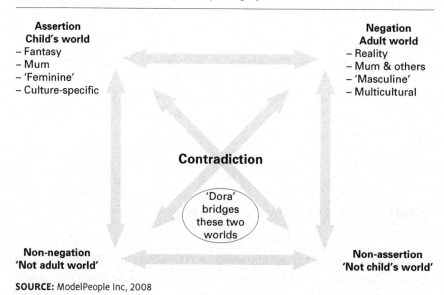

Assertion
Child's world
– Fantasy
– Mum
– 'Feminine'
– Culture-specific

Negation
Adult world
– Reality
– Mum & others
– 'Masculine'
– Multicultural

Contradiction

'Dora' bridges these two worlds

Non-negation
'Not adult world'

Non-assertion
'Not child's world'

SOURCE: ModelPeople Inc, 2008

Framework Four: decision-making

Figure 2.2 The purchase funnel

SOURCE: ModelPeople Inc

Traditionally, consumer decision-making was assumed to be rational and somewhat linear. For example, Aaker (1991) suggests that consumers develop relationships with brands in a number of stages: developing cognitive awareness and perceptions of quality and features; recognizing emotional benefits; forming a loyal, emotional relationship with the brand, based on repeated experiences and finally, identifying with the brand personality.

The journey towards purchasing a brand has been identified as a funnel (see Figure 2.2) and marketers have focused on converting consumers at each level of the funnel via the appropriate touchpoints: TV to drive awareness, for example, and point-of-sale activity to drive trial/purchase. Modifications to the funnel have been suggested, to reflect the new complexity of purchase channels and the consumer's 24/7 access to information about brands via social media and the internet. For example, McKinsey (Court *et al*, 2009) has suggested that consumers broaden their consideration set to take in brands of which they were previously unaware as they conduct online research for major purchases. This is true even for routine grocery brand purchases, with the availability of online coupons and social media promotions. However, the last two decades or more have seen heavy investment by brand marketing companies in shopper insights and marketing capabilities, driven by new research in the psychology and economics fields. This research indicates that consumer decision-making may not be this linear, and that decision-making at the point-of-purchase is less predictable than had been assumed, making the in-store environment more important for brands than had been thought. Marketing strategy should now consider shoppers discretely from consumers and develop complementary strategies for each.

Damasio (1994), building on the work of William James around bodily feelings and emotions, proposed that decision-making is influenced by 'somatic markers' of past experiences, which provide good or bad gut feelings about the outcomes of potential choices. When a negative somatic marker (eg a bad past experience or negative associations with a brand) is linked to a potential choice, the body, as it were, automatically rings an alarm bell to signal avoidance of this choice (Damasio measured this by way of skin conductance, a biometric response measure which we discuss in Chapter 6). Other research in the field of behavioural economics has supported the idea of automatic decision-making and challenged the classical economic theory that human beings make rational purchase decisions based on conscious reasoning. As early as 1957, Herbert Simon proposed the theory of 'bounded rationality'; that is, an individual does not exhaustively seek information to maximize economic benefit but 'satisfices (ie satisfy/suffice): looks for a course of action that is satisfactory or good enough'. This is because the mind (as we saw earlier) is 'bounded' by limits in cognitive processing capability (Simon, 1957). More recently, work in the psychology field on dual process theory posited that two distinctively separate cognitive systems underlying decision-making have evolved: one is an implicit (automatic), unconscious process and the other an explicit (controlled), conscious process. Stanovich and West (2000) coined the phrase 'System 1' and 'System 2' to describe these separate cognitive systems, which were later described by Daniel Kahneman (2002) as 'intuition' and 'reasoning' (see Table 2.1).

Table 2.1 The separate cognitive systems underlying decision-making

System 1: Intuition	System 2: Reasoning
Operates automatically and quickly Generates impressions	Operates in a controlled way and slowly Generates judgements
Looks for short cuts to decision-making (heuristics)	Monitors impressions; can endorse or reject heuristics: but is lazy
Is loss-averse Makes habitual purchases	Is prepared to take risks or make sacrifices Is prepared to evaluate new products

Adapted from Kahneman (2002) by ModelPeople

The reason why this theory has been so powerful in thinking about shopper behaviour is that, Kahneman suggests, System 1 is typically dominant at point-of-purchase. Shoppers do not typically make rational, linear decisions but decide automatically and quickly, relying on heuristics (cognitive triggers or short cuts to memory) to help them. 'There is no finite list of heuristics' according to Kahneman and research continues in both academic and marketing fields to develop a broader idea of how they work. Examples of heuristics are:

- **Availability:** the ease with which an idea comes to mind is an important heuristic which biases choice. Past purchase decisions are 'available' to the shopper, who therefore tends to make habitual purchases. Priming using consistent (emotionally resonant) marketing stimuli such as advertising or iconic packaging helps shoppers reinforce habit or conversely make a new decision at point-of-sale through high availability of the brand idea. This is especially true if there is a physical reminder of the emotionally resonant brand idea at point-of-sale, which is why a familiar pack design which is congruent with the brand positioning is such an important brand symbol. For example, Tropicana's sales plunged more than 20 per cent in 2009 when it completely redesigned brand packaging so that it no longer acted as a short cut to the brand idea.

- **Representativeness:** another key heuristic, which uses category similarity to short-cut reasoning: for example, when designing packaging, it's important to consider category conventions, such as the use of the colour green and plant imagery to denote 'natural' or 'healthy' food. Designs which do not contain 'representative' cues may be overlooked by shoppers because they don't offer a heuristic for the category benefits sought; conversely, breaking with category representativeness may make a brand distinctive within the category.

- **Framing:** shoppers make cognitive predictions about their expected emotions and therefore they are more likely to make a choice that is framed or presented as minimizing risk or loss (pain) rather than one which might maximize gain (pleasure). This is why new brands are often sampled or heavily discounted, or have generous warranties or return policies, to minimize the risk of trial.

- **Affect:** we have seen how marketing stimulus creates an affective ('emotional') response and this is also a heuristic. For example, a positive store environment puts shoppers in a positive mood which biases cognitive processing towards an expected positive outcome from the product purchased.

Figure 2.3 The path to purchase

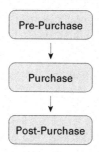

SOURCE: ModelPeople Inc

Rather than relying on the purchase funnel to describe a linear purchase decision-making process, I have found that it is more useful when developing brand and shopper marketing strategy to consider heuristics for the brand purchase decision throughout the path to purchase (see Figure 2.3). The path to purchase defines three stages of purchase decision-making: pre-purchase, purchase and post-purchase. Post-purchase has been found to be more important now consumers are empowered to share stories about brand experiences online and in social media. In an activation session for a pain relief brand, we used the dual processing framework as a model to understand heuristics and ideate shopper innovations throughout this path to purchase model. This included analysis of packaging heuristics which signal relief but also understanding how to design the store environment to create the correct affective heuristic for shoppers with different needs and emotional mindsets, based on the type of pain they were suffering (ModelPeople, 2013).

Context

Context – the environment in which consumers see your brand – is also a crucial influence on consumer decision-making. Context can be macro or micro. In Chapter 3 we explore brand macro-context (social/cultural, economic, technological or political) and its relevance to marketing strategy. Here we will consider several types of micro-context, but the list is not finite:

- **Needs-based:** studies show that consumers in many categories have a repertoire of brands and choose based on specific needs at the time. For example, in a US study (ModelPeople, 2014) with Millennials, they chose

McDonald's for a solo lunch when time was short, but a more upscale, fast-casual restaurant like Mendocino Farms or Panera Bread when with friends or with more time to relax and enjoy the experience.

- **Competitive:** consumers find it easier to judge relative than absolute value, and have been shown to display a preference for brands priced in the middle of a range. Competitive framing is also frequent, through 'compare to' pricing, for example. Research has also shown that framing brands as underdogs to mega-brands affects purchase intent and frequency (Paharia *et al*, 2015). For example, a coffee shop may emphasize it is a 'neighbourhood coffee house' to compete with Starbucks.

- **Tribal:** humans are social animals and often make decisions in a social or tribal context. Consumers may directly copy the behaviour of others whom they admire, which explains the diffusion of new fashion styles, for example. Or they may absorb others' opinions (consciously or non-consciously) which influences decision-making. Research (Rimé, 2005) indicates that humans share emotions 80–95 per cent of the time (although this effect declines over time and negative emotions are shared less often), which underlines the importance of the emotional narrative for brands. Sharing emotional stories elicits similar emotions in the listener which compounds the diffusion effect.

- **Visual:** brands have always sought to position themselves within complementary or aspirational media. This explains why mainstream fashion brands advertise in Vogue alongside couture brands. Social media now allows consumers to picture themselves with brands, which dilutes the marketer's ability to control the brand context (conversely the brand may benefit through viral exposure and positive word-of-mouth).

- **Geographical:** brands have in the past gained cachet from being seen as 'global' but as Millennial consumer values have shifted, they are trying to be seen as 'glocal'. For example, Absolut vodka launched a series of limited edition products called 'Chicago' and 'Texas' with advertising that speaks to local pride and distinctiveness.

- **Channel:** the context in which a brand is sold affects the way that consumers perceive the brand. For example, US consumers are more likely to trust the quality of vitamin brands purchased at upscale 'healthier' stores such as Whole Foods than those purchased at mainstream grocery stores (ModelPeople, 2013). This explains why brands seek distribution in specific accounts which are influential with consumers, and also why fashion brands open flagship stores: so they can control the context in which the brand is seen, rather than depending on other stores to list and display a brand to meet their own commercial objectives. Channel context also affects shopper mindset: how the shopper approaches the store and how much he or she is prepared to spend in that context (see the following mini case study).

MINI CASE STUDY
How club channel context affects shopper mindset and behaviour

Warehouse clubs like Costco and Sam's Club have grown faster than other grocery and mass retailers since the economic recession, and Costco is now the world's second largest retailer, despite charging annual membership fees of $50+. It's true that shoppers perceive low prices as the benefit of shopping in this channel; however, an ethnographic study, observing how shoppers behaved in this channel context, uncovered an emotional mindset which was only loosely related to low price. We (ModelPeople, 2011) observed shoppers becoming excited as they trawled through the aisles of the huge warehouse; not looking for bargains but for surprise treats for the family and supplies for social gatherings. Warehouse clubs are a destination for catering social events and this trip mission, combined with low prices and large pack sizes, created a unique channel context, which triggered non-conscious associations with nurturing family and friends. 'Everyone is always coming by', explained Sandy. 'The kids bring friends home from school or friends drop by for dinner unexpectedly. I'm going to have enough food!' 'I have a big family', said Nicole, 'there's always a birthday party. I know I'm going to buy a massive quantity; I grew up coming here with my mom doing the same thing... it's a tradition.' For these shoppers, the warehouse channel represented abundance, with low prices conferring permission to indulge social instincts. Free sampling of food items and the frequent introduction of new SKUs reinforced the sense of abundance and kept shoppers looking forward to the next party and the next trip!

Fournier (2015) has noted that many types of consumer research are framed in terms of the brand (or product or company) context. Moreover, big data simplifies and eliminates context. 'If we want strong brands', she says, 'we have to start with a deep understanding of the people and figure out where brands fit into their lives if at all... we have to bring context back into branding work.' In Chapter 3 we explore how to address context in marketing strategy, and then in Chapters 5–6 we explore methods and tools for deep understanding about the context of brands in our consumers' lives.

Future perspectives

On 2 April 2013, in the East Room of the White House, President Obama announced the launch of the BRAIN initiative (Brain Research through Advancing Innovative Neurotechnologies), with a remit to develop new technological approaches for the study of the brain. As part of this initiative, the Brain Activity Map (BAM) project aims to map the activity of some 90 billion neurons in the brain. Communication between these cells is thought to underlie brain function, but studying that communication has proved enormously challenging, because neurons form an almost unfathomable number of connections which are constantly in flux, based on what a person experiences. Current techniques allow neuroscientists to capture live signals either from just a few hundred neurons at a time or from large swathes of brain topography at once, but neither scale is sufficient to yield a comprehensive picture of brain activity. As a result, even after a century of study, neuroscientists lack a fundamental understanding of exactly how the brain gives rise to thoughts, emotions and behaviours. Significant claims have been made for the BAM project including therapies for diseases such as schizophrenia and autism and new technologies for 3-D imaging (and storage and manipulation of the massive data sets generated by brain-imaging). Biologist Edward Wilson (2014) describes BAM as trying to:

> ... connect all of the processes of thought – rational and emotional, conscious, pre-conscious and unconscious, held both still and moving through time – to a physical base. It won't come easy... each episode comprises mass neuronal activity so elaborate, so little of which has yet been seen, we cannot even conceive of it, much less write it down as a repertory of firing cells.

The BAM project may well create exciting future opportunities for deep insights research and marketing applications, but that future may be a long way off!

Neuromarketing

Neuromarketing (also known as consumer neuroscience) is a field of consumer research which uses neuroscience techniques such as magnetic resonance imaging (MRI) to understand how consumers react to marketing stimuli. It promises the holy grail of consumer research: empirical evidence of how consumers think and feel. However, some techniques (such as eye-tracking) have been around for decades and others (like MRI) are expensive to replicate. There is also a high degree of interpretation required to draw conclusions from the results in many cases. In Chapter 6, we will look at the major techniques currently in use, but this is a rapidly developing field. University College London (UCL) has launched a course on neuromarketing aimed at marketing and advertising executives. Perhaps we should leave the last word on the subject to course leader Dr Joe Devlin (2016), a neuroimaging researcher:

> There's much confusion and misinformation regarding neuromarketing in what it can achieve and measure, and there's a lot of 'bad science' being promoted in the hype surrounding it... We hope that in educating these major players, we can eventually reduce the amount of bad science being promoted, which is wasting people's time and money and developing misunderstanding of what neuroscience can achieve.

Empathy research

'Empathy research', the study of how other people's thoughts and feelings can affect our own thoughts, feelings and behaviour, is emerging as a multidisciplinary field of study with implications for marketing strategy (especially communications, as we discuss in Chapter 8). Biologist Frans de Waal (2009) states that empathy is an automated response over which we have limited control, which has developed biologically to ensure social cooperation and survival. For example, neuroscientists in Italy (Novembre *et al*, 2014) have discovered that 'social pain' (caused by events such as feeling excluded from social activities, the death of a loved one, a romantic break-up) activates the same brain regions regardless of whether someone was suffering personally or witnessing the social pain of another person (shown on video in the research). From an evolutionary standpoint, these pain responses fortify social connectivity. However, German researchers have proven that the way we feel ourselves can distort empathy for others. In a study (Silani *et al*, 2013) they identified that the part of the brain, called the right supramarginal gyrus, enables us to decouple our own emotional state from that of other people. But this only works if we are in a neutral state or the same state as the other person. The researchers found that when the neurons in this area of the brain were disrupted by incongruent stimuli, empathy plummeted: if we are feeling good ourselves, it is more difficult to empathize with another person's suffering. Designers understand this, and emphasize developing empathy with users as a process step in 'design thinking', which is defined as a 'human-centred approach to design innovation' (Kolko, 2015). We will discuss user research in detail, in Chapter 5.

In summary, exciting multi-disciplinary research fields are emerging which will have future implications for consumer understanding and marketing strategy.

Chapter 2 summary

There are four key frameworks which create a foundation for multi-disciplinary strategic learning:

1 **Framework One: emotions.** Basic emotions have evolved to allow satisfactory responses to positive or negative events (eg attack/anger/fight). Complex emotions can involve conscious appraisal of benefits with input from memory and reasoning; however, much non-conscious appraisal occurs provoking routine responses. Emotions can be primed and also socially defined and influenced. We remember emotional events better and for longer. These findings have implications for brand positioning, marketing mix and the use of insights tools to elicit emotional memories and observe non-conscious consumer emotions.

2 **Framework Two: needs, goals and values.** Needs and values are internal sources of motivation which influence goals and emotions. Consumers are generally held to have functional, emotional, self-expressive and self-actualizing needs.

3 **Framework Three: culture.** The purpose of culture has been variously defined by functional and structural anthropologists and sociologists as: fulfilling human social and physical needs; strengthening the collective ideas which give society its unity; and making meaning based on underlying, universal thought processes and codes of communication. The study of culture involves ethnography (recording everyday consumer behaviour in social context) and semiotics (understanding the codes which structure consumer behaviour and brand symbolism).

4 **Framework Four: decision-making.** Traditionally, consumer decision-making was assumed to be linear and complex. However, research in psychology (see Framework One) and economics points to much automatic, non-conscious decision-making based on heuristics (short cuts). Context (eg competitive or channel) also influences brand decision-making.

Research in all these fields is ongoing and offers exciting future opportunities for deep insights research and marketing applications.

References

Aaker, D (1991) *Managing Brand Equity*, The Free Press, New York

American Anthropological Association (2016) www.americananthro.org [last accessed February 2016]

Benveniste, E (1971) *Problems in General Linguistics*, p 218, tr M Meek, University of Miami Press

Boas, F (1920) The Methods of Ethnology, *American Anthropologist*, December

Chandler, D (2007) *Semiotics*, p 5, Routledge, Abingdon

Court, D, Elzinga, D, Mulder, S and Vetvik, O (2009) *The Consumer Decision Journey*, McKinsey Quarterly, June [last accessed February 2016]

Damasio, A (1994) *Descartes' Error: Emotion, reason and the human brain*, Putnam, New York

Devlin, J, www.ucl.ac.uk/lifelearning [last accessed February 2016]

Durkheim, E (1895) *Les Règles de la Méthode Sociologique*, Felix Alcan, Paris

Durkheim, E (1898) *Représentations Individuelles et Représentations Collectives*, Felix Alcan, Paris

Durkheim, E (1912) *Les Formes Elémentaires de la Vie Religieuse: Le système totemique en Australie*, Felix Alcan, Paris

Eco, U (1976) *A Theory of Semiotics*, p 7, Macmillan, London

Ekman, P (1972) Universal and cultural differences in facial expression of emotion, *Nebraska Symposium on Motivation*, pp 207–83

Fournier, S (2015) *Strong Brands, Strong Relationships*, p 397, Routledge, New York

Geertz, C (1973) Thick description: towards an interpretive theory of culture, *The Interpretation of Cultures*, p 323, Basic Books, New York

Giddens, A (1978) *Durkheim*, p 9, William Collins, Glasgow

Goffman, I (1959) *The Presentation of Self in Everyday Life*, Anchor Books, New York

Grandjean, D, Sander, D and Scherer, K (2008) Conscious emotional experience emerges as a function of multi-level, appraisal-drive response synchronization, *Consciousness and Cognition*, 17, pp 484–95

Greimas, A (1984) *Structural Semantics: An attempt at a method*, tr D McDowell, R Schleifer and A Velie, University of Nebraska Press, Omaha

Gueorguieva, V (2012) Subcultures as virtual communities, *Seminar BG*, May

Hatfield, E, Cacioppo, J and Rapson, R (1993) Emotional contagion, current directions, *Psychological Science*, 2, pp 96–99

Heuer, F and Reisberg, D (1990) Vivid memories of emotional events: the accuracy of remembered minutiae, *Memory and Cognition*, 18, pp 496–506

Jakobson, R (1960) Closing statements: linguistics and poetics, *Style in Language*, pp 350–377, Wiley Press, New York

James, W (1884) What is an emotion? *Mind*, 9, pp 188–205

Kahneman, D (2002) Nobel Prize Lecture

Kolko, J (2015) Design thinking comes of age, *Harvard Business Review*, September

LeDoux, J (1993) Emotional memory systems in the brain, *Behavioral Brain Research*, **58**

Lévi-Strauss, C (1945) Structural analysis in linguistics and in anthropology, *Word*, 1, August

Lévi-Strauss, C (1958) *Structural Anthropology*, Allen Lane, London

Lévi-Strauss, C (1964) *Le cru et le cuit*, Plon, Paris

Malinowski, B (1922) *Argonauts of the Western Pacific*, p 25, Routledge, Abingdon

Maslow, A (1964) *Religions, values and peak-experiences*, Ohio State University Press, Columbus

Merriam-Webster (2014) press release, http://www.merriam-webster.com/press-release/2014-word-of-the-year [last reviewed April 2016]

Mertz, E (2007) Semiotic Anthropology, *Annual Review of Anthropology*, **36**, p 343

ModelPeople Inc (2008) Creative Workshops with mothers of pre-school age girls

ModelPeople Inc (2011) Ethnographic research with club shoppers

ModelPeople Inc (2013) Healthcare shopper insights qualitative study

ModelPeople Inc (2014) Millennial eating out habits ethnographic study

Murray, H (1938) *Explorations in Personality*, Oxford University Press, Oxford

Nesse, R (2004) Natural Selection and the elusiveness of happiness, *Philosophical Transactions of the Royal Society: Biological Sciences*, **359**, pp 1333–347

Nesse, R (2009) in *Oxford Companion to Emotion and the Affective Sciences*, p 164, Oxford University Press, Oxford

Novembre, G, Zanon, M and Silani, G (2014) Empathy for social exclusion involves the sensory-discriminative component of pain: a within-subject fMRI Study, *Social Cognitive and Affective Neuroscience*, February

Ochsner, K (2000) Are affective events richly recollected or simply familiar? *Journal of Experimental Psychology*, **129**, pp 242–61

Paharia, N, Avery, J and Keinan, A (2015) Framing the Game, *Strong Brands, Strong Relationships*, pp 28–47, Routledge, New York

Panskepp, J (1998) *Affective Neuroscience: The foundations of human and animal emotions*, Oxford University Press, New York

Rimé, B (2005) *Partage Social des Emotions*, Presses Universitaires de France, Paris

Saussure, F de (1916/1983) *Course in General Linguistics*, tr Roy Harris, pp 15–16, Duckworth, London

Scherer, K (2005) What are emotions and how can they be measured?, *Social Science Information*, **44**, 4, pp 695–729

Scherer, K (2009) in *Oxford Companion to Emotion and the Affective Sciences*, p 17, Oxford University Press, Oxford

Schweder, R (2001) Deconstructing the emotions for the sake of comparative research, paper given at the *Feelings and Emotions Symposium*

Silani, G, Lamm, C, Ruff, C and Singer, T (2013) Right supramarginal gyrus is crucial to overcome emotional egocentricity bias, *Journal of Neuroscience Online*, 25 September

Simon, H (1957) A behavioral model of rational choice, *Models of Man, Social and Rational: Mathematical essays on rational human behavior in a social setting*, Wiley Press, New York

Stanovich, K and West, R (2000) Individual difference in reasoning: implications for the rationality debate?, *Behavioural and Brain Sciences*, **23**, pp 645–726

Tay, L and Diener, E (2010) Needs and subjective well-being around the world, *Journal of Personality and Social Psychology*, February

Tomkins, S (1962) *Affect Imagery Consciousness*, Springer Publishing Company, New York

Waal, F de (2009) *The Age of Empathy: Nature's lessons for a kinder society*, pp 4–11, Harmony Books, New York

Watts, A (1969) *The Book on the Taboo against Knowing Who You Are*, Jonathan Cape, London

Wierzbicka, A (1999) *Emotions across Languages and Cultures*, Cambridge University Press, New York

Wilson, E (2014) *The Meaning of Human Existence*, p 163, WW Norton, New York

Zajonc, R (1968) Attitudinal effects of mere exposure, *Journal of Personality and Social Psychology*, **9**, pp 1–27

Reshaping the marketing strategy template, based on Strategic Empathy

03

The purpose of a business is to create a customer.

PETER DRUCKER, 1954

With every product you purchase, TOMS will help a person in need.

TOMS SHOES BUSINESS MISSION, 2016

CHAPTER 3 OBJECTIVES

1 Review the elements of a marketing strategy template.

2 Explain how the marketing strategy template must be reshaped for competitive advantage, driven by new consumer priorities.

3 Explore a new model for defining the brand value proposition based on Strategic Empathy.

CASE STUDY   What's the purpose of a business?

TOMS was founded in 2006 after Blake Mycoskie noticed that many of the children in Buenos Aries, where he was volunteering, were running through the streets barefooted, with sometimes serious health consequences. Blake developed the alpargata, a canvas slip-on worn by local polo players, for the North American market, and pioneered the (now familiar) 'One for One' marketing strategy: for every pair sold the company would provide a free pair of shoes to youth in Argentina and other developing nations. Now TOMS are sold online and in hundreds of stores, including high-end retailers like Neiman Marcus and Whole Foods. TOMS' promotional strategy is sophisticated, involving university campus seeding, high-profile event marketing, social media and temporary pop-up stores. Mycoskie has maintained that a business approach and structure, rather than a charitable one, would best deliver against their mission, and this was validated in 2014, when Bain Capital acquired 50 per cent of the company, valuing it at $625 million. Mycoskie has pledged to use half of the proceeds from the sale to start a new fund to support social entrepreneurship and Bain has promised to match his investment.

Introduction

Philip Kotler (2013) notes that marketing has reinvented itself many times over the last 60 years, via new concepts and theories. Technology has been responsible for many of the changes in focus, driving innovation in online retailing, customer relationship management and consumer analytics. However, alongside that has been a major shift in the perceived purpose of a business, driven by emotional and spiritual consumer concerns. Peter Drucker (1954), often called the father of modern marketing, insisted that the purpose of a business was to create a customer. In discussing the TOMS business purpose, however, Daniel Pink (2012) noted that it creates consumers who are purchasing shoes *but also* mindfully making a purchase that transforms them into benefactors. Corporate social responsibility (CSR) is an important element in marketing strategy, such that the American Marketing Association (2016) now describes marketing as 'the activity, set of institutions and processes for creating, communicating, delivering and exchanging offerings that have value for customers, clients, partners *and society at large*'.

It's important to note, however, that CSR was not (as some cynics maintain) invented to make corporations feel good about themselves or avoid government scrutiny. Rather, CSR as an element in marketing strategy has emerged – as the TOMS case study shows – as a *competitive value-creating strategy* to address the changing emotional, moral and even spiritual priorities of consumers, especially consumers under 35. By purchasing TOMS, consumers feel that they are behaving responsibly and authentically, and demonstrating their values to others; in other words, these emotional and self-expressive benefits drive brand purchase and commitment, thereby creating brand value. Marketing strategy, at its core, expresses the architecture of brand value and the strategies and tactics to be applied to maximize brand value. *Marketing strategy formation must therefore be grounded in deep understanding of the social, cultural and psychological drivers of brand value to consumers; what we call Strategic Empathy.*

The objective of Chapter 3 is to review the elements of marketing strategy and contextualize them with reference to new consumer priorities and the theoretical frameworks explored in Chapter 2. We will suggest how the marketing strategy template must be reshaped for competitive advantage, based on Strategic Empathy, and we will propose a new model for defining the brand value proposition.

Time to reinvent marketing strategy for a new environment?

'The pace of change is accelerating', states Eric Schmidt of Google (Schmidt and Rosenberg, 2014). 'Speed has always been important but I think there is a real premium on speed today because of the competitive forces in the nature of business and the advent of technology and social media', says John Rice, Vice Chairman of GE (*Times of India*, 2015). *The Economist* (2015) notes that the adoption lag (the average time it takes slower countries to catch up with the use of a technology in pioneering countries) has shortened to 13 years for mobile phones. Technology, social media and online shopping with same-day delivery have given rise to consumer expectations of instant gratification. Consumers now exercise much of the power that brands themselves used to enjoy: they define the brand narrative through social media and purchase brands across multiple channels, identifying the lowest price using online tools. Considerable marketing effort is now expended on developing strategic and tactical responses to a flood of consumer analytics and real-time feedback from social media.

In Chapter 1, we argued that traditional annual strategy planning does not recognize the reality of emergent strategy formation as a response to a fast-changing environment. *Could it be that the time is now here, when nurturing emergent marketing strategy takes precedence over formal strategy planning?* If in fact this is the case, then it follows that nurturing broad and deep organizational understanding of how consumers think, feel and behave, and how the company can create superior value for them, is even more critical when lead-times to implementation are compressed, leaving little time for formal planning and hierarchical marketing management. In these new circumstances, Strategic Empathy acts like 'muscle memory', enabling employees across functions to deliver consumer and customer value at a faster pace. For example, Zara is a pioneer of fast fashion, shipping new products to its stores twice a week, but, unusually at this level of the industry, it produces all its designs in-house, relying on the tacit knowledge and consumer empathy of the 'marketing strategists' in their design department to produce what their consumers want. Percassi – the company which brought Zara to Italy – has founded a fast cosmetics brand called Kiko, which is only distributed through its own stores with dedicated brand salespeople, relying on their superior customer empathy to deliver brand value. Clearly, employees' empathy for consumers is regarded as an important competitive advantage by these 'fast' corporations. Additionally, now that consumer feedback has become instantaneous via new feedback channels like social media or online retail, and instant response is required, then employees at many different levels in the organization have become, de facto, 'marketing strategists', with the ability to adapt and implement marketing strategy on an emergent basis.

In order to avoid lack of direction and operational chaos, corporations must place high priority on creating a solid foundational marketing strategy, not as a fixed plan for the future but as a *roadmap for adaptive strategy formation*. This reshaped marketing strategy does not set strategies and plans in stone but brings the target consumer, customer or shopper empathetically to life and creates a vision for the future, in terms of how the company's differentiated value propositions (brands) will uniquely meet his or her needs. Corporations must also place high priority on communicating the marketing strategy roadmap to employees in a way that inspires consumer and customer empathy, so that they have the knowledge and motivation to execute the brand value proposition.

So what exactly are the key elements of the reshaped marketing strategy? Drucker (1954) stated that a business has only two functions, marketing and innovation, so it follows that marketing strategy is central to overall corporate strategy. Therefore, marketing strategy formation must go hand-in-hand with corporate strategy formation. In the next section, we will look briefly at the elements of a corporate strategy.

Corporate strategy components

A corporate strategy includes components which are more long-lasting like the Mission, Vision and Values statements, and also elements which are updated regularly – usually annually, as part of the formal strategic planning cycle – like Objectives and Strategies.

- **Mission statement.** The Mission statement is an overarching, timeless expression of the company's purpose and aspiration relative to its consumers, customers and other stakeholders, addressing what the company seeks to accomplish and how it seeks to accomplish it. It's a declaration of corporate ethics and values and how the company makes life better for its stakeholders. Stakeholders are those who have an interest in the company; for example, employees, consumers, customers, shareholders, suppliers. A statement of company culture may also be appropriate if there is something unique about it. For example, the UK retailer, John Lewis, states that 'The Partnership's ultimate purpose is the happiness of all its members, through their worthwhile and satisfying employment in a successful business. Because the Partnership is owned in trust for its members, they share the responsibilities of ownership as well as its rewards: profit, knowledge and power.' A Mission statement is ideally short like Facebook's: 'Give people the power to share and make the world more open and connected', or it can be developed into a longer manifesto of mission and values, like SC Johnson's 'This We Believe', a four-page statement first developed in 1886, which addresses five stakeholder groups including 'the world community'. The idea that society is a stakeholder for corporations has been expressed in the concept of 'shared value' (Porter and Kramer, 2011); that is the idea that business should generate value in a way that also produces value for society by addressing some of its challenges. For example, Nestlé redesigned its coffee procurement processes from small growers, providing advice and support on farming and then paying a premium for better beans. Higher yields and quality increased the growers' incomes, the environmental impact of farms shrank, and Nestlé's reliable supply of good coffee grew significantly, creating 'shared value'.

- **Vision statement.** A Vision statement is forward-looking and represents a viable dream about how the organization will look in five or more years. Vision defines what the organization aspires to be *and to do for its stakeholders. Consumers and customers must be central to the vision.* When working with clients on a Vision statement, I ask them to create a mental picture of the future, using words, images and stories. It's important that the vision is not just a pipe-dream but feels real and achievable, albeit at a stretch; and that strategies are designed with the vision in mind.

- **Values statement.** Values are enduring core beliefs. They're distinctive guiding principles for the operations of the organization, which never change. Values should be written in a way that relates to and inspires employees because, as we explore in Chapter 8, employees want to work for companies with a strong sense of purpose and values. For example, Coca-Cola's Values statement is as follows (Coca-Cola, 2016):

    Our shared values guide our actions and describe how we behave in the world:

    Leadership: The courage to shape a better future

    Collaboration: Leverage collective genius

    Integrity: Be real

    Accountability: If it is to be, it's up to me

    Passion: Committed in heart and mind

    Diversity: As inclusive as our brands

    Quality: What we do, we do well

- **Strategic objectives or goals.** These are long-term areas of strategic focus (usually spanning a three- to five-year time horizon) and create the strategic framework for annual strategic planning. They answer the question of what you must focus on to achieve your vision. Objectives are set based on the broad strategy selected by the company as to where to compete and how to identify and leverage sources of competitive advantage (what the company is best at doing) to deliver a differentiated value proposition. Kaplan (2010) recommends that objectives be set in four main areas:

    - Financial.

    - Consumer/customer value proposition.

- Internal processes (such as manufacturing, R&D or sales).
- Learning and growth:
  - **Human capital:** the skills, talent and knowledge that a company's employees possess. Kaplan and Norton (2004) recommend that companies identify the employee roles which most impact strategic implementation and concentrate learning development here.
  - **Information capital:** the company's databases, information systems, networks and technology infrastructure.
  - **Organization capital:** the company's culture, its leadership, how aligned its people are with its strategic goals, and employees' ability to share knowledge.

- **Functional or operational strategies.** These are the short- to medium-term strategies (usually one- to three-year) developed by each internal function which spell out the objectives and approaches which will be used to deliver the corporate strategy. Marketing strategy is a functional strategy. It will be evident from the areas of objective-setting recommended by Kaplan (2010) that there is substantial crossover between corporate and marketing strategy content in terms of defining the customer and the customer value proposition. However, Kaplan also identifies human and information capital as elements of corporate strategy, meaning that consumer knowledge and learning, and the way that consumer understanding is integrated into the company's information networks, is also an important area of shared responsibility. This is consistent with the process of strategic learning, which we described in Chapter 1.

- **Budget and resources.** Financial objectives, along with operational strategic priorities, will dictate the allocation of budget and other resources (eg human resources, investment capital) across the organization.

- **Scorecard.** Corporate strategy usually identifies the key performance indicators (KPIs) set for each strategic objective, so that performance can be tracked.

The reshaped marketing strategy

In its simplest terms, a marketing strategy must answer three key questions:

1 Where are we now?

2 Where are we going?

3 What direction should we take to get there?

Let's now look at the elements of marketing strategy which answer each of these questions. For simplicity, we will assume that the marketing strategy is being developed for a single consumer brand rather than for a portfolio of brands or an SBU (strategic business unit). We will also assume that the planning time frame is one to three years.

1. Where are we now?

Figure 3.1 Marketing environment

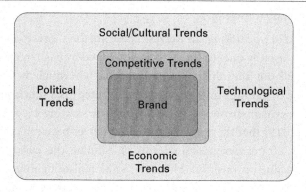

SOURCE: ModelPeople Inc

This strategic question is answered in the marketing strategy by an analysis which is often called 'current situation'. It summarizes the current position of the brand relative to its consumers, from multiple perspectives using financial assessment, brand analytics, consumer research and future trends analysis. For example, the analysis typically includes current market share, financial strength, channel distribution, market penetration, brand positioning and trends in target consumer perceptions (positive and negative) relative to competitors. However, in addition to looking at brand and competitive (micro) trends, it's also important to analyse trends in the marketing macro-environment, broadly defined as social/cultural, technological, economic and political trends (see Figure 3.1). Macro-trends can have a significant impact on the brand current situation. For example, the major supermarket chains in the UK have been hit by several changes in their marketing macro-environment in the last few years, including: technological (especially the shift to online for non-food purchases – in 2014, nearly 90 per cent of consumers aged 25–44 purchased online in the prior 12 months (ONS, 2014));

economic (squeezed incomes and reduced spending on food following the recession); and social/cultural (more eating out in fast casual restaurants and a decline in frequency of shopping). As a result of these macro-environmental changes, the supermarket chains are struggling for profitability. A SWOT (strengths, weaknesses, opportunities and threats) analysis may be developed to summarize the current situation and identify future marketing opportunities and challenges. Futuring may also be conducted to model further-out macro-trends which might impact the brand. For example, it's demonstrable that some of the macro-trends now impacting UK supermarkets could have been predicted some 15 years ago, particularly changes in shopping habits.

2. Where are we going?

This strategic question should be answered with a compelling vision for the future of the brand which explains brand goals. This vision is articulated in several important elements of a marketing strategy:

- target consumer or market segments;
- differentiated brand positioning;
- desired brand experience and consumer journey;
- brand objectives;
- financial projections.

We will explore each element in turn and identify models for expressing the key information.

Target consumer or market segments

As we explained earlier, bringing the target consumer to life empathetically is a key priority for the new marketing strategy. This process must start with describing the consumer or customer groups that represent the target market for the brand. Consumers can be segmented into groups based on many different variables of which some of the most common are: geographical market, demographics, attitudes and mindset, behaviour (eg product usage, purchase channel) and need states (functional, emotional and self-expressive). Decisions must be made as to the key variables to choose to define the segments. For example, luxury fashion brand consumer segments may be defined more by mindset and emotional and self-expressive need states than by geographical market (luxury fashion is a global consumer segment, though local cultural and social factors may still dictate variations in the marketing mix). Segment-defining variables and segment size must be modelled, for example, by doing a quantitative segmentation study and using regression analysis to identify discrete clusters of variables and estimate segment incidence within the consumer population. Other approaches include modelling product market segments (demand spaces) derived from conducting custom research or buying syndicated retail sales or product usage data from companies such as Nielsen or IRI. Increasingly, predictive analytics (Davenport, 2014) is used to model the most valuable consumer segments based on purchase behaviour data (derived, for example, from a loyalty card like the Tesco Clubcard or from unique customer records held by the corporation) and to identify (and target) the most valuable segments.

Defining segments is not, however, a purely quantitative exercise. As we argued in Chapter 1, quantitative data cannot help us *imagine who* our consumers and customers are or have empathy with *how they think and feel.* Therefore, once segments have been identified and sized in the marketing strategy, it is essential to bring them empathetically to life; that is to show the real people behind the data. In Chapters 4–8, we will explain how the strategy team can develop consumer empathy, and also how to develop media which will inspire the many 'emergent marketing strategists' in the organization to develop empathy with target consumers. Practically, there may be limitations on including empathy media (such as, for example, consumer documentary video) within a formal marketing strategy, although one can envision a future in which the entire marketing strategy is communicated in an entertaining and insightful medium like video. At minimum, the consumer should be brought to life via *personae*, or profiles of a representative consumer in each target segment: who they are and their relationship with our brand in the context of their everyday lives.

Differentiated brand positioning

Brand positioning is defined as *what the brand stands for in the mind of consumers* (Ries and Trout, 2001). Therefore, brand positioning must articulate *the way in which the brand delivers value to consumers, as distinct from competitive brands.* This is done by articulating the benefits which the brand uniquely delivers to consumers. As we saw in Chapter 2, consumer needs – and therefore desired brand benefits – are typically expressed in a hierarchy: functional (what the product does for me in practical terms);

emotional (how the brand makes me feel); self-expressive (how the brand makes me look); and self-actualizing (how the brand inspires me to fulfil personal purpose or values). However, a brand triggers many different, sometimes random, associations in the consumer's mind, built up over time through the consumer's own experience of the brand or through tribal associations. These associations include attributes (both functional and emotional), words, images, ideas, symbols, colours, logos, which tribes use the brand and how, and so on. Therefore, brand positioning must also articulate the key associations it wishes to embed in the consumer's mind: what facts, symbols and ideas define the brand? We must also define how we want to project the brand's 'personality', which indicates the type of relationship we are inviting consumers to enjoy with the brand.

Defining brand positioning, and ensuring that all elements of the marketing mix (eg product quality, design, price, service) are aligned with this positioning is a key priority for marketing strategy formation. If we have empathy with our target consumers, brand positioning should be simple, according to Drucker's famous quote: 'The aim of marketing is to know and understand the customer so well that the product fits him and sells itself' (Drucker, 1997). Marketing strategy must define *how the brand wants to deliver value to consumers* and *what key brand associations it wishes to nurture* by means of the marketing mix *over the long term*. This definition is made via an articulation of brand positioning architecture, which is therefore a key element of marketing strategy.

Brand positioning architecture is often expressed in the form of a Positioning Wheel or Positioning Pyramid which express key brand benefits and associations in slightly different ways (see Figures 3.2 and 3.3). The pyramid has the benefit of encouraging strategy teams to ladder attributes and functional benefits into so-called 'higher-order' emotional and self-expressive benefits. This approach is grounded in means-end theory (Gutman, 1982), which states that it is possible to link within a hierarchy (that is, to 'ladder' from bottom to top) product attributes, product consequences (consumer benefits) and an individual's values. However, this pattern of brand elements may not be so neatly arranged in the consumer's mind, which is reflected in the positioning wheel. Many corporations have a preferred model, but I have used both successfully. At the end of this chapter, we will explore a refined model developed by ModelPeople, which we feel better articulates the importance of social and cultural context for developing consumer empathy.

Figure 3.2 Brand positioning wheel

SOURCE: ModelPeople Inc

Figure 3.3 Brand positioning pyramid

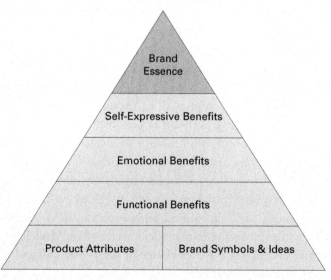

SOURCE: ModelPeople Inc

For ease of communication, brand positioning is also expressed in a written statement which identifies the target consumer and need, the product or category descriptor, the key differentiated benefits (sometimes called the discriminator) and the facts that support the benefits, called 'support' or 'reasons to believe' (RTBs).

Tool box

Brand positioning statement: template and example

Template:

> For [target consumer] who [need/want...], brand X is the [product or category descriptor] which provides [differentiated benefit/discriminator] because [reasons to believe].

Example:

> *For urban, health-conscious men and women who care about the quality and sustainability of what they put in their bodies, Trustworthy Tea is the only brand of ready-to-drink tea which offers tea refreshment you can feel good about, because it's brewed with organic, fair-trade leaf tea and less natural sugar (with none of the artificial additives) of other RTD teas.*

Brand positioning architecture is developed based on:

- Understanding what the brand *currently* stands for in the mind of the consumer, derived from:
  - quantitative attribute data;
  - deep qualitative insights into non-conscious brand associations.
- Strategic choices about the *future* development of the brand value proposition.

In Chapters 5–7, we explore methods for uncovering deep qualitative insights into the non-conscious emotional and cultural brand associations and explain the process for making strategic choices about the brand value proposition.

Desired brand experience and consumer journey

Brand positioning (how consumers see the brand) is impacted not just by tangible marketing mix elements such as product, price or communications, but by the complete experience (or journey) the consumer has with the brand, which includes many intangible elements. This journey includes shopping and post-purchase experiences as well as brand and product consumption experiences. Therefore, the desired *consumer journey* might also be articulated in marketing strategy, in order to identify critical pain points and opportunities that must be addressed in the marketing mix.

Tool box

Consumer journey mapping for brand positioning

Consumer journey (CJ) mapping describes the route consumers take as they interact with the company's products and services. It integrates quantitative research and company data (such as records of sales or service interactions) with qualitative experiential and emotional insights. A typical CJ map includes:

- Consumer actions/process, usually broken into sequential chronological phases (eg online research or shopping, store shopping, out-of-box product experience, service call, complaints). In the case of a leisure experience like Disney World, this may include interactions with the brand via staff, systems and property at multiple locations or day-parts throughout a visit as well as before the visit (booking a ticket). In the case of a hotel, it will include interactions from making a reservation through being welcomed at check-in and getting a good night's sleep and start to the following day.

- Consumer motivations, needs and behaviour at each step in the process. For example, La Quinta Inns has identified how its guests want to feel when they arrive, when they are in their room or public areas, and when they leave.

- Areas of particular importance in the overall customer experience.

- Brand satisfaction; pain points or dissatisfaction with the overall experience.

- Opportunities for emotional engagement. For example, a hotel chain will train desk staff to welcome guests in a specific way.

- Business touchpoints and process, including roles, systems and departments of the provider.

- Key performance indicators (KPIs): eg sales, abandoned shopping carts, complaints, social media sentiment.

Finally, brand objectives and financial projections must be expressed in answer to the question 'Where are we going?'.

Brand objectives

Objectives define brand goals over the designated time period, and how success will be measured (the KPIs). Objectives are related to brand financial performance, consumer conversion (eg trial, purchase frequency, based on company data or usage and awareness research) and key marketing mix initiatives (eg the launch of new products or increases in media budgets).

Financial projections

Projections will model sales, share and profits based on marketing assumptions. Predictive modelling is used to determine the optimum bundle of product, price and promotional support to achieve financial objectives.

3. What direction should we take to get there?

Once the future direction of the brand has been established, the strategy team must develop the detailed strategies and plans which are required to make progress towards brand objectives. This combination of functional strategies is called the 'marketing mix': defined as the set of variables which can be used to influence consumer response – if you like, the levers we can pull to deliver the chosen brand positioning and achieve the marketing objectives.

Kotler (2015) dubbed the marketing mix 'The Four Ps' – product, place, price, promotion – though many attempts have been made over the three decades since to add further Ps. Kotler himself has suggested that a fifth P, 'purpose' be added to reflect the importance of what he calls 'social responsibility marketing'. 'Purpose' defines brand responsibility over and above meeting consumer needs and making a return for shareholders: it defines responsibility to society (and sometimes beyond, to the natural world). These responsibilities are not necessarily dissonant: 'purpose' can be a compelling dimension of brand positioning for consumers, customers and employees. For example, UK brand The Body Shop was an early pioneer of 'social responsibility marketing'. (Body Shop founder, Anita Roddick (1991) famously proclaimed: 'I want to work for a company that contributes to and is part of the community. I want something not just to invest in. I want something to believe in.'). The Body Shop grew from a single shop in Brighton to a global corporation which was eventually sold to L'Oréal.

Especially for Millennial consumers (born between 1982 and 2000 and now the largest consumer cohort, representing over 90 million consumers in the US alone, and nearly 15 million in the UK), 'purpose' has become more than a lever to pull in order to influence consumer response. It has become an essential strand in brand and corporate DNA. Millennials want to work for a company which *inspires* them, as we will discuss in Chapter 8. Consumers are prepared to punish brands which fail to articulate and live up to their wider purpose, and reward brands which do.

MINI CASE STUDY

Consumers reward brands which deliver on their stated purpose and punish those which don't:

- Chipotle enjoyed a wave of publicity in 2015 when it refused to serve pork that had not been humanely produced, in contravention of their stated purpose. It's been calculated that the short-term sales loss was more than made up for by the long-term gain in brand equity. Chipotle (2016) now dedicate a whole section of their website to communicating their move to UK pig farmers.

- Protesters disrupted Primark and Benetton stores in London following the collapse of the Rana Plaza building in Bangladesh in 2013. A War on Want spokesman claimed that 'If Primark had taken its responsibility to those workers seriously, no one need have died this week (Metro, 2013). Primark paid worker compensation.

I conclude that 'purpose' is certainly an element in business mission and potentially also in the refined brand positioning model I introduce at the end of this chapter. Now, let's review Kotler's original four Ps: product, place, price and promotion.

Product/innovation

The 'product' (or service) associated with a brand name is often the primary element in terms of delivering the consumer value proposition. A product or service may have tangible (physical) elements, which can be readily identified and evaluated, and also intangible (non-physical) elements which are less readily identified. For example, I purchase a new car (tangible product) and also receive a free warranty (intangible product). Great brands have both tangible and intangible product elements which aim to create a multi-dimensional value bundle for consumers. For example, Hyundai vehicles are readily compared with other vehicle brands in terms of features and styling. However, during the recession, they launched the Hyundai Assurance scheme, which offered a return policy to anyone who had leased a Hyundai on approved financing and subsequently lost their job or became ill, thereby creating a highly valuable intangible product element which grew consideration and sales and also enhanced the brand's reputation for consumer empathy.

The product form can change over time – in fact it must do according to Levitt (1960) – to meet a changing marketing environment and evolving consumer needs but still deliver against its brand proposition. For example, Yellow Pages began in 1886 and still exists in print, but the online version has translated the brand's offline dominance in service listings and search into a new product form, making it one of the most frequently searched terms on the internet. Alternatively, a brand can act as a platform for the launch of brand extensions which offer variations in product form (eg milk chocolate and dark chocolate KitKat); or sub-brands which have a different product form and value proposition which are linked to the parent brand.

MINI CASE STUDY   Product proliferation: a cautionary tale

In the 1990s, Procter & Gamble transformed an old-fashioned skincare brand, Oil of Olay, into a 'prestige at mass' brand called 'Olay Total Effects'. In less than a decade the Olay brand surpassed $2.5 billion in annual sales, achieved by launching sub-brands including Total Effects, Regenerist, Definity and Pro-X, which attracted more prestige shoppers at vastly higher prices. However, over the past five years, Olay's sales have declined and now the brand is cutting its offerings by one-sixth and focusing its brand proposition around anti-aging. Says ex-CEO AG Lafley (*Wall Street Journal*, 2015), who has claimed credit for leading the product proliferation strategy: 'Consumers only spend a few seconds in front of any given shelf. They are trying to deselect as fast as they can and they just can't do it.' As we saw in Chapter 2, behavioural scientists have demonstrated that too much choice can confuse and deter shoppers from purchasing. For example, in one experiment (Iyengar and Lepper, 2000), conducted in a California grocery store, researchers set up a sampling table with a display of 24 jams to taste; on a different day they displayed just 6. Shoppers who took part in the sampling were rewarded with a discount voucher to buy any jam of the same brand in the store. It turned out that more shoppers stopped at the display when there were 24 jams. But when it came to buying afterwards, 30 per cent of those who stopped at the 6-jam table went on to purchase a pot, against merely 3 per cent of those who were faced with the selection of 24.

As Drucker implied several decades ago, innovation has become a key focus of corporate and marketing strategy and investment, and has therefore become a key application for the Strategic Empathy Process. In Chapter 2, we discussed 'design empathy' as a framework for developing product strategy and innovation and in Chapters 5–6 we describe research methodologies which are used to develop it.

Place (channel and shopper marketing)

Place refers to the distribution channel: where consumers can purchase the brand, whether it's a grocery, drug or mass retail store, a club warehouse like Costco or an online channel like Amazon. As we saw in Chapter 2, marketing strategists have for some years now realized the impact of channel context and of influencing shopper behaviour at point-of-sale to brand growth and have invested in specialist shopper insights, shopper marketing and key account resources. Using sophisticated data analytics, marketers are also able to identify patterns in channel and other brand interactions which are driving desired shopper behaviours. For example, a healthcare company identified that shoppers collecting prescriptions from drug stores were also likely to buy related OTC products such as painkillers or vitamins, and create appropriate linkages in shopper marketing approach.

Price

Price is a complex element of the marketing mix. Pricing strategy requires strategic choices to be made relative to other components of marketing and corporate strategy, such as, for example:

- the consumer value proposition (eg a premium product at a price premium to competition);

- market share strategy over time (eg penetration pricing is low at launch to build market share quickly, perhaps to create barriers to competition or to amortize manufacturing investment over a shorter time period);
- desired brand profitability.

Multivariate techniques are typically used to model consumer demand at different pricing levels and product value bundles, to support these strategic decisions. However, these models are prone to inaccuracy if a key variable is not properly estimated, for example, if a key retail account does not give the brand the expected level of distribution or shelf position. There may also be unforeseen macro-environmental trends which influence demand. In some categories, such as airlines or hotels, where supply is limited, dynamic pricing allows profit maximization by pricing products higher at times of peak consumer demand. Consumers may also prefer to fix pricing dynamically through sites such as Priceline.com or eBay.

Promotion (communication)

Promotion includes advertising and other brand communications (eg PR, social media) as well as sales promotion (eg discounting, promotions such as BOGOF). Tactical activities like these take up a significant proportion of marketing resource, and represent a significant cost to the brand P&L, both in terms of direct costs of media and agency fees and lost profitability from sales discounting. The promotion or communications strategy must articulate: the target consumer; the messaging strategy (what to say about the brand and how to dramatize the message); the media to be used and the budget.

Emphasis has shifted dramatically over several decades, from managing the brand message and medium (eg TV advertising and targeted media buys) to engaging the consumer in co-creating the message and finding the brand in a relevant and aspirational medium. Kotler (2013) has noted the emergence of three new types of marketing – co-creation marketing, social media marketing and tribalism – related to this:

- **Co-creation marketing.** Value creation used to be viewed as company-centric and, as Prahalad and Ramaswamy (2004) note, communications used to flow from the firm to consumers. Now, however, connected consumers are discovering that consumer-to-consumer communication is an alternative, and highly trusted, source of brand information which empowers them to co-create brand reputation and image, and requires marketers to respond. Co-creation is enabled by the internet which connects large groups of consumers and enables them to share views through social media, marketplaces like Amazon and forums like TripAdvisor.

- **Social media** has enabled every consumer to become media channel and content producer in one. Bloggers and YouTube content publishers command followings in the millions, but even consumers with small circles of friends can be influential in spreading a message. Moreover, consumers, especially Millennials, enjoy interacting with branded social media content. A survey (ANA, 2014) showed that one-third of consumers aged 19–35 say: 'When a brand uses social media, I like that brand more' (compared with only 16 per cent of consumers over age 35). Other consumers observe (and we assume, are influenced by) social media activity even though they do not engage. Also, branded social media can generate click-through to buy products. For example, cosmetics brand Urban Decay has aggregated all brand and consumer-generated content on a section of their website called 'UD All Access', where consumers can browse Instagram photos posted by consumers which feature UD looks and also shop for products. Hence, brands now need to develop social media and other online content which is compelling enough to be spread by millions of consumers. Berger (2013) suggests that useful information or stories with emotional content are shared by individuals because they want to look smart to others. However, Berger claims only 7 per cent of word-of-mouth consumer communication happens online, so marketers still need to pay attention to creating old-fashioned (offline) word-of-mouth. Mass media retains high potential to do this: for example, over 100 million Americans watch the Superbowl ads each year and share opinions, both offline and online.

- **Tribalism.** 'A tribe is a group of people connected to one another, connected to a leader and connected to an idea' (Godin, 2008). Brands can communicate with consumers in a highly targeted way by connecting with tribes and aligning themselves with the tribal 'idea'. For example, the athletic shoe brand ASICS sponsors marathon events and, by so doing, connects the brand in a leadership role with the 'tribe' of serious runners who are its core consumers, and for whom running (and their chosen apparel) is a key part of who they are. Tribes are also an essential source of consumer insight and empathy, as we discuss in Chapter 5.

A new brand positioning architecture

We argued in Chapter 2 that developing empathy with consumers requires deep understanding of how they think, feel and behave. The most powerful brands not only have emotional resonance with consumers, but also cultural resonance, that is they reflect back the way humans behave in their relevant social groups. Therefore, brand positioning has to reflect both emotional and cultural meaning to target consumers. Brands do not communicate cultural and emotional meaning in a rational way but by weaving an authentic story; what Holt (2012) calls an 'ideology'. A brand ideology is a heuristic; it helps the consumer choose between brands without engaging System 2 thinking. An ideology can tap a fact about the brand (eg according to Holt, the location of Jack Daniels' distillery in rural frontier country supports the brand's authentic whiskey ideology), or into a subculture or social movement (eg Chipotle's commitment to use only humanely produced meat). Or it can weave together emotional and cultural meaning, like Coca-Cola does when it expresses 'happiness' as both a feeling and the 'new world' optimism that's a key strand in the United States' DNA. A brand ideology can also break out of cultural 'orthodoxy': the way that competitors express cultural meaning (Holt, 2012). For example, Jack Daniels broke out of the cultural orthodoxy of 1960s' masculinity, by expressing whiskey authenticity instead of a classy modern lifestyle. Another example is Mini, which celebrated 'small' as a cultural idea, when it launched in the US, at a time when the best-selling vehicles were eight-seater SUVs with 5-litre engines.

Therefore, the core of our reshaped brand positioning model (shown in Figure 3.4 below) is 'brand meaning': that is, the emotional and cultural meaning of the brand to our target consumers. It asks the strategy team to consider cultural unorthodoxy: how can the brand create a distinctive emotional or cultural meaning from its competitors, like Mini? Additionally, our model asks the question: 'How does the brand inspire me?' We noted earlier that consumers want to buy brands that inspire them and people want to work for companies that inspire them. When consumers have all their basic needs met – as most in developed countries now do – they want the brands they buy to represent a bigger social or cultural idea, an idea that helps them self-actualize, or realize their own purpose and meaning on earth.

Figure 3.4 Reshaped brand positioning model

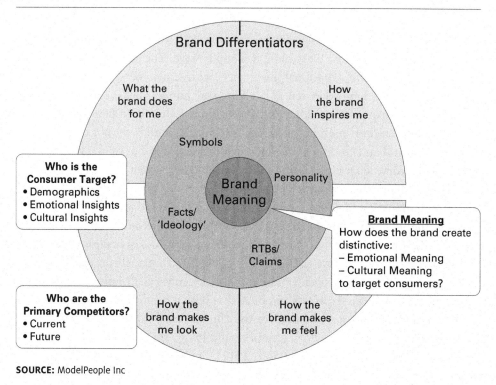

SOURCE: ModelPeople Inc

Truly powerful brand positioning enhances the value proposition and drives brand loyalty by engaging consumers in a narrative, which reflects their needs, emotions, culture and ideals: how consumers think, feel and behave; and their vision for the world around them.

Chapter 3 summary

1 Marketing is a core business function, defined as a process of value creation with the consumer or customer at the centre.

2 Marketing response lead-times are accelerating and marketing strategy is increasingly emergent (rather than planned). However, in order to avoid lack of direction and operational chaos, corporations must place high priority on creating a solid foundational marketing strategy not as a fixed plan for the future but as a roadmap for emergent and adaptive strategy formation.

3 The new marketing strategy brings the target consumer, customer or shopper and the brand proposition empathetically to life and creates a vision for the future.

4 Corporations must also place high priority on communicating the marketing strategy roadmap to employees so that they can implement the defined consumer value proposition (the brand).

5 Marketing strategy is central to overall corporate strategy. Therefore, marketing strategy formation must go hand-in-hand with corporate strategy formation.

6 In its simplest terms, the marketing strategy must answer three key questions:

   a) Where are we now? (current situation analysis)

   b) Where are we going? (brand objectives)

   c) What direction shall we take to get there? (brand positioning, marketing mix)

7 Brand positioning is *what the brand stands for in the mind of consumers*. Defining a differentiated brand positioning (how the brand delivers value to consumers as distinct from competitive brands) is a key priority for marketing strategy formation.

8 The consumer value proposition is expressed in brand positioning architecture. Two models are explained. A reshaped model is proposed which puts the brand's emotional and cultural meaning at the core and also asks *how does the brand inspire me?* with a wider social purpose.

References

American Marketing Association (2016) https://www.ama.org [last reviewed February 2016]

Association of National Advertisers (ANA) (2014)

Berger, J (2013) *Contagious*, Simon & Schuster, New York

Chipotle (2016) http://chipotle.com/carnitas

Coca-Cola (2016) http://www.coca-cola.co.uk/about-us/mission-vision-and-values [last reviewed February 2016]

Davenport, T (2014) A predictive analytics primer, *Harvard Business Review*, 2 September

Drucker, P (1954) *The Practice of Management*, Harper Collins, London

Drucker, P (1997) in Kotler, P, Standing Room Only: Strategies for marketing the performing arts, p 33, Harvard Business Press, Boston, MA

Godin, S (2008) *Tribes*, Piatkus, New York

Gutman, J (1982) A means-end chain model based on consumer categorization processes, *Journal of Marketing*, **96**, pp 209–25

Holt, D (2012) in *Handbook of Marketing Strategy*, ed V Shankar and G Carpenter, pp 306–17, Edward Elgar, New York

Iyengar, S and Lepper, M (2000) When Choice is Demotivating: Can one desire too much of a good thing?, *Journal of Personal and Social Psychology*, **79**, 6, pp 995–1006

Kaplan, R (2010) Conceptual foundations of the balanced scorecard, *Harvard Business Review*, Working Paper

Kaplan, R and Norton, D (2004) Measuring the strategic readiness of intangible assets, *Harvard Business Review*, 1 February

Kotler, P (2013) in The Thinker Interview, *CKGSB Knowledge*, 8 October

Kotler, P (2015) *Principles of Marketing*, Prentice-Hall, New York

Levitt, T (1960) Marketing Myopia, *Harvard Business Review*, July–August

Metro UK (2013) 27 April 2013

ONS (2014) Office of National Statistics, UK

Pink, D (2012) Drive: The surprising truth about what motivates us, p 134, Penguin, New York

Porter, M and Kramer, M (2011) Creating Shared Value, *Harvard Business Review*, January–February

Prahalad, C and Ramaswamy, V (2004) Co-Creation experiences: the next practice in value creation, *Journal of Interactive Marketing*, **18** (Summer)

Ries, A and Trout, J (2001) *Positioning: The battle for your mind*, McGraw-Hill, New York

Roddick, A (1991) *Body and Soul: How to succeed in business and change the World*, Ebury Publishing, London

Schmidt, E and Rosenberg, J (2014) *How Google Works*, p 10, John Murray, London

The Economist (2015) Time and the Company, 5 December

Times of India (2015), 9 January

Wall Street Journal (2015) 29 December

The Strategic Empathy Process for marketing strategy formation

04

Overview

Tell me and I forget, teach me and I may remember, involve me and I learn.

BENJAMIN FRANKLIN, 1706–90

CHAPTER 4 OBJECTIVES

1 Introduce the three phases of the Strategic Empathy Process: Immerse, Activate, Inspire.

2 Explore the importance of Pre-Planning, including framing the marketing strategic issue and deciding who should be part of the strategy team.

3 Explain how to design and implement a Strategic Learning Journey including:

   a) developing strategic objectives and scope;

   b) designing an immersive research methodology;

   c) activating insights into strategy.

4 Discuss the need for communicating insights to the wider stakeholder group to ensure collective learning and empathy.

CASE STUDY   Strategic learning: the culture and psychology of meal preparation in the US

'I was afraid to cook!' said Jenny, a Texas mom of two young children. We had just finished reviewing video footage of grocery store shoppers in a two-day activation session (ModelPeople, 2007). Two weeks earlier, we had run immersive ethnographic field research, incorporating Deep Visualizations of emotional memories of family meal preparation. 'I was afraid of disappointing my husband because his mom had great meals growing up and I didn't want to mess it up', confessed Jenny, giving us insight into the emotional pressures which shoppers face. 'But it's a great feeling when we sit down at the table as a family to eat a home-cooked meal, and talk about our day. A lot of families don't do that, but we do, every night.'

In the research, we had uncovered how essential it was to shoppers, emotionally, to bring their families together to eat dinner at the table, but for women shoppers, doing this had especial cultural relevance. As we reviewed dog-eared collections of recipes handed down from their own moms and other relatives, it became clear that learning to cook, and bringing the family together to the table to eat a home-cooked meal, were essential parts of making the transition from being a daughter and a wife to being a mom: the new 'clan matriarch', if you will. 'My momma died when I was just married' said Becky, showing us her mom's card index file of hand-written recipes. 'It brings me closer to her when I cook like she did.' In terms of Maslow's hierarchy of psychological needs, the family mealtime comprehensively addresses the bottom half of the pyramid: physical sustenance, shelter and safety within the clan unit and love/belonging. For many women, though, being a successful home cook also fulfilled the very top part of the pyramid at least in part: she self-actualized her chosen role as a mom, as a wife, and even as a daughter, strengthening the bond with her own mother as the cultural baton was successfully passed on.

In our ethnographies, we also explored the semiotics of 'family mealtime'. In US homes, the most important room is the open kitchen connected to the family room. A glance at any of the reality shows on HGTV (Home & Garden TV: an entire cable channel devoted to the achievement of a perfect 'family' home) confirms the importance of this 'open-concept' living space where parents can cook and have a clear sight-line to young children; or where a couple can entertain and not be disconnected from their guests. US families spend most of their time in this space. Huge fridge-freezers store packaged snacks and prepared fresh foods like pre-cut carrots and pre-grated cheese, so 'a meal' can be quickly produced, to meet the demands of a family who may be juggling shift work, different school

Figure 4.1 Framed sampler: 'A Kitchen Blessing'

SOURCE: ModelPeople Inc, 2007

hours and after-school activities and commitments to family, social or community activities (see Figure 4.1 for a framed sampler owned by one of the moms in our study). Data (CDC, 2011) showed that only about a third of children eat a meal with their families six to seven days a week and over one-quarter eat together less than three times a week. In the meantime, parents were exposed to a barrage

(Siferlin, 2012) of negative data reporting and imagery about the potentially devastating effects of kids eating alone, including obesity, depression and even drug and alcohol abuse.

The other interesting observation to be gleaned from surfing HGTV is that many Americans aspire to have 'a separate formal dining room'. This is a room which may only get used a few times a year, but always for gatherings of family and close friends. The archetypal family meal is Thanksgiving, which is a ritual meal usually cooked by 'mom' (the matriarch of the extended family). Hosting Thanksgiving for the first time at her house is a common rite of passage for a newly married or independent daughter. The Thanksgiving meal is deeply enshrined in US culture, even having been illustrated by artist Norman Rockwell as one of the Four Freedoms, a series of paintings reflecting the essential human rights described by FD Roosevelt in his 1941 State of the Union address. My son re-enacted pilgrims and Indians at the first Thanksgiving meal every year in elementary school in California, where we cooked turkey in the heat of a Santa Ana wind blowing from the desert. Thanksgiving is the time of the year when families are supposed to be 'home' together. Airports are jammed as everyone tries to fly home for the meal, and the Thanksgiving comedy forms an entire movie genre showing the trials of holiday travel on *Planes, Trains and Automobiles*. Many restaurants are closed for Thanksgiving; this is supposed to be the ultimate home-cooked family meal. Home goods stores sell huge platters for serving turkey and all the traditional trimmings, recipes for which are, as you might expect, handed down through family generations. Clearly, then, from a cultural perspective, family mealtime in the US may be a rushed affair most days of the week, but it is central to the American experience of home and family togetherness.

No wonder the women we spoke to felt under such emotional pressure to put delicious and wholesome family meals on the table. However, what the research also uncovered was how challenging it is in practice, to cook something that would please everyone, every day, and give the family 'something different' from time to time (especially after a day at work). 'My mom worked full-time and she had a meal on the table every day at 6 o'clock', said Patti, a part-time book-keeper in Nashville, and full-time mom to a nine-month old baby. 'I try to do that too, I'm learning. I look for recipes online and buy the pre-chopped veggies.' The strategy formation team, insights and shopper marketing executives from a global food company concluded that women wanted help in what they themselves saw as their essential role: nurturing the family unit by gathering everyone together to eat and connect as a family. They also realized that 'home-cooked' need not be fancy. For mom, the emotional resonance is in bringing the family together to eat something that everyone will enjoy, that she feels she has 'cooked'. A casserole made from pre-cut fresh meat, pre-washed veggies and a canned sauce is 'home-cooked' because mom made it and the family loves it. Even a large foil tray of frozen lasagne can be a meal, served family style in the centre of the table (like those giant Thanksgiving platters), if accompanied by 'sides': 'fresh-baked bread' from the store bakery, or a salad assembled from pre-washed ingredients.

In our research we also used Deep Visualization (see Chapter 6 for how to do this technique) to ideate new merchandising ideas to activate this insight. We asked shoppers to visualize their ideal store: what could the retailer do to help them bring the family together to eat? 'Have a display with a recipe and the ingredients', explained Jenny in the video which we were given permission to shoot in her local store. 'Keep it new and fresh. Here's a meal, a way you can get your family to sit down at the table and eat together. It says the store puts the needs of the family before the dollar.' 'That's a great idea', said the shopper marketing director. 'Let's develop that merchandising approach to present to this key account.'

As we saw in Chapter 1, learning has to result in action, to be called strategic learning. Therefore, as part of this Strategic Learning Journey, we ran a full-day Activation Session with the strategy formation team (insights managers, the brand manager and the key account manager for the store). The wider stakeholder team was primarily the mass retailer who had allowed the research to be conducted in their stores, a first for them and for their food suppliers. During the activation session, we created several new ideas for improving the merchandising of food products to support shoppers in putting meals on the table. These ideas were illustrated and presented to the retailer, along with the psychological and cultural insights which underpinned the strategy. Anticipating a presentation to the retailer which could transform their business and status as a trusted strategic partner, the client had invested in professional video which was edited to bring the insights to life in the form of the moving stories which women shoppers had told us. Following the presentation of the merchandising ideas, the company was given permission to set up in-store testing and was asked to present their strategy formation approach to competitive food companies, to encourage an industry-wide approach to shopper marketing innovation. They were also given responsibility for leading shopper marketing innovation across two product categories. For this marketing strategy formation team, their Strategic Learning Journey opened up the opportunity they had been looking for, to put together a category approach which would help an important retail customer build emotional loyalty with shoppers and also drive brand volume; and at the same time build their own relationship with a key account.

Introduction

In Chapter 1 of this book, we introduced the idea of Strategic Empathy, that is, the activation of empathy-based organizational learning into marketing strategy, as a powerful source of competitive advantage. In Chapters 4–8, we describe the Strategic Empathy Process, a leadership tool, with which marketing, strategy and insights specialists can develop Strategic Empathy, as a basis for harnessing and articulating emergent marketing strategy formation, and socializing it throughout the organization. We also noted that a key difference between traditional strategy formation processes and the Strategic Empathy Process is the deliberate inclusion of stakeholders from across functional departments, who are responsible for executing strategy, in a 'bottom-up', **collaborative strategy formation process,** based on **strategic learning** about the consumer or customer. We call the conscious design of a team-based learning approach a *Strategic Learning Journey* because the learning is designed to result in insights which can be activated into strategy; ie action results from the learning. Some successful corporations, like Johnson & Johnson, for example, (Brooks and Lawson, 2014) insist on this collaborative approach, believing that the team working on a specific strategic initiative needs to hear it from the consumer to ensure that initiatives are grounded in consumer insights. Not to do so is regarded as a potential risk of conflict within the team and also potentially detrimental to the business.

In Chapters 4–8, we explain the three phases of the Strategic Empathy Process and explain in detail how to implement the research, strategy planning and internal communication tools to design and implement the process in your own organization. In Chapter 9, we explain how to implement collaborative strategy formation in the non-profit sector, and show that there are some important differences in approach and timeline, when adopting a more democratic model of the Strategic Empathy Process in a non-profit context. The goal of Chapter 4 is to give a brief overview of the Strategic Empathy Process, to act as a roadmap for Chapters 5–9.

Overview of the Strategic Empathy Process

There are three phases of the Strategic Empathy Process, which follow a Pre-Planning phase (see Figure 4.2). These phases address the following questions:

1 Pre-Planning:
  - What are the marketing strategic issues that face the business?
  - What is the marketing strategy decision that must be made?
  - Who needs to be part of the strategy formation team?
2 Immerse:
  - What tacit knowledge or consumer data already exists?
  - What are the objectives and scope for new immersive research?
  - What is the right immersive research methodology?
3 Activate:
  - What new insights have we gleaned from immersive research?
  - What implications do these insights have for marketing strategy?
4 Inspire:
  - How can new insights and strategy be communicated to stakeholders outside the strategy team, so as to inspire empathy which will shape emergent marketing strategy formation?

Figure 4.2 Strategic Empathy® Process

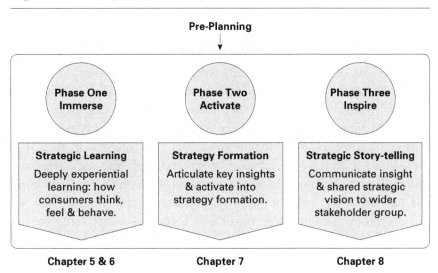

Phase One Immerse	Phase Two Activate	Phase Three Inspire
Strategic Learning	**Strategy Formation**	**Strategic Story-telling**
Deeply experiential learning: how consumers think, feel & behave.	Articulate key insights & activate into strategy formation.	Communicate insight & shared strategic vision to wider stakeholder group.
Chapter 5 & 6	Chapter 7	Chapter 8

SOURCE: ModelPeople Inc

Each of the three phases in the Strategic Empathy Process has a specific objective and output which builds on the prior phase, so it's important not to assume that a phase can be skipped to save time or budget. However, depending on the project goals, some phases may be de-prioritized. For example, if the strategy output of Phase Two: Activate is to be shared with a wider stakeholder group who are not close to the issues, but need to develop a high level of Strategic Empathy for successful implementation, then it may be important to invest time and budget in Phase Three: Inspire. However, in other situations, the stakeholder team might be comfortable that strategy and insights can be more easily or narrowly communicated, in which case time and resources can be focused on Phases One and Two.

Pre-Planning

The first goal of Pre-Planning is to ensure that the marketing strategic issue is clearly understood. This is defined as the key question that needs to be answered in order to make marketing strategy decisions. It's important to spend time defining what marketing decision needs to be made to address the marketing strategic issue; within what time frame the decision needs to be made; and who needs to be part of the strategy formation team and involved in the Strategic Learning Journey. It's also important at this stage to consider what might be the wider stakeholder group for the project: those people who don't need to be part of the project stakeholder team, but who will need to act on the outcome, for example, advertising or promotional agencies, retail customers, even shareholders. Consideration must be given to answering questions they may have and collecting the consumer content required to communicate the strategy to them (this is explained in Chapter 8). There is often a temptation to make the core strategy formation team large, so as to create a broad, cross-functional basis for interpreting and integrating learning and to encourage buy-in to the outcomes. In fact, the opposite effect may be achieved if strategy team members are not equipped to play a full role in the process because they lack skills, engagement or time. Clients often reflect that they wish they had kept the team smaller to enable the process to move faster and team learning to be integrated more smoothly.

Tool box

Example of Pre-Planning phase output

- **Marketing strategic issue:** a leading teen casual clothing brand has lost sales over the prior two years. Tracking data indicates a loss in salience (positive top-of-mind awareness) with teen males compared with two more recently launched competitors. Feedback from retailers indicates that product is outdated and offtake of competitor SKUs is higher.

- **Marketing strategy decision:** develop a new competitive brand positioning strategy, to refresh the brand's image and give direction for a new product design approach.

- **Time frame:** for implementation in a new ad campaign starting in the key back-to-school sales season, in six months' time.

- **Strategy formation team:** brand team, product design and merchandising teams.

- **Wider stakeholder team:**
    - ad agency account and creative teams who will implement the strategy (they are often part of the core strategy formation team);
    - key retail account buyers who will decide how to slot the new product into their store merchandising plans.

Phase One: Immerse in the consumer's world

Figure 4.3 Phase One: Immerse

SOURCE: ModelPeople Inc

We noted in Chapter 1 that empathy, as well as data, is required for strategic learning which forms the basis for marketing strategy formation. In order for the strategy formation team to develop real empathy for consumers or customers, they must *immerse* themselves in the consumer's or customer's world; not just *imagining* how they think and feel, but actually walking with them in the context of their daily lives. As we saw in Chapter 2, anthropologists have taken this contextual approach to understanding human culture and behaviour for centuries, living with the subjects of their ethnographic research for months at a time, but corporate executives might find that kind of timeline and budget hard to justify. In the commercial world, walking with consumers is achieved through designing and fielding deeply immersive and experiential research. That's why we call Phase One of the Strategic Empathy Process *Immerse*. Phase One typically takes three to six weeks. It should not be rushed, because if learning is superficial or incomplete at this stage, strategy formation and organizational learning may be compromised. There has been considerable focus recently on 'agile research', defined as using an iterative approach to fast-track research results. An 'agile research' approach may well be used to collect data or refine research stimulus during a Strategic Learning Journey (see Chapter 6) but it is not an excuse for rushing the overall process of developing deep insights and understanding. Empathy can take time.

Tool box

There are three steps in Phase One: Immerse:

1 Review existing learning (data and tacit knowledge) and define strategic learning objectives.
2 Define immersive research scope.
3 Design an immersive research methodology.

Step 1: review existing learning and define strategic learning objectives

The first step in Phase One is to review what existing learning and tacit knowledge is held by team members and to question where this might be outdated or incomplete. It's important to allow enough time to discuss learning, and especially to share tacit knowledge within the strategy team, as this can lead to breakthrough thinking about what new learning is needed. In the teen fashion brand example above (see page 79), the mental models which the team has about teen males, and on which prior marketing decisions have been made, may be outdated. It's important to review existing data and consumer research that exists and to create hypotheses which might explain the marketing strategic issue: why might the brand have lost salience? Behavioural data might show a drop in online repeat purchases during the critical back-to-school period in primary DMAs (but not in secondary) and a drop in click-through from young male content websites. Brand tracking data might show, for example, that 'has the latest styles' measures have dropped. Channel sales data might indicate a drop in department store sales. The design director's teen son may have told her that the 'cool kids' no longer wear the brand. Some recent focus groups with teens in primary DMAs may show that they don't mind wearing the brand on family occasions but feel it is not stylish enough for school. All this information can give us some clues about what may be happening and help to define strategic learning objectives. The goal is not to develop hypotheses which are to be proved or disproved, but to reflect existing data and tacit knowledge into the research objectives and instrument. For example, in this case, the strategy team might decide that the strategic learning objective is to understand changes in how teen boys develop personal style relative to their peer group, and the key influences on apparel purchase and style perceptions in peer group situations, relative to the brand and competitive set positioning and product offering.

Step 2: define immersive research scope

After reviewing existing learning, the next step in Phase One is to design immersive experiential consumer research, which begins with defining scope and designing methodology. The scope of the research means: *'who do we talk to?'*; and *'where: what's the research context?'* Research methodology answers the question *'how do we conduct the research?'*

When defining scope, it's common to assume that we need to speak to the users of our brand and competitive brands, but there may be good reason to speak to a broader group of people: as we saw in Chapter 1, searching outside the usual places for knowledge is a practice of successful 'learning organizations', which deliver superior performance. It can be useful to speak with 'trendsetters' or with experts in the category, such as journalists, designers or retailers to get an alternative perspective.

Trendsetters, consumers who are early to adopt or encourage the spread of new consumption behaviours, have been a focus for marketing and consumer research since the late 1990s (Brooks, 2001). Trendsetters can be an important source of insight because their current behaviour can offer clues to the future behaviour of mainstream consumers. Trendsetters are often recruited for research purposes through personal networks (Brooks, 2003), because they are hard to pinpoint in recruiting databases (see Chapter 6 for more on recruiting techniques). Gladwell (2000) offers a qualitative definition of three types of trendsetter who are influential in diffusing trends, and their traits can be reflected in recruiting criteria: connectors (people who know a lot of other people); mavens (people who can be relied on for expert advice); and salesmen (charismatic people whose behaviour or attitudes are highly influential). Rogers' (2003) theory about the diffusion of innovations identifies five groups of people based on the speed with which they adopt trends and the level to which they influence others: innovators, early adopters, early majority, late majority and laggards. Of these, innovators (about 2.5 per cent of the population) are risk takers who initiate new ideas or behaviours; and early adopters (about 13.5 per cent of the population) adopt new ideas and are influential in persuading the mainstream to adopt them too.

For example, in an automotive design concept study, we spoke to three groups in order to understand how mainstream consumer design perceptions might evolve: design experts such as an editor of a home design publication and a product design creative director; young adult trendsetters with a strong design aesthetic or a professional involvement with design; and mainstream car buyers of all ages.

It's also important to consider *context*, as part of the scope. As we saw in Chapter 2, context is key to understanding consumer behaviour and decision-making. Context includes geographical markets, subcultural context (eg sports car enthusiasts, gamers), social context (eg at work among colleagues, in a bar among friends), retail channel (eg JC Penney vs Apple stores). How can we design a research methodology that lets us observe and understand the way in which our consumers make decisions related to our brand? Observing and interviewing in context not only offers immersive, experiential learning but also avoids some of the methodological issues we have discussed, such as limits of memory and System 2 thinking.

Step 3: design an immersive research methodology

Designing an immersive research methodology requires us to think creatively about objectives and scope. How can we observe and speak with our consumers in the right context so as to uncover truly new insights? Budget, timeline and practical constraints also come into the equation. In Chapters 5–6, we describe and illustrate, using case studies, many observational and interview techniques that allow deep learning about how consumers think, feel and behave to unfold. It's essential for the strategy team to be creative and push the envelope in terms of using new methodologies, tools and multi-disciplinary approaches to understand their consumers, as we explored in Chapter 2.

Whilst the scope and methodology, in a commercial setting, must be identified upfront, for reasons of timeline and resources, it's essential to allow the consumer's world to unfold naturally and for the strategy team to be alert to observations which may hold new and deep insights. Time should be allowed for additional exploration in Phase One; we may decide we need to broaden the scope or objectives to answer questions that have arisen during the research process. Time should also be allocated to coaching the strategy team to be effective consumer or customer observers, interviewers, note-takers and analysts. As Benjamin Franklin might have said, strategy team members must be involved with consumers, so they can learn! It's a missed opportunity for developing consumer empathy, to abandon research to external specialists. Immersive research requires active participation from the strategy team. Chapters 5–8 offer ideas and tools that enable the strategy team to conduct consumer observations and interviews themselves.

Phase Two: Activate insights into marketing strategy

Figure 4.4 Phase Two: Activate

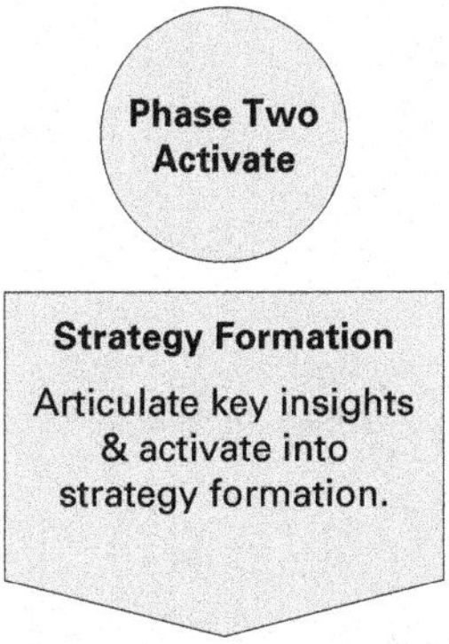

Phase Two
Activate

Strategy Formation

Articulate key insights
& activate into
strategy formation.

SOURCE: ModelPeople Inc

Having immersed in the consumer's world, the strategy team then uses the empathetic understanding they have developed **to articulate the key insights (or nuggets of learning) and to use them in collaborative strategy formation; a process we call** *activation* of insights into strategy. This is done in strategy team activation sessions. It's essential to spend time upfront in this type of session to work through observations, identify new learning and reshape currently accepted insights about the consumer. If this is not done, the strategy team can fall back into a familiar comfort zone, and stop short of thinking deeply about what they have seen in immersive research and developing new insights which might lead to breakthrough new strategies.

The timing of activation sessions is important to capture and activate the stakeholder team's learning while it's still fresh. A half-day activation session held immediately after fieldwork is complete can be very useful in capturing fresh impressions and identifying priorities for research analysis. A longer activation session should be held within two to three weeks following field research, which allows time for analysis of research findings while ensuring that the team's first-hand impressions are still fresh. In Chapter 7, we describe the approaches to defining key insights and how to design and run collaborative activation sessions to help the stakeholder team to activate insights into strategy. We also look at how to design activation sessions around ideation for brand innovation.

Phase Three: Inspire empathy among the wider stakeholder group

Figure 4.5 Phase Three: Inspire

SOURCE: ModelPeople Inc

In Phase Three, the strategy team must communicate the insights and shared strategic vision developed over the course of their Strategic Learning Journey to the wider stakeholder group. We saw in Chapter 1 that turning individual learning into collective organizational learning is critical to the process of developing marketing strategy. Successful companies are those that consistently create new knowledge, disseminate it throughout the organization and then activate this new knowledge into new products (Mintzberg, 2007). For this reason, I encourage clients to think as much about how to communicate or 'socialize' insights and strategy *at the outset of a project*, as about how to design the right methodology to address the research question.

Phase Three is called *Inspire*, because communication must be done in a powerful way so as to inspire the same kind of empathetic understanding which the core stakeholder team has experienced, as a basis for strategic action. For example, in the case study on page 16 at the end of Chapter 1, we saw how a global home networking corporation needed to help its engineers understand the difficulties consumers faced when trying to shop for and install home networking solutions. Intellectually, the engineering team knew that most consumers were less technically adept than they themselves, but actually *seeing* video of consumers struggling to shop and to install the company's products inspired them with understanding and empathy, and led them to develop new product solutions like the Valet router, which has an interactive user interface to guide the consumer through the installation process, and sells at a premium price to the base model. In Chapter 8, we give detailed suggestions on how to define communication objectives and create media which communicate insights and inspire learning and strategy activation among the wider stakeholder group.

Strategic Empathy Process checklist and timeline

Weeks 1–2 Pre-Planning:

- Frame the marketing strategic issue faced by the business.
- Identify the desired outcomes and the marketing decision to be taken.
- Identify:
  - strategy team members;
  - wider stakeholder group: required outcomes.

▶

- Identify strategic learning objectives.
- Timing of Strategic Learning Journey to deliver required strategy outcomes.

Weeks 3–6 Immerse:

- Determine what tacit knowledge or consumer data already exists.
- Identify research objectives and scope.
- Design research methodology and tools.
- Develop fieldwork plan and timeline.
- Implement strategy team member coaching in observation/interview.

Weeks 4–9 Activate:

- In-field activation session.
- Research analysis.
- Post-field activation session design and timing:
  - key consumer insights definition;
  - collaborative strategy formation.

Weeks 6–12 Inspire:

- Define communication objectives.
- Design, produce and launch communication media.

CASE STUDY   The Strategic Empathy Process in action: global oral healthcare brand innovation

The brief

The client, a global oral healthcare company, wanted to put together a Strategic Learning Journey for their whole organization, to gain empathy and deep insights into the consumer experience of and treatment for gum disease (ModelPeople, 2006). Learning was to be activated in new product development. Video was an important part of the brief, to ensure that insights could be socialized across the entire organization, in order to inspire empathy for the consumer as a basis for executing a major new strategic initiative. While it was expected that learning would be shared among a very wide stakeholder group including operational management in the US, corporate management in the EU, and the company's customers (dental professionals), the core marketing strategy team was relatively small and included representatives from insights, product marketing, professional marketing and R&D.

Pre-Planning

The **strategic marketing issue faced by the company** was over-reliance on a narrow product portfolio, which missed the opportunity to leverage additional sales volume from a leading, high-quality brand name in oral healthcare, which had high consumer and customer awareness. Therefore, the **desired marketing decision** was to identify specific opportunities for brand extension via new product development.

Phase One: Immerse

A great deal of **data and tacit knowledge** already existed within the organization but there was less understanding around the consumer experience of gum disease and their emotional response. The client also wanted to understand consumer motivations to seek treatment and the extent to which dental professionals would be prepared to recommend existing and new products and how they would approach it with patients. These goals defined **research scope and objectives**. It was decided that a combination of ethnographic interviews and in-depth interviews with patients, in-depth interviews with dentists and mini focus groups with dental hygienists was the optimum **immersive research methodology**. Ethnographic interviews gave us the opportunity to observe the role and significance of oral care within the consumer's overall healthcare behaviour, and to observe and discuss in detail oral care regimes. Depth interviews with consumers allowed us to use techniques such as Deep Visualization to uncover the emotional experience of gum disease. Depth interviews with dentists allowed a candid discussion about the clinical and business aspects of recommending new products. Mini groups with hygienists encouraged the sharing of concerns and approaches to patient treatment and counselling. Strategy team members observed all the research phases and were coached on how to observe ethnographic interviews and take verbatim notes for the planned activation session.

Phase Two: Activate

Two weeks following the fieldwork, the strategy team held a full-day activation session at the client's HQ. I presented insights into the consumer experience and emotional response at different stages of progression of gum disease and identified the points at which consumers sought treatment, based on both patient and professional feedback, and their attitudes, motivations and behaviours at those points. The team built on new insights and their own tacit knowledge to arrive at a shared viewpoint of the consumer pain points and needs regarding gum disease treatment. Then they worked through group exercises to identify differentiating product benefits and RTBs (reasons to believe) which would form the basis of a product development brief and targets for clinical claims to address pain points and needs. Subsequently, the team developed new product concepts for further exploration.

Phase Three: Inspire

A half-hour video was produced using footage from interviews and text slides to communicate and illustrate the consumer experience of gum disease throughout different stages of its progression, and their emotional response and treatment approaches at each stage. This video was used for several years afterwards for internal training purposes, to inspire consumer empathy and understanding of the entire experience of gum disease: how and why consumers seek products and treatment and their unmet needs.

Outcomes

The activation session resulted in the development of about 10 new product concepts which were taken into 'Agile' qualitative research. Concepts were explored and then refined by the strategy team between consumer focus groups so that each new group built on learning from the last group, resulting in fully refined and ranked concepts at the end of two days in-field. These new concepts resulted in new products and new patient and professional advertising approaches.

Chapter 4 summary

- There are three phases of the Strategic Empathy Process, which follow a Pre-Planning phase: Immerse, Activate and Inspire.

- The goal of Pre-Planning is to ensure that the marketing strategic issue which the business faces is clearly understood; that the marketing decision to be taken is defined; that the right people are on the strategy team to enable learning to be interpreted and integrated efficiently; and that the needs of the wider stakeholder group are understood when it comes to designing research and communicating insights and strategy.

- The goal of Phase One: Immerse is to develop empathy for the consumer or customer by conducting deeply immersive, experiential research. This requires the strategy team to do the following:
  - Step 1: review existing learning and define learning objectives.
  - Step 2: define immersive research scope (consumer type and context).
  - Step 3: design an immersive research methodology (type of research, location and number of interviews).

- The goal of Phase Two: Activate is to use the empathetic understanding gained in Phase One to articulate the key consumer insights as the basis of collaborative marketing strategy formation in team activation sessions.

- The goal of Phase Three: Inspire is to share strategic learning with other stakeholders who need to act on the insights, through video and other media.

- The entire process takes more than six weeks. It is essential not to skimp on strategic learning, which could compromise effective strategy formation. However, an agile research approach can be used in places to fast-track output.

References

Brooks, C (2001) *Targeting Trendsetters*, Account Planning Group Conference, 2001

Brooks, C (2003) interviewed by Grossman, L (US) and Chu, J (Europe) The Quest for Cool, *Time Magazine*, 13 September

Brooks, C with Lawson, D (2014) *Influencing the Corporate Strategy Agenda with Research Insights*, Conference presentation at the US Market Research Association Corporate Researchers Conference

CDC (2011) Centers for Disease Control and Prevention, National Center for Health Statistics, *National Survey of Children's Health*, http://www.cdc.gov/nchs/slaits/nsch.htm [last viewed February 2016]

Gladwell, M (2000) *The Tipping Point*, Little Brown, New York

Mintzberg, H (2007) *Tracking Strategies: Towards a general theory*, Oxford University Press, Oxford

ModelPeople Inc (2006) Strategic Empathy Process, oral healthcare

ModelPeople Inc (2007) Strategic Empathy Process, meal preparation and grocery merchandising

Rogers, E (2003) *Diffusion of Innovations* (5th edn), Simon & Schuster, New York

Siferlin, A (2012) Why families who eat together are healthier, *Time Magazine*, 24 April

The Strategic Empathy Process Phase One

05

Immerse – immersive research methods

CHAPTER 5 OBJECTIVES

1 Explain what immersive research is and how to design it, so that the marketing strategy team develops a deeply intuitive understanding of the target consumer or customer.

2 Describe core immersive research methods and explain how to use each one.

3 Illustrate, with global case studies, how to combine immersive research methods in a multi-disciplinary approach.

CASE STUDY   Milk: India and the US

When I get tired cycling or at karate I need milk. I need strength to learn, it's for memory. I have to help my mother, I like her very much. I need memory to learn.

Boy, aged 10, Bangalore

Today's world is competitive, they will succeed... they will be bold, active and fresh. The child will get strong because of Bournvita.

Mum of child, aged 10, Mumbai

Food and beverage brands evoke consumers' deeper emotional and cultural associations. This is because food is essential for survival; food is also social and pleasurable to the senses. Our US-based client marketed a delicious chocolate 'milk modifier' brand, which, added to hot or cold milk, was positioned for pre-tween children on a platform of 'fun nutrition'. In the US, the cultural code for milk is 'mother nurture'. However, by the time they go to elementary school, American kids aspire to swap milk for the juice drinks, soda and water preferred by older children. Therefore, 'fun' is an essential element in brand positioning, to reinforce milk's status with kids as they mature.

In India, however, 'milk modifiers' are called 'milk food drinks' (MFDs), with the key competitors – British legacy brands such as Bournvita and Horlicks – positioned on a platform of child nutrition, with vitamin fortification as the functional RTB. Our client (ModelPeople, 2014a) saw an opportunity in the vast Indian market, but needed to address the marketing strategic issue of how to competitively position their brand in India. Therefore, they commissioned a multi-disciplinary research project to understand how the Indian consumer thinks, feels and behaves, prior to market launch. The strategy team (representatives from the US global brand team and local marketing executives) embarked on a Strategic Learning Journey, which generated some completely unexpected 'Ahas' and altered the shape of local brand positioning and competitive strategy.

The research methodology was designed to enable the strategy team to understand the cultural place of milk in the Indian family and then to explore brand positioning and product formulation concepts. These two stages of research are often conducted separately but the US-based team needed to make the most of their immersion journey. The team began by interviewing a paediatrician (as they are trusted advisors regarding child nutrition) and then held three-hour ethnographic interviews in Mumbai and Bangalore, followed by three-hour Creative Workshops to explore concepts (see later in this chapter for details of how to conduct each methodology). We recruited middle-class mums of kids under the age of 10, the core buyers of MFDs, defined according to a standard socio-economic classification (SEC) as women in families where the male head of household had at least some college education and was a middle or senior executive or professional business owner. Prior to the interviews, women produced a scrapbook using pictures and words to illustrate the meaning of milk to them (this format was chosen over a digital format because the target consumer does not always have regular access to a computer).

The first surprise for the strategy team was the cultural importance of milk to an Indian mum. Giving milk to children is a morning ritual, rooted in the long-established importance of household dairy production for family sustenance.

Traditionally, the cow (which is sacred to the majority Hindu population) is a critical food source in rural villages. Processing milk into dairy products like curd, paneer and ghee that form the (protein-rich) basis of Indian meals is a traditional skill. Even in India's mega-cities like Mumbai, a few urban families still keep cows. For other families, buffalo or (lower-fat) cows' milk is delivered unpasteurized, daily, to most households, and processed traditionally (see Figure 5.1), though this is changing as packaged dairy products offering flavour variety and taste become available and aspirational to children.

Milk is boiled in the morning to ensure it's safe for consumption, and to separate cream for processing. Curd (yogurt) is made from the milk by adding a live culture, and the cream is skimmed and heated to make ghee (clarified butter) or paneer, a soft cheese used to add protein to vegetable dishes. Giving children warm milk in the morning is part of this daily milk processing ritual which provides protein-rich food for the family. Therefore, for the Indian mum, milk is tied in with family nurturing.

Figure 5.1 Household milk processing in India

For mums, physical growth has been a measure of her success at nurturing. Paediatricians use growth charts with mums from an early age to indicate norms, and schools send children for a height/weight check-up on admission to elementary school.

> *The parental concern is that my child is not growing as well as his peers, he*
> *is the shortest in the class, so I will show them he is growing per the curve.*
> *Paediatrician, Mumbai*

Mums have been told by paediatricians that milk delivers calcium and protein, needed for growth and so for the Indian mum, milk is both culturally and emotionally associated with being a good mum. However, it's not always easy to get a child to drink milk, and so flavoured MFDs, which make milk more palatable to a child, have become part of an unbreakable morning ritual in many homes. Fortified MFDs have historically been positioned on a physical growth platform, and made available in affordable small-serve sachets for lower-income households.

In modern India, food scarcity has receded for the emerging urban middle class and physical and mental demands on children to succeed in a highly competitive emerging economy have increased. Just as in the West, middle-class Indian women are having fewer children and focusing intense effort on nurturing one or two children to ensure their success (and, they readily admit, to ensure their own welfare in old age!). There is intense competition for Indian children to get into good elementary and senior schools to 'get ahead' in a booming economy, where education is seen as a route to future success; near-perfect exam scores are required for entry to a prestigious college. Parents also want their children to do out-of-school activities like extra tuition, sport or dance to compete on all fronts as sports accomplishment may also be a route into a top school with lower grades. Now, Indian mums see their nurturing role as preparing children to get ahead in a competitive world that has changed out of all recognition since they grew up, and their nutritional priorities have shifted from growth to **physical energy** and **mental performance to win.**

> *We want our children to be something more than us, to have something*
> *extra... extra qualifications, to be good at sport. If you're a sportsperson you*
> *get a seat in the college because preference is given to sports people.*
> *Mum of child aged 9, Mumbai*

Milk is still at the heart of the new nurturing rules. Children typically start the school day early from the age of 5, so they can be cranky and may not want to eat before school starts. The morning milk is seen as a good substitute for food:

a 'complete food' that fills the stomach until a hearty breakfast tiffin can be eaten at school. Mums see milk as essential in kick-starting the child's day and giving him/her the physical energy/vitality and mental focus to perform until tiffin-time.

The mum feels relief that the kid drank the milk and will be energetic.
A happy child will achieve; he will feel energetic; he will perform his best
if his stomach is full.   *Mum of a child aged 6, Mumbai*

Since milk is still central to mums' newly defined nurturing role, vitamin-fortified MFDs have remained central too, not so much nowadays in helping her ensure her child survives and grows, but in fulfilling her ambitions for her children to succeed materially in life. MFD brands have evolved their brand positioning to reflect this new cultural reality. A TV ad for Cadbury's Bournvita shows a mum training her son (who appears to be about 10) to sprint competitively. 'My son will learn the habit of winning when he defeats me', says mum. We see the son crying with fatigue and frustration, as he trains over and over, in all weathers. Finally, we see him edging ahead of mum in a flat-out race to the finish line. 'So the day he defeats me, I will win', she says.

However, while there is strong competition from heritage brands like Bournvita for the morning day-part, the team also identified strategic opportunities in the after-school day-part. At this time of day, mum is open to trialling new brands and indulging the child's preference. She may also encourage independent snacking on cereals, frozen or packaged snacks or other dairy products like yogurt or packaged lassi. Forming independent preferences is important for kids' food or beverage brands because tween brand preference will carry forward into teen age (and beyond) and will trickle down to younger siblings. Aspirational tween brands, in any culture, are different from the brands offered by mum, reflecting the tween's emotional need to gain distance from his childhood self. While children of school age in India are typically given milk when they return from school or evening activities, there is no ritual surrounding this occasion. Mum is more relaxed about nutrition as the child has eaten during the day, and sees her nurturing role at this time of day as rewarding the child and letting her relax and have fun, but energy is still important so the child can do evening activities and bridge the nutritional gap between lunch and dinner.

At 7 pm they have their evening milk, after their tennis coaching or her
dance lesson. They are really hungry but I can't give them too much before
dinner at 8.30 pm. They need extra energy to finish their studies.
                                      Mum of children aged 9 and 11, Bangalore

Afternoons they have juice or a shake, ice cream, curd also. Something from milk: curd or buttermilk. Cold chocolate or warm. Anything is OK in the evening depending on the season. It depends on their choice.

Mum of child, aged 12, Bangalore

These findings offered the US brand team an opportunity for immersive strategic learning about the Indian market and identified rich new positioning territories to explore with their local marketing colleagues.

Introduction

Figure 5.2 Phase One of the Strategic Empathy Process

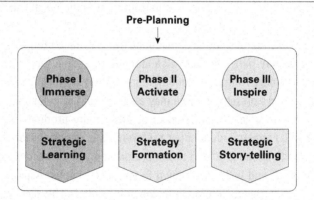

SOURCE: ModelPeople Inc

We saw in Chapter 1 that the Strategic Empathy Process starts with a conscious approach to learning which must be shared by the team as a basis for strategy formation. We called the conscious design of a team-based learning approach *a Strategic Learning Journey* because the learning is designed to result in insights which can be activated into strategy; ie action results from the learning. A Strategic Learning Journey leverages all available forms of data and insight to support learning, but at its core is *immersive, experiential consumer research* which develops a deep understanding about our consumers or customers and the way our brands fit into their lives.

Chapter 5 explores the principal immersive research methodologies that are used in Phase One (Immerse) of the Strategic Empathy Process, to support marketing strategy formation by promoting strategic learning within the strategy team. The methods discussed, though well established in both academic theory and consumer insights consulting practice, are adapting, and will continue to adapt over time, as new technologies emerge and evolve new insights tools. Many of these new methods, like mobile ethnography or MROCs (market research online communities), for example, build on and enhance well-established theoretical approaches and consumer research practices. Some methods (like eye-tracking) have been around for decades but are gaining new traction through integration with other research methods, as a result of vastly cheaper technology. None of these new methods is a game-changer on its own merits. However, many of the new methods add to the Strategic Empathy Process toolkit, when applied to creating deep insight into how consumers think, feel and behave, within a multi-disciplinary research approach. Therefore, the methods described in this chapter, both long-established and newer, should be regarded as a reliably grounded launch pad for the student or practitioner to continue to learn and adopt new approaches in order to bring fresh insight to research questions. The goal of Chapter 5 is to explain *how to design an immersive research project* in a multi-disciplinary approach to strategic learning. In Chapter 6, we go on to explain how to *manage an immersive research project*, and *design a research protocol*, and we explain how to use specific immersive research tools to uncover non-conscious consumer attitudes, brand perceptions and motivations.

What exactly is immersive research?

There is no widely accepted definition of immersive research in academic or marketing consulting communities. Some definitions frame immersive research as understanding 'in the moment' how consumers use a product or service in context and the frustrations they experience (Wilson and Macdonald, 2011). Others (Crossman, 2016) define immersive research as a deliberate act on the part of a researcher to immerse him- or herself into a specific subculture: ie to 'go native' over a period of time to make an in-depth, longitudinal study. An even narrower definition of immersive research is the use of virtual store simulations (ARF, 2008) to measure shopper reactions to new products, packaging and merchandising approaches.

For the purposes of this chapter, I will define immersive research as a *multi-disciplinary research approach* which allows the team responsible for marketing strategy formation *to develop a deeply intuitive understanding* of the target consumer or customer *by observing and exploring behaviours, experiences, deeply held beliefs, emotions and perceptions in the relevant context.* Let's unpack this definition:

- 'Observing in the relevant context' requires the team to look at how and where the consumer experiences the product or service. This might happen 'in the moment' by going out to where the consumer experience is taking place (for example, observing a usage occasion). However, 'in the moment' is a costly approach which is not always necessary because we can ask the consumer to provide information which allows remote observation. For example, in the home networking case study in Chapter 1, we had consumers bring in photographs of the design context for their network devices, which enabled us to observe (and explore with consumers) the problems with the existing design and the parameters for a new design brief.

- 'Exploring in the relevant context' requires the researcher to work with consumers (using the range of tools we will describe in this chapter) to uncover deeply held beliefs, emotions and perceptions *relative to a specific context.* For example, in the meal prep case study in Chapter 4, we had respondents visualize memorable meal experiences, which enabled the team to understand the deeply held beliefs about a mom's role and the emotions and cultural importance surrounding the dining table.

- Selecting 'the relevant context' is essential to designing the right immersive research methodology and tools. Framing the context too narrowly can lead the team to miss out on essential understanding. For example, in the meal prep case study, if we had framed the context as the client's products, rather than exploring the wider cultural and emotional context of meal preparation, then we would have missed the rich detail required to execute marketing campaigns and new product development. Wilson and Macdonald (2011) also make the point that understanding the context around product usage may help identify profit opportunities for offering integrated solutions. For example, by studying consumers' entire dental care regime, rather than just brushing, Philips Sonicare recognized a need for help with dental flossing and designed an electric flossing device to complement their existing electric toothbrush range. This helped the brand to enhance its positioning with consumers and dental professionals as an advanced dental care brand.

Because of the depth of insight required to understand how consumers think, feel and behave, immersive research methodologies are usually qualitative.

However, they can also be quantitative: new technologies (eg for textual, video and image analysis) are enhancing the ability to elicit and analyse complex responses with a quantitative sample. In the next section of this chapter we will look at a number of immersive research methods and tools and how they can be applied to allow the team responsible for marketing strategy formation to develop a deeply intuitive understanding of the target consumer or customer, by observing and exploring behaviours, experiences, deeply held beliefs, emotions and perceptions in the relevant context.

Ethnographic research methods (in business)

The first immersive research method we shall look at is ethnographic research, in a business context. We learned, in Chapter 2, that ethnographic research (grounded in anthropological approaches) is the fieldwork-based study of human behaviour in the context of socio-cultural systems and everyday practices. Using this definition, many of the methods we describe in Chapter 5 can take an ethnographic perspective. However, many theorists regard ethnographic research as requiring the researcher to be immersed, in-person, in the participant's regular activities, so as to observe and record data first-hand. This is the definition that we will use here. Ethnographic research methods have been well established in the business world for at least 20 years and the last 5–10 years have seen wider usage of online and mobile ethnographic tools which enhance the researcher's ability to 'observe' without being present, and to design studies which are more longitudinal in approach, while remaining cost-effective and deadline-sensitive.

'Classic' ethnographic research is longitudinal, that is, it happens over a period of time to allow for observation of how the context, socio-cultural dynamics and product or service experiences differ over time and place. In business, however, researchers are rarely given the luxury of weeks or months to immerse with participants! Consumer ethnographic research engagements typically last from three hours to a day, spent with the participant in the relevant context. Many clients are interested in longitudinal methods and may request several encounters with consumers over a longer time period.

Choosing the context is important. There is a tendency to rename ethnographic research engagements as 'in-homes' or 'shop-alongs' or 'drive-alongs', driven by the need to plan ahead to observe a specific product usage or consumer activity in a narrow time frame. Clients are familiar with consumer ethnographic research and will typically be prescriptive in the RFP (request for proposal): 'Ten 3-hour interviews including a visit to the store where they buy groceries' is a typical brief. However, this degree of context specificity can disguise the importance of thinking about the wider context of the consumer's life, and allowing, as far as possible, ethnographic observations and interviews to unfold naturally. Therefore, consumer ethnographic research must be both planned and spontaneous in approach. Planning happens before and during the recruitment stage and spontaneity while engaging with participants, both in-person and online.

Designing and planning an ethnographic research project

Ethnographic research projects are more complex to plan than other types of qualitative research. Allow at least four weeks to plan and recruit for ethnographic research in a business context, depending on the sample size and complexity of the context (longer if consumers are likely to be hard to recruit or several geographic markets are involved).

There are multiple ways to design an ethnographic research project and it is worth taking the time to think creatively about how to approach it. Consider doing some initial exploratory research, such as a Semiotic Scan (see Chapter 6 for how to do this), small-sample online ethnography or 'netnography' (see later in this chapter). In particular, it is essential to think through the research scope (who to talk to) and context (where). We reviewed this in Chapter 4. For example, an apparel company trying to understand changing consumer behaviours which are affecting the sales of jeans deliberately designed a broad scope and context. As well as brand consumers, we (ModelPeople, 2015a) broadened the scope to speak with leading-edge consumers who were not users of the brand but made style choices that reflected fashion trends that might trickle down to the mainstream consumers who did buy the brand. We designed a broad context for the ethnographic research, looking at everything their consumer wears across occasions, rather than just looking at jeans and traditional jeans occasions. The ethnographic observations took place in-home (observing wardrobe and outfit choices for different occasions) and during a social event, to understand both the personal style and social context. Pre-work included a diary of outfit choices for work and social occasions. And we explored the culture and emotion of denim using some of the tools described in

Chapter 6. This broad context was essential to understanding the complex factors behind the sales decline.

ModelPeople typically includes **online ethnography** as an element in an ethnographic research protocol. This enables us to collect more data, collect data over a longer period of time, and also preview and select the most insightful and participative recruits. Online ethnographic tools include, for example:

- Online diaries in which participants write about, photograph and video what they are doing, thinking, feeling, wearing, cooking etc.

- Mobile video – collected by the participant on a mobile phone – of 'in the moment' activities, such as a shopping trip, or experiences, such as an arthritic pain episode.

- Mobile written description of brand encounters, recording each time the participant comes across a brand or category touchpoint which might influence behaviour or perceptions:

  - We used this in a gaming project, for example, to understand marketing influences on game consideration in the pre-holiday period (ModelPeople, 2010a).

- Online communities, in which a group of participants are engaged over a period of one month or more in a number of encounters allowing longitudinal data to be collected. Encounters might be individual or social, or a mix of both. For example, in an apparel study, we asked participants to do an e-collage of their graphic T-shirts and then opened up the e-collages for comments from other participants, which enabled us to observe what types of design were admired by this fashion subculture (ModelPeople, 2015b).

Researchers usually employ an online platform to collect online ethnography, display results to the strategy team and allow tagging and analysis of the data. My company has maintained a custom online platform (called PeopleBlogSpot) for over 12 years, but more recently commercial platforms, such as Recollective, have been developed for short-term rental. Such platforms allow multiple observer logons, so that the strategy team can be engaged in observing online ethnography as well as in-person ethnography. This is important because rich data, both ethnographic and semiotic, is produced. The team can also come to consensus on which participants to engage in in-person observations.

Once the project has been designed and the decision made regarding whom to interview, a screener can be written and recruiting participants can begin. Qualitative research screening and recruiting is covered in detail in Chapter 6. However, a special note must be made regarding recruiting for ethnographic research. The observation context may require the participant to do something private or personal, such as changing in and out of clothing, shaving, brushing teeth or even showering in front of the observer team! Additionally, the participant may be asked to wear glasses which track and record eye movements (during a shopping trip, for example), to allow deeper analysis of what attracts shoppers at point-of-sale.

When recruiting participants for ethnographic research, ensure that the recruiter is completely clear about what the respondents will be required to do and that written instructions for the protocol are included in the screener to avoid unhappy surprises for the participant which may compromise the engagement.

Conducting an ethnographic encounter

We have already noted the constraints of conducting ethnographic research in a single three-hour encounter with a participant. I have found that the best way to overcome these constraints is to have a semi-structured research protocol; that is one which asks different kinds of ethnographic question in sequence, but allows time for contextual observation and unstructured conversations which arise spontaneously and which may offer key insights. The other reason for having a structured protocol is that it ensures that the same data points are collected from all participants in a study, enabling analysis across interviews.

Spradley (1979), in a short book which I recommend, identifies three core types of ethnographic question, which I have illustrated here with examples from an ethnographic study into 'lunch' among working consumers:

- **Descriptive questions,** which ask the participant to paint a picture of their culture or everyday lives, in their own language. Spradley describes different kinds of descriptive questions including:
  - Grand Tour questions (eg 'Tell me about a typical work day.').
  - Specific Grand Tour questions, which focus in on specific occasions or places (eg 'Tell me about what you eat and drink during a typical work day.').
  - Guided Grand Tour, an essential question which asks the participant to show us something relevant to the topic and offers an opportunity for observation (eg 'Show me where you keep your lunch items for the work day.').

– Task-related Grand Tour questions, which ask the participant to do something to illustrate the topic (eg 'Show me a till receipt from the last time you purchased lunch items for the work day and tell me more about each item.').

– Mini Tour questions, which focus in on a specific aspect of the topic (eg 'Tell me how you heat food at work.').

– Experience questions, which ask for specific relevant experiences (eg 'Tell me about some unsatisfactory work day lunch experiences.').

– Native-language questions, which probe nomenclature, essential for input to marketing communications (eg 'What do you call each of the times when you eat or drink food during the day?').

• **Structural questions**, which ask the participant to show us how they organize domains, essential for understanding consumer taxonomies (eg 'How would you categorize the different kinds of things you eat and drink at work? What other categories exist?').

• **Contrast questions**, which ask the participant to describe differences between terms used (eg 'What's the difference between a snack and a meal?').

At the outset of an ethnographic interview, it's important to build rapport and put participants at their ease by setting up the interview and letting them know what to expect. I start by introducing myself and any observers. I then engage in some light, affirming conversation to get the participant used to chatting with me. It can help to accept refreshments if offered, and always accept them if they have been specially prepared for you. (You don't have to actually finish them!) I ask the participant where he or she would like the interview to take place, and choose a space where we won't be disturbed by other family members. Always ensure that the participant chooses where he or she wants to sit, so as to feel comfortable and in control. I explain early on that my professional code of conduct, as a member of the US Market Research Association (or equivalent), requires me to protect the privacy of research participants. I ask permission to take audio recordings and photographs, and I confirm that any notes or photos will be used only by the research team and not for public purposes. If video is to be taken, specific protocols apply to setting up the interview, and these are covered in Chapter 8. Then we can begin the interview, using our semi-structured interview guide.

I always regard an interview as an informal conversation. I move from general to specific descriptive questions so that the participant explains as much as possible in his own language without prompting from me. If we get stuck on a topic, we move on and then circle back round from a different angle because, as the interview progresses the participant becomes more relaxed and able to articulate her experiences, thoughts and feelings. Spradley notes the importance of expressing interest, which is critical to encouraging the participant; and restating what they say to encourage them to expand on the initial description. He also advises expressing ignorance to encourage detailed descriptions. This is easy for me as I can explain that an English person does not understand everything that Americans do! I regard an ethnographic interview as like unravelling a ball of string. The string can become knotted and require untangling. Relevant information does not flow in a straight line, which is why it's important to keep an interview guide semi-structured and allow specific topics to resurface again and again until we have reached the core of the research question.

In Chapter 2, we discussed the importance of a multi-disciplinary approach to immersive research, and I typically use multiple tools (explained in Chapter 6) which explore a topic from multiple perspectives, emotional as well as cultural. In this sense, I am, unapologetically, conducting a hybrid form of 'ethnographic' interview and some practitioners have been resistant to this type of approach (eg Sunderland and Denny, 2003). However, although I believe it's important not to be rigid about designing ethno-graphic protocol in business, it's essential that the core of an ethnographic interview is descriptive questioning and observation in cultural context. The tool box below describes how to structure a three-hour ethnographic interview guide for a consumer interview, asking different types of questions, and suggests an example, but the ultimate structure of the interview guide will depend on the strategic learning objectives.

Tool box
Sample ethnographic interview guide flow

1. Before the interview begins

Goal: build rapport with the participant:

- Make easy conversation on general, non-controversial topics.

2. Setting up the interview (5 mins)

Goal: communicate what will happen during the interview to put the participant at their ease:

- Explain the interview time-length, what the participant can expect, ask permission to record audio or video and take photographs.

3. Getting to know the participant (25 mins)

Goal: understand the participant's personal context, values and goals:

- Ask personal descriptive questions, eg:
  - 'Tell me about yourself.'; 'Tell me about your life.'
  - 'Tell me about when you were growing up.'; 'What are the things you remember?'; 'How did that shape who you are today?'
  - 'How would a close friend describe you and what's important to you?'
  - 'What is most important to you personally, in your life?'
  - 'Do you have a philosophy or mantra that you live by?'
  - 'Where would you like to be in, say, five years' time?'

4. Asking descriptive questions (50 mins)

Goal: understand culture and behaviour in context through descriptive questioning:

- Start with Grand Tour descriptive questions (eg 'Tell me what you do/ how you do it.')
- Probe specific areas with Mini Tour questions (eg 'Tell me more about what/how.')
- Ask specific experience questions (eg 'Tell me about a great/bad experience shopping at that store.')
- Use structural and contrast questions to clarify (eg 'How do you categorize... sort these products into groups and name each group?'; 'What's the difference between...?')

▶

5. Guided Tour questions (90 mins)

Goal: observe culture and behaviour in context through Guided Tour descriptive questioning:

- At a suitable point in the interview, ask Guided Tour descriptive questions to enable observation and questioning within relevant context ('Show me (eg) your vehicle, where you store food products, how you install the router.').

- This section may include a lengthier observation such as a ride in a vehicle, examining kitchen cupboards/fridge and recipe collection, demonstrating a dental care regime.

- If we can't observe an experience or a context (eg a family holiday) then we may use visualization or metaphor to enable participants to enrich response.

6. Wrap up (10 mins)

Goal: wrap up the interview:

- A good question at this stage is 'Is there anything more you'd like to tell me?'

- Thank the participant, let them know how they will be paid and say goodbye.

Design research

As we saw in the home networking case study in Chapter 1, ethnographic research is commonly used to create designer empathy for product or service users, by allowing designers to observe first-hand the tasks which the user has to perform, their experience with the product or service, and also any difficulties and work-arounds that the consumer is using to resolve difficulties. Not only can this lead to new ideas for improving design, but it can also suggest completely new product ideas which meet previously unrecognized consumer needs, like the Valet router.

It's important when conducting ethnographic observations for design activation to develop what Carlopio (2010) calls an 'activity analysis': that is, to map all of the tasks which the user performs in relation to the product.

To do this, we design the research protocol so as to observe each stage of product usage in context. For example, in an ethnographic study for which the marketing decision was a brief to redesign packaging for a cola brand (ModelPeople, 2014b), we went to the store with the users to buy the product (a large 2-litre bottle), accompanied them home to watch them unload and store the product, observed a mealtime or event at which the product was served, and then the bottle disposed of. Several issues were observed, including difficulty in storing the bottle on pantry shelves or in a fridge, and difficulty pouring cleanly when the bottle was full. This led to a redesign of the bottle. We also developed a usage occasion-based taxonomy of brand sizes which was used in an innovation session with the brand's marketing and packaging teams and representatives from independent bottlers, to ideate new pack sizes and multi-pack configurations.

It can be helpful to observe user behaviour over a period of time. IDEO (Battarbee *et al*, 2012) cite the example of State Farm Insurance who wanted to understand how to create better services for Millennials, so they opened up a coffee shop in Lincoln Park, an upscale Millennial neighbourhood in Chicago, and offered free consultations along with the coffee, enabling the company to learn about how Millennials perceive and use insurance services.

User Experience (UX) research is a specialized field of user research which involves applying user observation, experience-based feedback and prototype or site interface usability testing to website design.

Recording what happens in the ethnographic interview

Taking systematic notes of field observations is considered to be a core task in ethnographic research (Emerson *et al*, 2011). In a consumer setting, verbatim transcripts of the ethnographic interview, field notes, photos and video are all essential in the analysis process:

- **Verbatim transcripts**, done after the interview from digital audio preserve original consumer ('native') language. This is important, as written notes can filter what was actually said through the lens of our own perceptions and language, thus losing nuances which may be critical.

- **Field notes** are written down by the researcher during the interview and include observations of body language, behaviour and context and other observational nuance which may not be captured on audio or video.

Connections between individual participants often occur to me while I am interviewing and I write these down in the margin of my pad. It can be tough to take extensive notes during an interview and also engage fully with the participant so I jot down the most important notes and then listen to audio very quickly after the interview to extend and type up my notes, so they can be shared with other members of the team.

- **Photos** are essential to record the interview and I take as many as possible, asking permission again if the image is sensitive (like a woman's 'muffin-top' belly in her jeans!). It is useful to make a list of photos that must be captured for each interview to enable comparison across participants. For example, we always photograph a car owner with his vehicle as the stance in relation to the car can be revealing of the nature of the relationship with the vehicle. Men with super-duty trucks stand four-square in front of the vast grille, arms crossed, grinning confidently. Men with sports sedans strike a pose, one hand rested casually over the engine. Men with mini vans try to shrink into the background. You get the idea.

Tricia Wang (2015) recommends sharing ethnographic field notes on social media. She feels this empowers participants by allowing them to feel more of a participant in research. We opened up individual digital diaries to all the participants in a Millennial casual dining study and found that the group did indeed enjoy commenting on each other's dining venues. This project was, however, social in nature. Opening up diaries of pain episodes doesn't give the same result, since pain is a more personal experience which consumers are less willing to share.

Netnography, social media ethnography and digital ethnography

The internet and particularly mobile technologies have resulted in new types of social behaviour and new ways in which consumers connect with brands. These technologies also offer new ways of conducting ethnographic research.

Netnography, a term originally coined by Robert Kozinets (2010) is a web-based ethnographic research methodology that allows a researcher to immerse herself into online conversations between consumers in an empathetic way. It involves the researcher gaining entrée into computer-mediated communities (CMCs), much like an ethnographer would in a specific geographical cultural milieu. CMCs can be brand communities (eg branded fan pages on Facebook or brand-sponsored forums like Dell World) or independent user communities (like Mumsnet for parents). It's important for the researcher to gain entrée to a community in an honest and respectful way by being open about identity and purpose, much as the ethnographic researcher would treat a participant in an in-person ethnographic encounter. Netnography has proven to be both productive and cost-effective at:

- gaining specific feedback from users via branded communities;
- crowd-sourcing co-creation for new product designs, flavours or names;
- uncovering latent needs through broader participation in communities related to a topic such as beauty.

However, a study conducted by ModelPeople (2010b) revealed there are negatives to the netnographic methodology, compared with online or in-person ethnography, primarily:

- expression in a CMC is often geared towards positive aspects of the self (unless the user is completely anonymous), whereas in-person observation can observe and query negative aspects;
- forms of expression can be contrived, whereas the in-person ethnographer who has built rapport with the participant is more likely to get a genuine response;
- responses to questions from the researcher can be controlled or limited, and it can be hard to probe for details because rapport can be limited online;
- responses to questions can be misunderstood without the ability to observe intonation gestures or body language.

Social media ethnography is a rapidly developing field and definitions and practices are still evolving, driven in part by the academic community. It includes exploring and interacting with social media discussions, analysis of online networks to model the most influential users and discourse analysis, which can be directed at consumer content and the identities that consumers create for themselves online (Postill and Pink, 2012). In practice, consumer brand corporations use enterprise-level social media monitoring services to track consumer sentiment (mentions, both positive and negative) of their brands, but open-source tools such as Social Mention exist for independent researchers to use.

There is some linguistic confusion between 'online', 'social media' and 'digital' ethnography. Some academics (Caliandro, 2015) suggest that **'digital'**

ethnography is focused on emergent culture found on the internet and comprises both quantitative (eg network analysis) and qualitative (eg sentiment analysis) techniques. This definition of 'digital ethnography' seems to encompass social media ethnography and netnography, but does not encompass 'online' ethnography, the latter being a method to gather 'offline' ethnographic data online. In practice, the terms 'digital', 'virtual' and 'online' ethnography are all used by practitioners at this time to describe the use of an online platform to capture consumer ethnographic data. It remains to be seen which descriptor wins the war.

Tool box
Ethnographic research checklist

- The ethnographic interview is designed to uncover consumer behaviour and attitudes through the lens of culture and takes place in a relevant context, such as the home.

- Allow at least four to eight weeks to design, plan and implement the project.

- Review all existing sources of data and do initial semiotics or trends analysis to understand the relevant context for the study.

- Create hypotheses around the research question based on existing data review, to help design the research participant screening criteria and context.

- Thoroughly consider the relevant context and be creative in designing where and how to design the consumer encounter.

- Ensure recruiters are fully briefed as to what you want the participants to do during the observation to avoid unhappy surprises!

- Build in a longitudinal component to the project, pre- and post-fieldwork: pre-work enables selection of the best participants and a mix of contexts; post-fieldwork study elements enable more detailed observation over time.

- Write a semi-structured protocol but don't over-control the participant; encourage her to do whatever she usually does or wants to do so the observation unfolds naturally.

- Record (with the participant's prior permission) the context using photography and video (see Chapter 8 for details). Take the same type of photo shots for each participant as this often reveals insights derived from comparison across interviews.

- Field notes are essential. Write down observations about participant and context. Get verbatim transcripts of interviews to preserve native language. Write up field notes as soon as possible following an interview and share with the team.

In-depth interviews

An in-depth consumer interview (IDI) is an informal conversation between a researcher and a single individual, with the goal of uncovering deeply held or non-conscious beliefs, attitudes, perceptions, motivations and behaviours. Therefore, IDIs are particularly effective when conducting research into topics which evoke complex emotions and require deep probing, such as healthcare. IDIs are also a great methodology for business or professional immersions where confidentiality may be a requirement for a productive conversation. In-depth interviews usually take place in a central location such as a research facility, rather than a contextual situation, as is the case with an ethnographic interview, and are typically one to two hours in length. However, they can also be conducted remotely if the participants (business executives, for example) are geographically far-flung. For example, if we decide to interview experts as part of a design study, this would typically be done by phone or Skype. Custom platforms can also be rented for conducting and recording webcam interviews. Unlike ethnographic interviews, for which observer numbers are limited, multiple observers can hear the same interview, for example, behind the glass in a research facility or via a Skype group call.

While the interview is not conducted in a contextual situation, it may still be important to understand the context of the participant relative to the research question. If this is the case, consider setting an online ethnographic pre-work exercise to enable discussion of context where relevant. For example, for a low-budget project (Brooks, 2002) we ran IDIs with plus-size teen girls and asked them to upload to our digital platform photos of themselves in favourite outfits with their friends, so we could observe and explore the emotions around shopping for and wearing plus-size clothing brands vis à vis skinny friends.

In-depth interviews can also form part of a longitudinal study. For example, we (ModelPeople, 2008) ran IDIs with menopausal women about their experiences of menopause and then we engaged with them online through weekly diaries as they trialled a new supplement, designed to alleviate the physical symptoms which can accompany menopause. Finally, a group discussion brought the women together to exchange views about their experiences and explore packaging concepts.

The protocol for a depth interview can be more structured than for an ethnographic interview because the context (an interview room) is known; we don't have to explore physically or face any unexpected situations! However, time should be allowed to explore subjects that come up, perhaps unexpectedly, *in-depth*. The interview should also include a number of the immersive research tools (such as metaphor elicitation or visualization) which are described later in this chapter, to help the interview participant to express difficult ideas in non-verbal form and to uncover non-conscious mental models. Standard batteries of images or words can also be used to structure an interview and compare data across interviews.

The interviewer's goal is to sustain a rich, deep and highly nuanced conversation in which the participant feels uncritically supported in expressing personal emotion. It is common for an IDI participant to thank me at the end of an interview and to tell me, 'It was fun!' Or, rather sadly, 'No-one has ever listened to me this way before.' To achieve this, the interviewer must build rapport with the participant and establish mutual trust and respect over the course of the interview. There are several ways to reinforce this:

- When the interview starts, seat the participant in an armchair, facing the interviewer but slightly offset. If sitting at a table, set the chairs at right angles (rather than facing), which avoids the impression of a formal interview and the risk of stifling informal conversation.

- Make eye contact with the participant, but give them space to look away when it's comfortable for them to do so.

- The interviewer should listen more than she talks. Silence encourages the participant to say more. Mirror body language and facial expressions to cue non-verbal listening.

- The interviewer should also use 'reflective listening', what Carl Rogers (Miller and Rollnick, 2013) calls 'accurate empathy'. This involves helping participants explore their own experiences and perceptions more deeply, by reflecting back to them what they said based on how the interviewer understood it. People don't always say what they mean; they encode meaning in words. Therefore, the interviewer has to decode (or 'make a guess' about!) the meaning in the words she hears.

- The decoding reflection is made as a statement and not as a question because a question can evoke the participant to rationalize what they said and to become defensive, while a neutral statement encourages a helping response and a more honest evaluation of behaviour. The following example is from a study about the reasons why patients take too many OTC pain killers, and uncovered common 'rationalizing' patterns which needed to be addressed in safety communications.

Tool box

The following example of reflective listening using decoding statements is from a study about the reasons why patients take more than the recommended dose of OTC pain killers (ModelPeople, 2013), and uncovered common 'rationalizing' patterns which needed to be addressed in safety communications.

Participant: 'I take the recommended dose.'

Researcher: 'You take the recommended dose on the label.'

Participant: 'Well, I guess I don't read the label every time. I don't know, I suppose, I just know.'

Researcher: 'You just know what works for you.'

Participant: 'That's right! I'm a big guy. I need to take a bigger dose.'

- As the above example shows, reflective listening also moves the interview forward in my experience (what Miller and Rollnick call 'continuing the paragraph'). I am able to offer the participant a slightly reframed way of understanding what he or she has just said that can be illuminating for us both and can nudge the conversation to a deeper level. I will say, 'Please tell me if I did not get that right', from time to time, to affirm that it's OK to correct my continuation.

▶

- Miller and Rollnick also recommend other interviewing approaches which I have found useful, defined by the acronym, OARS:
  - Asking **O**pen questions, which require a long answer, rather than closed questions which prompt a short or yes/no answer. For example: 'Tell me about your daily diet,' rather than 'How many servings of veggies do you eat every day?'
  - **A**ffirming, or encouraging the participant to keep going with the conversation. For example, I may say 'I appreciate you giving me such a good description' or 'You have given me so much useful information that I want to move on to discuss something else please.'
  - **R**eflecting (see above).
  - **S**ummarizing pulls together what the participant has already said, which is a good way to confirm understanding and also to ask 'Is there anything else that we have not mentioned?' Summarizing can also be a method of affirming, since it shows that the interviewer was listening.

Dyads and friendship pairs

A dyad is an in-depth interview with a pair of participants who are strangers. The pairs can be matched in terms of demographics and other screening criteria or they may be different. If matched, then we expect a degree of consensus within the conversation. If different, we may wish to create 'conflict' to generate debate. In my experience, dyads are considerably less productive than individual depth interviews because there is natural constraint between the two participants, whereas an interviewer who takes time to build rapport can overcome this with a single participant. The exception to this is the friendship pair, where participants are known to each other. This type of dyad can uncover additional insight via discussion between people who know each other's habits and can add perspective or call out less honest responses. For example, we (ModelPeople, 2007a) ran a study with tween gamers and recruited pairs of girls who knew each other and gamed together. These paired interviews were richer in terms of understanding social gaming motivations than would have been the case in a one-on-one interview. In this study, we also ran parent–child friendship pairs to uncover how parents monitor gaming behaviour and how game purchase decisions are negotiated. These interviews reflected both conflict and consensus!

Tool box

In-depth interview research checklist

- An in-depth consumer interview (IDI) is an informal conversation between a researcher and a single individual, with the goal of uncovering deeply held or non-conscious beliefs, attitudes, perceptions, motivations and behaviours.

- A dyad is an in-depth interview with a pair of participants who are strangers.

- Friendship pairs, where participants know each other's attitudes and behaviours in relation to the study topic, can elicit information which may not have come out in a one-on-one interview.

- Allow at least three to four weeks to plan and implement an IDI project.

- Consider a homework exercise to bring context into the interview.

- Use a semi-structured research protocol to allow the conversation to unfold naturally.

- Use immersive research tools such as metaphor elicitation, to help the interview participant to express difficult ideas in non-verbal form or visualization, to uncover non-conscious mental models (see Chapter 6 for details).

- Use standard image or word batteries to explore commonalities across interviews.

- Most importantly, build mutual trust and encourage honest communication by using OARS techniques.

Group discussions

Consumer group discussions (usually called focus groups), whether conducted in-person or online, are not as appropriate for immersive research as observation or ethnographic depth interviews, for the following reasons:

- It is clearly difficult to have an informal conversation with four to eight people at once, and to achieve the level of depth of exchange possible in individual interviews.

- Social desirability bias is more pronounced in a group setting. It has long been recognized (Edwards, 1957) that research participants report behaviour or attitudes in a socially acceptable direction.

- Limits of memory: most people don't pay attention to routine consumer tasks, such as shopping for household items and so they can't remember their behaviour or decision-making process. This is why ethnographic observation 'in the moment' is helpful.

- Tendency to rationalize what we do to avoid appearing irrational or inconsistent.

Design and moderation of the group can address these issues in part, for example by:

- Keeping group size small, and minimizing social desirability bias through group composition, for example by matching gender, income and behaviours. This is commonly done, especially for sensitive topics like healthcare.

- Using an online pre-group exercise which can be discussed in the group. Participants are often more willing to share personal thoughts in the 'privacy' of an online post, although as we have seen, a different kind of bias can be introduced in online exercises with a social component. A pre-work exercise can also be useful to observe context, as we did with the home networking case study in Chapter 1. Asking focus group participants to undertake a shopping trip and record it using mobile video, prior to coming to the group, cannot only offer useful insight but also get around limits of memory issues.

- Asking for 'private commitment': thoughts about specific questions or responses to marketing stimulus (eg concepts) are written down before being shared with the group.

- Using indirect research techniques instead of asking direct questions. For example:

  - Expressive techniques, such as asking participants to use images or objects to help describe something sensitive (eg a picture of a knot can help a participant with IBS illustrate how her symptoms feel without feeling so embarrassed in front of the group).

  - Descriptive story-telling that lets the participant unfold the story rather than get on the defensive and rationalize behaviour (eg 'Describe how you usually go about shopping for x brand...' rather than 'Why do you buy x brand in y store twice a week...?').

   – Projective story-telling, where the group participant imagines the reactions of another (similar) consumer (eg 'Tell me about the kind of person who'd buy this brand.'), the idea being that the participant's non-conscious perceptions are projected onto the imagined consumer.

• Using reflective listening (though this is harder in a group because of the complexity of remembering multiple responses). For example, in the early stages of the group, I take extensive notes about what a participant reports that they do (purchase habits for example). Later on in the group, I will often get an answer (typically after using an indirect technique) that seems inconsistent with what a participant reported earlier, and then I will gently restate my impression of what they said earlier. Sometimes I get a red-faced shrug or a confused shake of the head. More often, the participant will give me more helpful detail on why they feel this way, or will confirm that their original response was right (or wrong).

Despite their disadvantages, and regular attacks on their validity in the marketing press, consumer groups remain popular to support marketing strategy development. This is probably because they are a cost-effective and fast way to get broad insight into a topic, or to get early input to the development of marketing mix components such as advertising, new product or shopper marketing concepts. Perhaps equally importantly, the strategy team can easily observe focus groups *as a team*, and integrate tacit knowledge and observations iteratively, which is essential to developing shared strategic learning. It's harder to integrate learning when only two people saw a specific ethnographic interview. I suspect this explains the relatively lower usage of online focus groups, which have cost advantages over in-person groups. It is also possible to conduct up to five groups in a single day which can expose the team to up to 50 consumers, allowing them to quickly come to consensus around a marketing problem. Observing a broad sample of individual interviews (IDIs or ethnographies) takes much longer (I am not directly comparing these methodologies with group discussions, as their goals are different, but these are considerable practical roadblocks). It's now common for focus group reporting to be turned around in two to three days, with a strategy team debrief held in-field or a couple of days after, to enable the strategy development process to proceed at a fast pace. This poses analytical challenges for the researchers, and up-front preparation is needed to produce notes and transcripts overnight and synthesize insights within the team in-field (see Agile Research in Chapter 6).

   Group research is most effective, in my experience, when used to explore topics in-depth including cultural context and non-conscious emotional perceptions, using creative expression, ideation and co-creation. ModelPeople often uses extended (three- to four-hour) Creative Workshops, of 8–12 participants each. The workshop protocol is designed to minimize social desirability bias, elicit non-conscious responses to stimulus and maximize expression of social and cultural context. The group protocol uses a combination of immersive research tools, to elicit non-conscious responses; and creative ideation using imagery to express perceptions which are grounded in the individual participant's cultural and emotional perceptions and memories. A series of exercises, lasting 30–40 minutes each, keeps participants moving and looking forward to the next task, so energy remains high. Participants work individually or in matched pairs before presenting their thoughts to the group, to minimize bias. 'Creative Workshops' can be used for foundational research, with the goal of learning as much as possible in a short period about how consumers think, feel and behave relative to a specific topic. They are also particularly well suited to innovation research, because expressive techniques used enable us to understand category semiotics and explore non-conscious reactions to new concepts.

MINI CASE STUDY
'Craft' food and beverage – Part 1: Creative Workshops

A foodservice company was interested in gaining foundational deep insights into the emotional and cultural drivers of Millennial consumer preference for craft products, as a basis for product and branding innovation. The online store, Etsy, was the first to widely promote craft products and producers and was an instant destination for Millennial consumers. Now retail stores in the US, from Whole Foods to Nordstrom, routinely stock local 'craft' products, representing a significant cultural shift away from mass-produced brands and towards more personalized choices. Existing data and the tacit knowledge of the strategy team (marketing and insights executives) indicated that their Millennial target consumer was eating out at least five times a week and seeking, from their favoured 'fast casual' eateries, a purposeful philosophy around ingredient quality and source, and brands with a human face and authentic sense of hand and place. 'Craft' perceptions had become for Millennials a discriminator of choice for food and beverage brands, which was reflected in marketing strategies such as 'locally produced', 'uses only sustainable seafood' and 'real sugar'.

Our first step (ModelPeople, 2013–14) was to run three-hour Creative Workshops to provide foundational learning about the dimensions of 'Craft'. Prior to the workshops, participants completed an online 'semiotic opposites' exercise, creating an e-collage of images to define 'Craft in Food and Beverage': what it is and what it is not. This was explored at the beginning of the workshop, to set a benchmark against which to co-create new product concepts. For the rest of the workshop, participants worked in pairs to sort and prioritize new product concept ideas on flashcards, and then co-create (using an imagery battery, words and drawings) the idea, flavours and packaging for their favourite concept. The top co-created concepts were fleshed out by the branding agency, and positioning look–feel boards (collections of images to represent a new brand) were developed. Then mini focus groups were set up to explore and further co-create branded concepts prior to quantitative testing.

Executive panels

Executive panels are a form of consumer group at which executives (any number from a handful upwards) are present in the room to observe the panel, and may ask questions. These offer a concentrated form of consumer immersion for time-poor senior operational executives, but importantly, can also be used to integrate or institutionalize learning among senior stake-holders. The case study below illustrates two alternative approaches. In the unedited approach, executives observe the consumer group as it happens and learning is *integrated* immediately after the group. In the edited approach, strategy team learning is synthesized and the consumer group is scripted for executives so that learning is institutionalized among executives.

Tool box

Two approaches to designing executive panels

1. Unedited: purpose is to integrate learning

The client, an import automotive brand, wanted to engage mid-level and senior executives from the two geographic markets – responsible for design & engineering and marketing & sales – in immersive research which allowed them to ask as many questions as they wanted of US consumers. We (ModelPeople, 2012) recruited a panel of eight Millennial sporty coupé intenders and asked them to complete several online

▶

e-collages, showing photos of their lifestyle and style preferences, prior to attending a full-day Immersion. In front of an audience of 20 executives in an auditorium space at the Architecture & Design Museum in LA, the eight consumers discussed how lifestyle and style preferences influenced choice of car, and responded to questions about future design ideas, presented by the product planning team. Small teams of executives then accompanied an individual participant on a car tour and ride. At the end of the panel, executives discussed what they had heard and a learning summary was drafted in real time to *integrate* the day's learning. Learning was used to inspire design of a new sporty coupé for the US market.

2. Edited: purpose is to institutionalize learning

The client, a fashion retailer, wanted the brand's top design and merchandising executives to hear the voice of the customer relative to key marketing strategy issues. So we (ModelPeople, 2007b) effectively scripted prior consumer learning for an executive panel. First we ran observations of in-store purchase occasions, including interviews in the back room of the stores. The strategy team spent a day distilling down the key learning and insights which they thought executives should hear. Then we invited the women back to a hotel suite for afternoon tea. With the executives watching, we recreated over an hour, the four days of discussions we had already held to highlight key points, and then women showed us their purchases and told us why they'd chosen these items. Finally, we took questions from the executives, before they took afternoon tea with their customers and enjoyed an informal chat about what they'd heard. Executive learning was used to springboard approval of new merchandising and product strategies for the retailer's stores.

Online communities

Online communities, also known by the acronym MROCs, have become a well-established immersive insights tool. An online community is a screened sample of consumers retained over a period of time, specifically to provide longitudinal feedback on marketing questions. Many organizations use MROCs for a wide range of activities, from doing a quick check of new packaging to co-creating new products (see Table 5.1).

Table 5.1 Advantages and disadvantages of MROCs

Advantages	Disadvantages

• Flexibility:
   – Quick feedback from pre-recruited panellists.
   – Longitudinal feedback: ability to track behaviour or develop ideas over time.
 • Ability to segment panel (eg by age).
 Can be more cost-effective than commissioning a new project.
	• Refreshing panel to maintain quality and response rate.
	 • Bias: panellists wish to give positive answers to remain on the panel.
	 • Probing for depth of emotional response is limited.
	 • Limited ability to observe context.

MINI CASE STUDY
'Craft' food and beverage – Part 2: online community

In Part 1 of this case study, we (ModelPeople, 2013–14) described the foundational Creative Workshops conducted for a new foodservice 'Craft' brand. We left that case study at the point where a branded product concept had been developed.

Having developed the product concept, the strategy team decided they needed further input to the brand positioning architecture so ModelPeople re-recruited the Creative Workshop and mini focus group participants into an online community (MROC). Over the course of the following 12 months, the community engaged in a number of exercises. For example, we conducted online ethnography to learn more about Millennials' affinity with specific positioning dimensions of 'Craft' food and beverage brands. We also posted concept stimulus to gain feedback on: product recipe and flavours; elements of positioning architecture such as brand personality, values, emotional and self-expressive benefits and back story, to help with the design of packaging and communications. The benefit of using the same participants was their engagement in developing every aspect of a brand they wanted to experience. In addition, because we had met and knew a lot about these participants, we had deeper understanding of what consumer profile responded well or badly to specific elements of the brand concept. The final detailed brand concept emerging from longitudinal MROC input was tested quantitatively with a clean sample and scored highly.

Chapter 5 summary

1   A Strategic Learning Journey leverages all available forms of data but at its core is ***immersive, experiential consumer learning*** which develops a deep understanding about consumers or customers and the way specific brands fit into their lives.

2   Principal immersive research methodologies described in this chapter are:

   a) ethnographic research in a business context, including user research, online ethnography and digital ethnography;

   b) in-depth interviews (IDIs);

   c) focus groups, Creative Workshops and executive panels;

   d) online communities.

3   The methods discussed, though well established in both academic theory and consumer insights consulting practice, are adapting, and will continue to adapt over time, as new technologies emerge and evolve new insights tools.

4   Insights tools which can be applied within these methods are described in Chapter 6.

References

ARF (2008) *Shaping Retail: The use of virtual store simulations in marketing research and beyond*, https://kelley.iu.edu [last reviewed February 2016]

Battarbee, K, Suri, J and Howard, S (2012) *Empathy on the Edge*, available from IDEO

Brooks, C (2002) IDIs with plus-size teens

Caliandro, A (2015) Ethnography in digital spaces, in *Handbook of Anthropology in Business*, Left Coast Press, Walnut Creek, CA

Carlopio, J (2010) *Strategy by Design*, p 72, Palgrave Macmillan

Crossman, A (2016) *Immersion*, http://sociology.about.com

Edwards, A (1957) *The Social Desirability Variable in Personality Assessment and Research*, Dryden Press, New York

Emerson R, Fretz, R and Shaw, L (2011) *Writing Ethnographic Fieldnotes*, p 5, University of Chicago Press, Chicago

Kozinets, R (2010) *Netnography*, Sage, New York

Miller, W and Rollnick, S (2013) *Motivational Interviewing*, The Guilford Press, New York

ModelPeople Inc (2007a) Friendship Pairs with tween gamers (console and hand-held)

ModelPeople Inc (2007b) Executive panel with female shoppers of a mid-tier store chain

ModelPeople Inc (2008) IDIs and online qualitative with menopausal women

ModelPeople Inc (2010a) Dyads with young male purchasers of console video games

ModelPeople Inc (2010b) *Evolving Ethnographic Techniques for the Social Media Generation*, paper presented at the EQRC Annual Conference

ModelPeople Inc (2012) Executive panel with young male sporty coupé enthusiasts

ModelPeople Inc (2013) Ethnographic research and IDIs with OTC pain killer users

ModelPeople Inc (2013–14) Creative Workshops and online qualitative with Millennial craft food and beverage purchasers

ModelPeople Inc (2014a) Immersive research with purchasers of MFDs for children in India

ModelPeople Inc (2014b) Ethnographic research with purchasers of 2L soda

ModelPeople Inc (2015a) Ethnographic research with female denim purchasers

ModelPeople Inc (2015b) Online ethnographic research with young male purchasers of graphic Ts

Postill, J and Pink, S (2012) Social media ethnography: The digital researcher in a messy web, *Media International Australia*

Spradley, J (1979) *The Ethnographic Interview*, Wadsworth, Belmont, CA

Sunderland, P and Denny, R (2003) Psychology vs. anthropology: Where is culture in marketplace ethnography? in *Advertising Cultures*, ed TD Malefyt and B Moeran, Berg, Oxford

Wang, T (2015) Live fieldnoting: creating more open ethnography, in *Handbook of Anthropology in Business*, Left Coast Press, Walnut Creek, CA

Wilson, H and Macdonald, E (2011) Immersive Market Research, *Admap*, November

The Strategic Empathy Process Phase One (continued)

Immerse – immersive research tools and techniques

CHAPTER 6 OBJECTIVES

1 Give detailed guidelines for how to manage an immersive research project.

2 Demonstrate how to develop an immersive research protocol and discussion guide.

3 Describe how to implement techniques to uncover the non-conscious emotional and cultural drivers of how consumers think, feel and behave.

4 Illustrate, with global case studies, how to combine immersive research methods and these new tools, in a multi-disciplinary approach to marketing strategy formation.

CASE STUDY
Managing a multi-cultural immersive research project

'Walking is like a sunrise', said Nami, showing the interviewer the picture she had chosen of a vibrant sunrise over a rich turquoise ocean. 'Just sea and sky, nothing else; walking represents "inside me". I feel refreshed, liberated, it heals my mind and spirit. I can walk at my own pace, go where I want and I can control my own pace.' We (ModelPeople, 2010) were sitting outside a café in the Yokohama Port area of Tokyo, talking to a 34-year-old mum who walked four miles around the local park twice a week, as an escape – we learned from the Metaphor Elicitation and Deep Visualization exercises which we did with her – from her small apartment and caring for her young daughter; to regain some sense of personal focus and control. We had been asked to study 'walking' in the US, Europe and Asia as foundational research for a global sporting goods brand who wanted to develop a marketing strategy for their walking apparel and footwear division.

We found a 'walking' project surprisingly complicated to design and plan, considering it's an activity that most of us do every day! The first challenge we had was to develop the scope and methodology for the project. In terms of scope (deciding who to talk to and in what context), data showed that footwear was purchased primarily by people who walk for fitness, but also people such as nurses or waiting staff who are on their feet for long periods and need cushioned footwear. Walking for fitness also differs in place and intensity, including hiking off-road, urban power walking, and just 'walking' to get somewhere! This made developing the screening criteria complicated. German and Japanese consumers use different words for hiking, fitness walking, Nordic walking and 'taking a walk', which we had to reflect in our screener. Clearly, we needed to understand a complex linguistic taxonomy reflected in different geographically-based walking cultures in this category. Therefore, we decided to select a mixed methodology which combined observation of 'purposeful' walking practices and ethnographic interviews with small consumer groups to explore common definitions. We also used metaphor elicitation in a pre-work exercise, asking people to record their walking practices over a couple of weeks, and select pictures to represent the most important meaning of walking to them. In the interviews, we used Deep Visualization to uncover the non-conscious emotions associated with walking, both positive and negative.

Over the course of our study in these three key markets, it became clear that many consumers shared Nami's passion for 'me-time' during their walks; but also that they felt walking was not serious exercise, because everyone does it.

Walking lacks the pride of serious athleticism. 'Walking is great, and it's more for a mental thing rather than a physical thing', said Todd in Chicago. 'For me walking is just to get outside and get balance, but the gym is more important. I need to get those endorphins out. If I only went for a walk I would still feel sluggish.' The use of different linguistic forms for 'walking' is an attempt to resolve this confusion: in Germany and Japan, the English word 'walking' is used to replace 'gehen' and 'sanpo' – the words for 'going for a walk' – to make it clear that walking for fitness is intended. In these markets, the English term 'Walking' was often used with some pride to reflect the superior technical knowledge and athleticism involved:

> I was slow when I walked. I started to think that I am taking a walk not **Walking**. People around me were walking fast and swinging their arms so I thought that's what real walking is about. **Real walking** is so different from what I was doing.   Male, Tokyo

Some consumers are embarrassed by walking and aim to graduate to running instead of walking:

> I know a woman who jogs to the park, she does not want the neighbours to know she walks.   Katrine, Hamburg

However, others take pride in being **walkers**, and do not want to run because they lose the emotional benefit of me-time:

> Running is hard, it's the breathing; it's not fun. I guess I am more focused on what my body is doing. I can't clear my head. I can't get my mind on issues I'm thinking about.   Kim, Chicago (Deep Visualization)

A scan of category semiotics in each country showed 'walking' as seriously unsexy compared with running and other fitness categories. Imagery showed middle-aged couples pottering along. Moreover, the 'walking' section in a shoe store is often dominated by orthotic footwear, which reinforces the impression that walking is not athletic! Observations showed that donning specialized footwear and apparel, and using intensity measurement devices such as a pedometer were important to consumers, to differentiate 'fitness walking' from 'walking'. Yet consumers were largely unaware that walking footwear and apparel existed and, as we have seen, lacked stylish, aspirational choices.

After pulling together the commonalities and differences between the brand's key markets, the strategy team presented the findings to a wider stakeholder group of product design and marketing managers and conducted a half-day activation session to develop brand positioning architecture and product strategy.

Introduction

In Chapter 5, we explored how to select and implement immersive research methodologies; that is, research methods and tools which develop a deeply intuitive understanding of the target consumer or customer by observing and exploring behaviours, experiences, deeply held beliefs, emotions and perceptions in the relevant context. In Chapter 6, we build on the research methods and tools explored in Chapter 5, by explaining how to *manage an immersive research project*. Then we explore how to *design a research protocol* using some highly effective immersive research tools like Deep Visualization and metaphor elicitation to uncover *non-conscious* brand perceptions and motivations for consumer behaviour. By the end of Chapter 6, readers will have the skills and techniques to enable them to design and implement Phase One of the Strategic Empathy Process.

Immersive research project management

Research project management is defined as managing the process of (in this case, consumer or customer) research in order to ensure a successful outcome within the planned budget and timeline. Once the Learning Journey scope, objectives and overall approach are decided (see Chapter 4), and the specific methods selected (see Chapter 5), a project plan must be developed and managed. The principal steps in managing a research project are:

1 design sample size, screening criteria and location;
2 confirm the budget and create a project plan and timeline;
3 design a recruiting screener;
4 manage the recruit and project logistics.

Sample size, screening criteria and location

Sample size is the number of participants to be included in our research project. In quantitative research the sample size can be statistically derived based on the degree of confidence desired from the study. In qualitative research, however, sample size relies more on practical criteria such as budget and how many different types of people (sub-samples) we want to include. In academic settings (Baker and Edwards, 2012) a saturation approach can be used (researchers stop when they are not hearing anything new) but this does not work in a commercial context, because we need to define and recruit for a specific sample size upfront, for budget and timeline reasons. The usual approach is to decide first how many different sub-samples we want to include based on the scope of the project and then let that decision guide the sample size. Budget constraints also come in here because, in qualitative research, sample size hugely influences project cost. I prefer to prioritize quality over quantity and ensure we prioritize finding and remunerating the best people. As we saw in Chapter 5, this approach may include recruiting more people than we want to talk to and then previewing and selecting the most insightful and participative recruits by means of an online qualitative pre-interview exercise. In practice, 10–25 individual interviews and 4–12 group workshops are typical ranges for a single country study.

Screening criteria are the variables chosen to define the different sub-samples to be included in research. This decision is based on the strategic learning objectives, as discussed in Chapter 4.

Tool box
Typical screening criteria

- Demographics such as: gender, age, personal or household income, ethnicity, education, social class and employment status.
- Category/brand purchase, usage or intention to purchase over a specific time period. It is usual to exclude rejecters: people who say they *would never* buy a category/brand.
- Purchase habits: for example, the channels where the brand is usually purchased.
- Perceptions: for example, are they positive or negative towards a brand or category?

In qualitative projects, where the sample sizes are smaller, it's important not to be too prescriptive about screening criteria or you end up looking for very specific consumer profiles: for example, a Caucasian woman in her 30s with kids and a household income of $50–70,000 who buys Campbell's soup at

Walmart. This makes recruiting time-consuming and expensive. The best approach is to set broad categories of screening criteria and then look for a mix of the best people who meet the broad criteria. For example: women aged 25–39 with a household income of over $50,000 who buy soup (mix of brands: Campbell's, Progresso, Heinz, private label) at mass stores.

Location of the research project is the final decision. This is usually based on where the brand's key or potential markets are located. More than one market may be selected to account for variations driven by geographical culture, climate, historical brand dominance or other variables such as the type of distribution or store format. However, other factors may drive choice of location, particularly for innovation strategy development. In most geographical markets there will be one or more influential urban markets where trends start and this may be important for design innovation, especially in style-driven categories like fashion, alcohol or automotive. For example, in the US, we typically go to New York (especially Manhattan) and Los Angeles (coastal cities and Hollywood) to do this kind of research, but other cities may be influential in specific ways (eg San Francisco for tech and Austin for music). If working in an unfamiliar global market, it's essential to take advice from local recruiters as to which markets to select to reach specific types of participant.

Budget, project plan and timeline

Once the screening and location decisions are made, the budget can be put together. The choice of recruiting method is a key factor. A company may have lists of consumers or customers who have opted in to be approached for research projects. However, it's common to use an established field recruiting specialist to recruit for in-person research as they maintain databases of pre-screened, opt-in consumers with whom they have established trust to facilitate unknown researchers to engage with them. In some countries, like Russia and India, field recruiting agencies may be less experienced with ethnographic recruits and it's common to recruit through personal networks (Brooks, 2012). In India, for example, upscale consumers may be reluctant to agree to an extended period of time in their homes unless it is by personal request. Other hard-to-find consumer sub-samples are also recruited via personal networks. For example, my company retains a global network of Millennial trendsetters (GlobalCultureBlog®), leading-edge consumers in major cities around the world, who recruit local young adult trendsetters, enthusiasts and influencers for research studies. The budget should allow for a drop-out rate among recruited participants. It's typical to over-recruit by 10–20 per cent. 'Floaters' (participants who agree to stand by for a specific time period in case a scheduled participant cancels) may also be required to cover last-minute drop-outs. It's not uncommon to turn up on a participant's doorstep for an in-home ethnographic interview and find that the participant has forgotten you were coming or changed his or her mind!

Bid requests are sought from recruiters to define recruiting fees, location rental for IDIs (in-depth interviews) or groups and incentive payments to participants, which enable the budget to be confirmed. Once the 'winning' recruiter is identified, create an overall project plan, working back from the fieldwork date, which takes into account time for: screener development, recruiting, previewing, selecting and confirming participants, developing a research protocol and briefing researchers. Allow at least four weeks, though this time period can be compressed if necessary.

Recruiting screener

The next step is to write the screener, the tool which recruiters use to screen a population of potential research participants and select the consumers or customers whom we have chosen to include. This can take several days as it needs to be discussed and piloted by the strategy team and then piloted by the field recruiting agency. A screener is an ordered list of questions designed to be read out to potential participants during a phone screen. More often now, a partial screener is e-mailed out to a recruiter's database to pre-qualify participants. Questions are mostly closed-ended (inviting a single response which can be coded for easy analysis). Sometimes, a segment 'typing tool' (developed in quantitative research) is included to define which target consumer segment a respondent belongs to. Include one to two open-ended questions, which should be asked verbally over the phone (not by e-mail) to check the articulacy of the recruit and the internal consistency of their responses. For example: 'Think about the last time you purchased lipstick. Describe the shopping experience in detail.'

It's important to consider the order and format of questions, which should be:

- Logical. For example, put category usage questions before specific brand usage questions.
- Clear and concise, so as not to confuse the respondent.

- Disguised to avoid deliberately fake responses. For example, hide the activity, category or brand you want to recruit for in a list of other options and be wary of respondents who answer 'yes' to everything.

The field recruiter should be able to give practical advice on how to write a usable screener.

Recruit and project logistics

The rapport with the participant, which we described in Chapter 5 as essential to a successful interview, starts to be built at the recruiting stage. It's important to build the participant's trust and enthusiasm to take part in the interview. Always let participants know who will be conducting the interview and provide them with a way to check your credentials, such as a link to the recruiter's or researcher's website. Reassure participants that you adhere to the UK MRS (2016) Code of Conduct or the US MRA (2016) Code of Marketing Research Standards (or international equivalent). Try to have the same person make each contact with the participant and try to use female recruiters if the participant is female. The cost and time commitment of ethnographic research sessions demands extra attention to screening, and it may be worthwhile for the researcher to rescreen participants informally and quickly over the phone, to gain additional detail about the context we will be observing and the ability of the participant to articulate the topic. This rescreening is an opportunity to further establish trust with the participant and confirm what will happen during the research session. Let participants know what will happen during the research, how many people will be observing (and of what gender) and if video is to be taken. In markets less familiar with ethnographic research, where field agencies may not have adequately briefed participants, this step is essential.

As recruiters fill the interview slots, they should send participant profiles which record the answers each participant gave to the screener. It's important to check that these details correctly reflect the screening criteria set, as sometimes the recruiter may have misunderstood what's required. Finally, make sure all team members know where to go for the research. If the research is away from a facility, it's important to double check location addresses with participants and to ask about any special instructions for parking, gated community access and so on. Provide observers with instructions of where to meet and at what time so that researcher and observers meet the participant all together and don't arrive in piecemeal fashion.

Managing global research

Developed and major emerging markets all have an infrastructure of the kind described above for recruiting participants. In smaller emerging markets, it's essential to work with a tried or professionally recommended local provider, to ensure participant quality, as the value of recruiting fees and incentive payments has been found in some instances to encourage dishonest screening practices. Some global markets have a different approach to recruiting and scheduling, so it's essential to allow enough lead-time to accommodate this. For example, when scheduling professional interviews in Japan, respect for professional participants' status dictates latitude in choice of interview times, which can make it difficult to run as many interviews in a single day as is possible in the US or Europe. Some markets, including Japan, may also be less comfortable with short recruit lead-times. Finally, if there's a significant time difference between your time zone and the recruiter's, this can add to communication time. It's essential to create a project plan and allow at least six weeks if more than one country market is involved.

Immersive research tools

Having selected an immersive research methodology and recruited the project, the next step is to design the research protocol, which is the form that the consumer or customer interaction will take. The protocol is described in a Moderator Guide or Discussion Guide. In this section we will explore some important tools which allow researchers to explore the non-conscious emotional and cultural drivers of consumer perceptions, beliefs, attitudes and behaviours. These tools are methodology agnostic: they can, mostly, be incorporated into either individual or group methodologies, and some of them can also be used in a quantitative research phase to validate qualitative learning.

Deep Visualization

We saw in Chapter 2 that brand representations in the mind are dynamic patterns of associations and emotional memories (derived from experiences of the brand within different contexts). Non-conscious brand associations are embedded in implicit memory, and can be primed by marketing stimuli. Therefore, it's essential to understand these associations and emotional memories for the purposes of forming marketing strategy and measuring its effectiveness. More narrowly, Rapaille (2006) has argued that *the combination* of the *earliest* product or brand experiences *with a specific emotion* creates what he calls an 'imprint' on the mind, which influences future thoughts and actions relative to a brand or category. Imprints, Rapaille contends, are influenced by culture, and can differ between cultures, which must be understood in developing marketing strategy. Deep Visualization is a tool which I use often in consumer and customer research to access the deep-seated emotional memories and non-conscious brand associations which are formed by brand experiences, whether the experience was early, good or bad. The technique was developed by Richard Maddock (Maddock and Fulton, 1996) and Charles Kenny, and taught to me by a master: one of their former associates, Clare Grace (1998). I have applied it in thousands of interviews across multiple categories.

The principle behind Deep Visualization is that the interviewer uses relaxation, visualization and repetition to uncover non-conscious associations and deep-seated emotional memories, until the core expression of a brand is arrived at. These types of interviews are most effectively conducted in a comfortable and relaxing setting. Firstly, participants are asked to close their eyes, take a deep breath and relax, putting them into a state of heightened Alpha brain wave activity, in which the mind is clear of intrusive thoughts and sensory input is minimized, to aid concentration. The participant may be asked to do a quick 'practice' visualization of a recent event, which should be emotionally neutral (eg taking a walk along the street outside your house) to avoid priming. Then the interviewer will ask the participant to go back in time to a specific experience. Maddock suggested having them visualize a clock going backwards or leaves flying backwards on a calendar. Typically, we select a memorable (good) experience to uncover positive brand associations, but a good experience is often contrasted with a bad experience in order to understand the full dimension of brand perception.

Researcher notes by Clare Grace

I have done many of these interviews in dimly lit one-on-one rooms, with the respondent leaning back in a recliner if possible, with their eyes closed or covered with a sleep mask. It's important that people can actually place themselves back in time and relive (rather than remember) an experience, so that they can recall 'first-hand' all the associated experiences and emotions. I will say 'you are really there, you can feel it', to encourage them to do this. They will usually start to speak in the present tense, telling me what they are doing and seeing right now in their visualization. Participants really seem to enjoy this and will often thank me at the end of their interview.

Once the participant has let the interviewer know that they are 'there', in the experience, the interviewer will gently and repetitively probe the narrative to reveal deeper levels of motivation and meaning. Typical probes are 'What do you see?', 'How does that make you feel?', 'What's important about that?' and, when we are reaching the core of meaning we can ask 'What does this brand/experience represent to you?' It can also be helpful to ask participants to imagine that their favourite brand has been taken away: how do they feel about that and what will they do now? This helps us understand the depth of attachment to a brand and how consumers see, and feel about, alternatives.

Deep Visualization is particularly insightful when used to:

- Uncover the deepest levels of brand motivation and emotional connection. The interviewer does this by repetitively probing for the meaning behind important associations with a brand or product experience.

- Explore the earliest experiences of a brand within a cultural context. For example, Rapaille (2006) gets people to go back to the earliest experiences they can remember of a brand or product, believing that these early experiences 'imprint' or help to form culture-specific brand associations which solidify over time.

- Understand the sensory dimensions of a brand experience (both positive and negative) which might inspire or give direction for innovation or communications: eg colour, texture, taste, mouth feel or sound. We do this by asking a participant to describe 'in the moment' everything they are experiencing as they consume or use a brand.

- Help research participants co-create innovation ideas by asking them to imagine something new within the context of a visualized experience. For example, after discussing likes/dislikes of a brand, or exposing various stimuli for improving a category shopping experience, I might ask the participant to put themselves in a store situation and imagine a new brand on the shelf or a new aisle experience and describe it.

MINI CASE STUDY
Using Deep Visualization to differentiate consumer segments

A year-long project with a global beverage company (ModelPeople, 2005) required us to bring 21 beverage segments to life for marketing activation. A quantitative study had identified specific 'need states'; that is, what consumers were looking for in terms of functional and emotional benefits, what beverages they tended to drink and when/how often. We had run a series of ethnographic interviews and IDIs with each segment, to understand the cultural and emotional drivers of beverage and brand selection, and now we were doing IDIs with a segment of consumers who drank soda up to eight times a day, often with fast food.

In my interview with Albert, he admits that he drinks about six cans of 'coke' a day, starting in the car on the way to work, in place of breakfast, and finishing up late at night on his way home from an evening out. He seems reluctant to talk about what he describes as his 'harmless addiction', so I ask Albert to visualize drinking his favourite brand of 'coke' with fast food. I instruct Albert to close his eyes and relax; and then to 'see' himself drinking his favourite brand. The idea of the visualization is to put Albert into a state of light relaxation and increase his Alpha brain wave activity, so as to allow him to more easily access emotional memories about brand experiences. Albert describes his day as a clerk in a busy town planning office, handling numerous calls and site visits. 'It's stressful', he says, frowning and shaking his head in an agitated way. The height of his day is lunch, when he gets to sit down and enjoy a taco or fried chicken sandwich. I ask Albert to tell me how the soda feels as it goes down his throat and he describes how he is anticipating the sensation of the bubbles and the rich, warm flavour in his mouth. As he savours the familiar salty, crunchy comforting flavour of his sandwich contrasting with the refreshing acidity of the cola, he feels the lift of the calories and caffeine; the cares of the day recede. As he talks, Albert's face relaxes and he smiles to himself. 'This is my time', he says, 'my escape'. It's the time of day when he gets to call the shots and tell the world to go away and stop hassling him for a few minutes. A personal oasis. The soda and food heighten the moment for Albert. It's game on for the remainder of the day. 'What does the brand represent?', I ask him. 'A moment in my day', he replies. 'A moment of pure happiness.'

'Now, your regular brand is not available on the soda fountain today but there's a new brand available; what will you do now?' I ask. 'Go elsewhere', he shoots back. 'The food won't taste right. I can't go back to work disappointed. I won't be able to make it through the rest of the day.' I ask him to project himself into another scenario: 'It's another time in the day. You had your coke with lunch but this time you'd like something different. What kind of new version can you see in your mind's eye? Taste it, what does it taste like? What's the sensation of the drink as you swallow it?' Albert considers. 'It might be nice to have something just a bit different, yeah. Something sweet, the same carbonation that burns as it goes down, but sweeter, maybe fruity.' I ask Albert to open his eyes. 'What did I say,' he asks anxiously, 'did I do a good job?' 'Yes', I reassure him. The brand manager agrees. She got an idea for a new line extension while listening to Albert describe flavour combinations. The advertising creative director nods too. He heard rich, new language about the brand experience and how it relates to the consumer's emotional relationship with the brand, which has inspired the new creative brief his team is working on.

Semiotic Scan

In Chapter 2, we discussed the potential of semiotics analysis for immersive exploration of cultural, social and emotional context. An applied version of it, called a 'Semiotic Scan' has long been used in design and communications research, or to pre-select a battery of images for metaphor elicitation work (see next section). I often do a 'Semiotic Scan' at the outset of a consumer research project, especially in categories with a strong, style-based intangible element to brand equity, such as automotive, fashion or consumer electronics.

Tool box

How to do a Semiotic Scan

- The purpose is to deconstruct category and related semiotics ('signs'): both textual (consumer discourse such as social media) and visual (such as ads and photographic imagery), in order to explore category or brand cultural codes as a basis for immersive consumer research.

- Firstly we look at category and brand semiotics and also related category semiotics (eg for an automotive study we might look at automotive category ads, consumer photos and film imagery; but we may also look at related categories such as architecture, fashion and electronics).

- Then we identify key themes which define the category and build a battery of images and/or words for use in metaphor elicitation and projective exercises (we explain below how to do this).

A Semiotic Scan can also be conducted during a strategy team working session. This is a great way to get a new team grounded in the category, to provide input to a brand SWOT analysis or to identify positioning opportunities for a new brand:

1 The team works with imagery and textual materials, using its own tacit knowledge to identify key ideas.

2 Ideas are then clustered into themes to define category values and symbols.

3 Category brands are mapped against theme clusters to give a picture of the category and identify white space for meaningful, differentiated brand innovation or positioning.

MINI CASE STUDY   Innovation in flavoured malt beverages

A white spirits brand had been approached by a major beer brewer to form a joint venture (JV) and produce a low-alcohol flavoured malt beverage (FMB) to be marketed to young adults of legal drinking age (LDA). The sophistication of the spirit brand needed to be translated authentically to the FMB in a way that would differentiate it from other FMBs in the market. The JV strategy team along with the appointed ad agency (Brooks, 2001) needed to decide how the new brand would be positioned relative to the parent brand. The JV strategy team, comprising representatives from both JV partners, attended a working session in a Chicago hotel suite for two days. In two teams of four people, we firstly reviewed marketing communications imagery from both white spirits and FMB categories, and identified brand and category codes and messages on Post-it notes. Then the teams clustered the Post-its into themes and produced a single cluster map, which identified themes across the two categories. The strategy team then plotted FMB and spirits brands against these clusters. The map revealed the positioning landscape for licensed FMB brands and identified positioning white space for our new FMB. We were also able to predict positioning direction which might be taken by other spirits brands entering the category to ensure we would remain differentiated in our chosen space. The new FMB was launched, positioned as we had ideated during the strategy team working session, and rapidly became the number two brand in the category with about one-third of the marketing budget and sales capability of the number one brand.

Metaphor elicitation

Metaphor, defined as expressing the unfamiliar in terms of the familiar, is used widely in qualitative research to explore both unspoken and unconscious meaning, beliefs and experiences. Metaphor as a research tool is effective in part because human beings are accustomed to using and seeing spoken and visual metaphor in everyday life: even little children use metaphor to help them describe or make sense of unfamiliar phenomena (eg using 'big bird' as a metaphor for a plane). Lakoff and Johnson (1980) argue that the human conceptual system is 'fundamentally metaphorical' in character. Metaphors can be personal or widely used and are derived from our experiences: physical, social or cultural. They note three types of metaphorical concept which are realized by very many linguistic expressions:

1 **Orientational** metaphors, which relate to spatial relationships (eg up/down as in 'Things were looking up but now we are going downhill again').

2 **Ontological** metaphors which project entity status onto something that does not have that status inherently (eg Mind as Machine: 'My mind is rusty today'; 'The cogs are turning').

3 **Structural** metaphors, which structure one experience in the form of another (eg Life is a Lottery: 'He's a real loser'; 'If I play my cards right I could be in with a chance').

Advertising often uses metaphor as a means of transferring associations from one object to another in an indirect way. When we see the plane take off over the Saab in the TV ad, we infer the power, speed and emotional freedom of the driving experience. When we see Julia Roberts in an ad for *La Vie Est Belle* perfume, we transfer the aspirational qualities of Julia and her own 'beautiful life' to the fragrance.

Thus, eliciting metaphor, either verbal or visual, in research can:

- Explore social and cultural codes which form the framework of meaning for a brand:

  - For example, in a project for an entry-level luxury car brand (ModelPeople, 2006a), we explored the meaning of luxury using visual metaphor. When we analysed the images and accompanying words chosen we were able to identify several unspoken dimensions of luxury that were essential to these buyers, among them: personal expression (not social at all), sensory pampering, technology empowerment and exciting creative vision, exclusive place and harmonious aesthetic. Not only were these metaphors helpful in terms of inspiring design direction; they also clearly indicated direction for advertising execution and brand partnerships.

- Elicit non-conscious brand perceptions, including those which have been deliberately and consistently created by brand communications:

  - For example, Gap ran a famous TV campaign in the 1990s with the tagline 'Everybody In...' (cords, vests etc). When doing metaphor-based research in this category, some 10 years later (Brooks, 2003), consumers repeatedly selected an old print ad of this campaign to represent Gap. Unfortunately, the metaphor 'Everybody In...' now meant ubiquitous, mass and lacking individuality. The brand had lost its cool and become commoditized, largely because of merchandise and store experience, we found as we explored further, but the metaphor remained in the non-conscious mind.

- Identify perceived brand relationships, cultural archetypes or personae. Because humans are social animals, much of a brand's emotional connection can be expressed in personal relationship terms. Sometimes if you dig deeper, the connection can be traced back to an actual relationship – eg 'my mum used' the brand; 'my glamorous friend told me about' the brand:

  - For example, a common exercise is to ask the participant to look through a battery which shows images both of famous people and archetype images such as mother, father or child.

- Help consumers describe emotions that are hard to put into words. For example:
  - 'I feel like I'm breathing underwater', was a common metaphor used by heavy sinus sufferers in a healthcare study (ModelPeople, 2014), which was used in a TV ad.
  - Encouraging women in group research on menopause (ModelPeople, 2008a) to draw their feelings elicited much stronger emotions than would have emerged through discussion alone.

Figure 6.1 Vicious circle

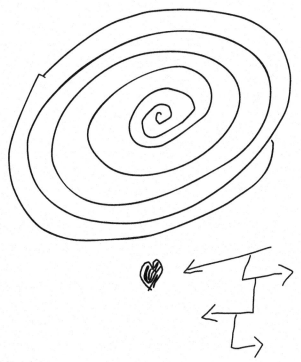

SOURCE: ModelPeople Inc

Like a vicious circle that never ends, the symptoms keep coming and coming.
It's just not going anywhere, it's just there. Then I drew a heart because usually I'm a kind loving person, but I drew a **black heart because I'm not my sweet loving self.** Then I drew arrows going in different directions, because I feel like I'm going in all different directions.

Peri-menopausal woman, Chicago

- Uncover non-conscious associations, which cannot be elicited through questioning:

  - For example, we (ModelPeople, 2004) used imagery to help US mothers define 'healthy childhood' and discovered that obesity was a huge concern, not so much for physical health reasons but because parents were frightened that their children would be negatively labelled and ostracized by other children and would be unhappy, even depressed as a result. The social and mental impact of obesity was of more concern than the physical impact, an insight that was subsequently used in a TV ad by a no-sugar kids' cereal brand.

- Explore sensory dimensions of a brand experience:

  - For example, we (ModelPeople, 2007) ran a project with a foodservice bakery supplier to determine the key elements of an in-store bakery experience. First, we had focus group participants visualize a memorable trip to a bakery, focusing on the sensory aspects: the sights, sounds, smells etc. Then we asked them to pick from a battery a picture that best reflected this experience. Four pictures were selected again and again and, by analysing the images and related stories from the visualizations it became clear what the important do's and don'ts were: the smell and feel of warm, soft fresh bread was key, but also the sight of bakers working behind the counter (even though they were putting pre-prepared frozen product into the oven!); the ambience of the bakery was also key, it needed to be set apart a little from the loud bustle of the store so that it felt homely, warm and soothing. These insights were activated into store design strategy for a global grocery retailer.

- Identify ideas or concepts that can be reflected in brand innovation. When exploring innovation concepts with consumers, it can be difficult to explore brand fit. Consumers tend to state, if asked, that 'of course' a specific brand could bring this new product to them. Building metaphorical representations of a new concept can identify points of congruence or dissonance with the master brand strategy:

  - For example, a yogurt brand wanted to launch a probiotic brand extension. A Semiotic Scan of the probiotic landscape (ModelPeople, 2006b) had revealed that the dominant code was 'medicine' and the marketing team was considering a serious, functional positioning for this new brand. We exposed focus groups to a short, branded product concept and asked them to use images and words to create a metaphor-based representation of the new brand. From these representations, it became clear that the key point of differentiation for the consumer for this line extension was taste and enjoyment first and efficacy second. This was perhaps not surprising, given the master yogurt brand's established equity in taste, but the metaphor exercise helped the strategy team decide between positioning alternatives.

- Explore the differences between segments:
  - For example, in a study for a vitamin and supplement brand, we (ModelPeople, 2008b) asked participants in ethnographic interviews to show us images that represented 'healthy' to them; and then to select images which represented the client's brand. One segment selected images showing youthful, body-con athleticism; another selected images showing wellness as part of a confident, balanced approach to life. Brand imagery was more consistent: associating the brand with balanced, natural nutrition and wellness; appealing to the needs and values expressed in the metaphors of the confident group but lacking a performance edge for the body-con segment. This insight led to the innovation of new products for energy and performance, with a more youthful, body-con positioning.

Over the course of at least 10,000 interviews in which I've used the metaphor and visualization tools, I have found that some metaphors reoccur frequently regardless of category or geography. For example:

- **Balance** is a desired state of physical, emotional or spiritual equilibrium and harmony. This idea goes back to Aristotle's mean or middle way between excess and deficiency, which influenced not only classical ethics but also architectural design and art. The balance metaphor crops up in categories as diverse as automotive design ('Luxury is harmonious design, nothing out of place'), beverages and healthcare ('I want to feel balanced: calm and centred'). Consumers who express this desire are generally past (or trying to emerge from!) the frenetic young adult life-stage and find a settled place in life. Balance is more grown-up and confident. Affluent consumers also express a feeling of balance as a reflection of their pride and satisfaction with what they have achieved. They might seek to reflect this feeling of balance by seeking ethical balance: 'giving back' through charitable giving or social or environmental advocacy. Much luxury design aims to project a sense of quiet balance. Balance can be a means of redressing an imbalanced situation (or redressing guilt): for example, giving kids a healthy breakfast to make up for giving them a packed lunch full of convenient, processed food.

- **Belonging** is a primal human urge. Maslow gives 'belonging' second place in his hierarchy of needs. We see the belonging metaphor crop up in categories which express ritual social connection (eg beer or food); also in categories where identification with other people is important (eg in fashion, as we saw with the Gap 'Everyone In...' case study). In some categories, including fashion, there can be a tension between belonging and being individual, often expressed as 'I want to stand out, but not too much'. The degree to which a consumer wants to 'stand out' will often define a segment in fashion categories. Fashion brands also have to manage being identified with 'belonging', as we saw with Gap. For example, we (ModelPeople, 2009) spoke with consumers and lapsed consumers of a brand of premium jeans, popular with teen girls. These women, now in their 20s, had all loved the brand when younger, but now rejected it because they saw themselves as older, wiser and more successful. The brand represented 'belonging', but for teen girls; they had moved on, in denim as in life. Other consumers of the same age, however, relished the brand as representing who they had wanted to be when they were teens (and now could afford to be). Many brands try to harness 'belonging' as part of their brand essence: for example, the American Girl doll brand has just launched a new campaign, 'The Pledge', which answers feelings of isolation among young girls by dramatizing how girls can be more powerful if they act together 'for all'; social media is promoting 'Us-ies' as the alternative to 'Self-ies'.

- **Control.** From the earliest age, humans are strongly motivated to gain control: over their environment and actions. Control therefore is the dominant metaphor in categories where consumers feel either out of control (as in healthcare) or vulnerable (as in automotive). In a study with chronic pain sufferers, the desire for control was expressed by seeking a regime of multiple products: the act of rubbing on a topical lotion or applying a heat pad gives the illusion of control. Some consumers prefer pain killers that allow four doses a day, rather than two, because they feel more in control of pain. 'Power is nothing without control' pronounces an ad for Pirelli, showing a rubber fist made from tyres smashing through water on a road.

Zaltman and Zaltman (2008) identify seven types of what they call 'deep metaphors', that is 'human universals' which start developing at birth and are shaped by social environment: transformation, journey, control, balance, connection, resource, container (keeping something in or out).

Tool box
Implementing the metaphor tool

- Metaphor can be elicited in two ways: unaided or aided.
- In the unaided approach, the researcher asks participants to choose words or images which represent the brands, experiences or concepts being explored (eg 'Choose images which represent all the aspects of luxury to you personally' or 'Choose images and words which represent Infiniti, Lexus, BMW, Acura and Mercedes'). The researcher may ask for either:
  - Individual combinations of images and words.
  - A collage of pictures and words pasted/written onto stiff paper.
  - An online e-collage. I prefer to use our PeopleBlogSpot e-collage function because it allows participants to select images from their own photo galleries, as well as images published online, and also resize images to reflect their relative importance.
- In the aided approach, the researcher gives participants a battery of pre-selected images and/or words to choose from. Depending on the research question, this battery could be derived from client brand assets combined with images derived from a Semiotic Scan, for example:
  - Brand images, used in communications (unbranded).
  - Brand images and key words used by client internal or agency design teams (brands typically have a 'style guide' which incorporates visual articulation of brand essence and personality collections of images, called brand 'look-feel').

▶

- Images or words chosen by the strategy team to reflect dimensions of brand and competitive brand essence or personality.

- Common archetypes. We have a standard image battery including people (some famous such as John Wayne) and emotions archetypes such as mother, father, child, innocent, carefree, stressed, sad, happy, alive etc. It's helpful to have a standard battery as this often enables useful comparisons across different types of exercise: for example, the different brands in a corporate portfolio; or competitive brands within a category.

- Values and goals: Miller *et al* (2001) have devised a battery of 100 values which can be printed onto index cards for research participants to sort into piles according to importance. This resource has been generously published online.

- The unaided approach allows participants latitude in coming up with the exact images which they feel are representative, perhaps enabling new strategic perspectives. The aided approach enables the team to explore brand, competitor and category symbols with consumers in a focused way, including new ideas or details that consumers may not have readily articulated on an unaided basis. Ideally both unaided and aided approaches are used (perhaps setting an unaided exercise as pre-work for a research session).

- It's essential to consider how to frame a metaphor question: narrowly (eg by brand or category) or more generally. Framing the question more generally or widely may offer up crucial related contextual or emotional insight. For example, it may be more insightful to ask consumers for metaphors relating to 'family time' than just to 'mini-vans'.

MINI CASE STUDY
Healthcare branding using metaphor elicitation and visualization

A joint venture between two brands in the healthcare space had resulted in a unique new product concept which had scored well in quantitative evaluation. The clients now needed to make decisions regarding branding and positioning. To add complexity to this strategic question, the two brands were positioned differently from each other; and one brand had different brand equities in its two key geographic markets in the US and Germany. The opinions of healthcare professionals who would recommend the brand were also important. Therefore, we (ModelPeople, 2013) designed a mixed methodology including IDIs with healthcare professionals and Creative Workshops with consumers in both the US and Germany.

In the consumer workshops we used aided metaphor elicitation: participants established separate baseline brand metaphors and personae for the two JV brands. The battery of images was assembled from the two brands' style guides and other images, selected to represent both brands' known functional and emotional benefits. Then participants were exposed to the new product concept (unbranded) and undertook a projective visualization exercise to imagine a consumer learning about, purchasing and using the new product. They were asked which of the given brand approaches they most associated with the visualized person and usage experience. Then they created another brand metaphor and persona for the new device, branded as they had decided. Comparing both brand metaphors and personae revealed areas of fit between non-conscious associations with the existing JV brands and with the new product concept. This identified clear areas of equity, in both the US and Germany, which each of the JV brands could bring to the new brand and resulted in development of a common US/Europe brand positioning architecture. Exploring visualizations also gave insights into the expected purchase decision process, including the role of the healthcare professional. Brand positioning was subsequently validated using an online brand metaphor exercise for the new product with a quantitative sample.

We were also able to do similar exercises in the IDIs with healthcare professionals. Personae were used to establish the kinds of patients that professionals expected to have a dialogue with regarding the new product which was very useful input for the professional marketing team. I had been nervous about using non-conscious approaches with, usually sceptical healthcare professionals, but it worked extremely well.

There has been some criticism of the metaphor elicitation technique, on the basis of the difficulty of validating the researcher's interpretation of the research output. For example, Hofstede *et al* (2007) demonstrated the congruent validity of a visual brand metaphor exercise and a personification exercise in terms of discriminating between beer brands; but the discrimination could not be translated to verbal personality dimension scores. This result is hardly surprising. The power of metaphor is in its ability to illuminate shared consumer meaning, and reflect brand or cultural symbolism, where it may be difficult to express meaning verbally. In deep insights research, visuals can be more precise than words.

Laddering

Laddering is a technique of the means-ends chain model theory (Gutman, 1982) which, in a marketing context, helps researchers explore deeper levels of consumer-perceived benefits within the hierarchy of brand benefits. The researcher guides the participants to articulate attributes, functional benefits and emotional or self-expressive benefits. The technique uses repetition, similar to the way it's used in Deep Visualization. In an IDI, the researcher can verbally guide the participant as shown in Example 1 below. Laddering can be combined with metaphor to create rich emotional responses. For example, in a bottled water study conducted in the US and India (ModelPeople, 2011), which we discuss in Chapter 7, we used laddering to create distinct positioning spaces for the brand. We asked pairs of participants to brainstorm reasons for drinking bottled water on Post-its and then ladder the ideas from basic to more important. This resulted in four distinct benefit spaces, articulating functional, emotional and self-expressive benefits and personal values, which were used to create brand positioning concepts for quantitative research.

Tool box

Example 1:

'Why do you drink [bottled water brand]?'

'Because it's more clean and pure than water from the tap.' [attributes]

'What's important about clean and pure?'

'Well I want to put only good things in my body.'

'Why is that important to you?'

'I feel better. [How?] I feel calmer, less jittery.' [functional benefit]

'What's the result of feeling less jittery?'

'I feel balanced, at ease with everything and everyone.' [emotional benefit]

'How does water do that?'

'Water is natural. I feel calmer when I'm outdoors by water, at one with nature.' [values]

Example 2:

'Why do you drink [bottled water brand]?'

'Because water is hydrating.' [attributes]

'What's important about hydrating?'

'I need to hydrate after I work out at the gym to replenish my body.' [functional benefit]

'Why is that important to you?'

'I will look good and have the energy to do well at work.' [self-expressive and emotional benefits]

'Why is that important to you?'

'I want to succeed. I want to do well financially.' [values]

Projective techniques

Projective techniques are sometimes used in qualitative research to help participants to articulate repressed or withheld feelings by projecting these onto another character. Many researchers invent their own projective exercises, but examples are:

- Bubble drawings, in which the participant fills in 'thought' and 'speech' bubbles for a designated character (eg a purchaser of instant coffee).

- Writing a script in a third person, again as a designated character.

- Sentence completion (eg *'Brand X Tomato Soup...?'*).

- Word association. Participants are asked to say the first word that comes to mind in response to a given word. Jung was the first to use this in psychoanalysis.

The concept of projection originated with Freud, who conceptualized projection as a defence mechanism by which people unconsciously attribute their own negative personality traits to others, and was adapted by clinical psychologists using tools such as the Rorschach 'ink-blot' technique, incomplete sentences and imagery. In an early study, Haire (1950) showed two almost identical shopping lists of items to different samples of housewives who were asked to describe the putative purchasers of each list: one list included instant coffee and one included non-instant coffee. The housewife who was said to buy the list containing the instant coffee was more frequently described as lazy and sloppy; the housewife said to buy the list containing the non-instant coffee was more commonly said to be thrifty and a good housewife. Haire subsequently correlated negative responses about the instant coffee purchaser with non-instant coffee users.

There has been criticism of the use of projective techniques, centred on inconsistent interpretation of projective responses, attributed to researcher subjectivity (Boddy, 2005). I sometimes use these exercises in group situations to help overcome social desirability bias. It is also important to listen for participants using projective phrases to express an opinion indirectly. For example: 'A person who does not know about this may find it useful' ('And so do I but I don't want to say so!').

Consumer neuroscience methods and tools

Consumer neuroscience opens up the possibility of observing a consumer's neural and physiological responses to marketing stimuli *and using this to identify how consumers feel and predict how they will behave*, somewhat of a holy grail for immersive research. The field is evolving very rapidly, but adoption and expected adoption of methods and tools is still niche according to the GRIT Trends Report (2015). The main methods listed by the GRIT report in order of adoption are:

- **Eye-tracking.** Eye-trackers have been used in marketing for decades to explore how consumers look at marketing stimuli such as packaging, print ads or direct mail and more recently web pages. A common output is a heat map, which shows the areas that consumers looked at most often or for longest. Eye-tracking can be done in a lab, but is also applied to shopper marketing research in a simulated (built or virtual) environment like a store aisle, or in a real store environment. For example, our ethnographic studies have incorporated eye-tracking to observe how shoppers in a supermarket scan an actual shelf set and what catches and retains their attention. We have also incorporated it into observed shopping tests within a simulated store environment, built out by a major consumer brand corporation to test new packaging and shopper marketing approaches. Eye-tracking explains *what* the consumer is looking at but cannot explain *why*, so it is increasingly combined with neuromarketing measures such as EEG.

- **Facial analysis.** As we saw in Chapter 2, the facial analysis coding system (FACS) was devised by Paul Ekman (2004), based on data about the activation of facial muscles to produce emotional expressions. Coding of facial expressions is now done automatically using software and camera or webcam, resulting in fast analysis of large sample sizes. For example, participants in an online advertising effectiveness study using aFAC (automatic facial action coding) react to stimuli, during which their facial expressions will be measured via webcam. The limitations with the method are that the range of universal emotions is mostly negative and lacks nuance; it's also common for participants to suppress facial expressions. Some quantitative studies also ask participants to select an individual face, from the range of universal expressions, to indicate their emotional response to stimulus, rather than using a verbal scale which may be more open to interpretation.

- **Neuromarketing** measures. Neuromarketing is a branch of decision neuroscience: research which studies the brain's response to marketing stimuli such as advertising. EEG (electroencephalography) measures (albeit crudely) patterns of electrical brain activity in the cortex, using sensors placed on the head. fMRI (functional magnetic image resonance) uses magnetic fields to track the blood flow throughout the brain as participants respond to marketing stimulus, including the deeper levels of the brain, which are not accessed by EEG measures. fMRI has practical disadvantages: equipment is scarce, expensive and has limitations (participants have to lie still for extended periods of time in a claustrophobic environment). Various studies have caused excitement by accurately predicting the future performance of an ad or product based on fMRI tests; for example, Berns and Moore (2012) correlated activation of the nucleus accumbens in teenagers, measured by fMRI as they listened to music tracks, with the eventual success of the track. However, it's claimed (Satel and Lilienfeld, 2013) that scientists cannot yet form reliable causal links between brain-imaging data and consumer behaviour. For this we need complementary psychological, social and cultural analysis. For example, Karkamar (Nobel, 2012) notes that, while the neural response measured may be consistent across cultures, the marketing activation may be very different. She cites the example of the way happiness is expressed in Eastern and Western cultures. For this reason, neuromarketing methods may be combined with other methods, to further explore a measured neural response.

- **Biometric response**. This involves measuring the body's non-conscious responses to marketing stimuli, such as heart rate, galvanic skin response (sweating) and pupil dilation. Biometrics measure the level of emotional arousal but do not measure the type or valence of the emotion so they are typically used in combination with other measures.

- **Wearables.** Biometric data can be collected using loaned equipment or the participant's own equipment, such as a fitness band with a heart-activity monitor.

Agile research

Agile Consumer Research was inspired by *The Agile Manifesto*, written by US software developers (in 2001), which promotes iterative and incremental software development among cross-functional teams. The manifesto stated that continuous user involvement is very important, as needs cannot be fully collected at the beginning of the development cycle. It is of interest to consumer researchers because data (qualitative or quantitative) is gathered quickly, but also offers the opportunity to refine a research instrument or stimulus iteratively to reflect insights as they are gathered. For example, in the oral healthcare case study we discussed at the end of Chapter 4, the strategy team refined new product concepts iteratively in between a series of focus groups so that the final product concepts reflected learning from all the groups, avoiding the need to commission more research to review refined concepts. Agile research is now more often done online, facilitated by custom platforms which integrate fast turnaround panel recruiting.

Chapter 6 summary

1 Research project management involves managing the process of consumer or customer research, in order to ensure a successful and cost-effective outcome.

2 A project plan, with the following key steps, must be defined and managed, allowing at least four weeks; at least six weeks for projects with more than one country market:

   a) design sample size, recruiting criteria and location;

   b) confirm the budget and create a project plan and timeline;

   c) design a recruiting screener;

   d) manage the recruit and project logistics;

   e) design the research protocol (often called an Interview, Moderator or Discussion Guide).

3 **Sample size** is the number of participants to be included in our research project and is based on project scope (how many different consumer sub-groups are there?) and budget.

4 **Recruiting criteria** are the variables chosen to define the different types of consumers whom we wish to include. This decision is based on the learning objectives.

5 **Location** of the research project is usually based on where the brand's key or potential markets are. More than one market may be selected to account for variations driven by variables such as the culture, climate or type of distribution. Leading-edge urban markets may also be chosen, especially for innovation strategy research.

6 **A recruiting screener** is the tool which recruiters use to screen a population of potential research participants against recruiting criteria and select those whom we have chosen to include.

7 The **immersive research protocol** must include tools which allow researchers to explore deep-seated emotional memories and non-conscious emotional and cultural associations which drive how consumers feel and behave. These tools include: Deep Visualization, metaphor elicitation and laddering. Tools can be combined within any research methodology.

References

Baker, S and Edwards, R (2012) *How many qualitative interviews is enough? Expert voices and early career reflections on sampling and cases in qualitative research*, ESRC National Centre for Research Methods, University of Southampton, http://eprints.ncrm.ac.uk/2273/4/how_many_interviews.pdf [last reviewed February 2016]

Berns, G and Moore, S (2012) A neural predictor of cultural popularity, *Journal of Consumer Psychology*, **22**, 1

Boddy, C (2005) Projective techniques in market research: valueless subjectivity or insightful reality?, *International Journal of Market Research*, **47**, 3

Brooks, C (2001) Positioning workshop: beer/liquor

Brooks, C (2003) Immersive research with mainstream fashion shoppers

Brooks, C (2012) Successfully Recruiting Global Ethnographic Research Participants, *MRA Alert Magazine* (June), http://www.modelpeopleinc.com/press [last reviewed February 2016)

Ekman, P (2004) *Emotions Revealed: Understanding faces and feelings*, Phoenix, London

Grace, C (1998) Clare Grace & Associates, Memphis, TN

GRIT Trends Report (2015) http://www.greenbook.org/grit/ [last reviewed February 2016]

Gutman, J (1982) A means-end chain model based on consumer categorization processes, *Journal of Marketing*, **96**, pp 209–25

Haire, M (1950) Projective techniques in marketing research, *Journal of Marketing*, **14**, 5, pp 649– 56

Hofstede, A, van Hoof, J, Walenberg, N and de Jong, M (2007) Projective techniques for brand image research: two personification-based methods explored, *QMIRJ*, **10**, no. 3

Lakoff, G and Johnson, M (1980) The metaphorical structure of the human conceptual system, *Cognitive Science*, **4**, pp 195–208

Maddock, R and Fulton, R (1996) *Marketing to the Mind/Right Brain Strategies for Advertising and Marketing*, Quorum, Westport, CT

Miller, W, C'de Baca, J, Matthews, D and Wilbourne, P (2001) *Personal Values Card Sort*, University of New Mexico, http://casaa.unm.edu [last reviewed February 2016]

ModelPeople Inc (2004) Focus groups with mothers of elementary school age children

ModelPeople Inc (2005) Immersive research with beverage segments

ModelPeople Inc (2006a) Immersive research with entry-luxury car buyers

ModelPeople Inc (2006b) Focus groups with probiotic dairy drink consumers

ModelPeople Inc (2007) Focus groups with in-store bakery shoppers

ModelPeople Inc (2008a) Immersive research with peri-menopausal and menopausal women

ModelPeople Inc (2008b) Immersive research with vitamin user segments

ModelPeople Inc (2009) Creative Workshops with premium denim consumers

ModelPeople Inc (2010) Immersive research with fitness walking consumers in the US, Japan and Germany

ModelPeople Inc (2011) Creative Workshops with bottled water consumers in the US and India

ModelPeople Inc (2013) Creative Workshops with dental consumers in the US and Germany

ModelPeople Inc (2014) Focus groups with congestion relief users in the US and Canada

Nobel, C (2012) What neuroscience tells us about consumer desire, *Harvard Business School Working Knowledge* (March), http://hbswk.hbs.edu [last reviewed February 2016]

Rapaille, C (2006) *The Culture Code*, p 6, Crown Business, New York

Satel, S and Lilienfeld, S (2013) *Brainwashed: The seductive appeal of mindless neuroscience*, p 150, Basic Books, New York

UK Market Research Society, www.mrs.org.uk [last reviewed February 2016]

US Marketing Research Association, Code of Marketing Research Standards, www.marketingresearch.org [last reviewed February 2016]

Zaltman, G and Zaltman, L (2008) *Marketing Metaphoria*, p xvi, Harvard Business Press, Boston, MA

The Strategic Empathy Process Phase Two

Activate insights into strategy

CHAPTER 7 OBJECTIVES

1 Explain the three steps of the Insight Activation Process.

2 Explore different approaches to analysing learning developed in Phase One.

3 Define what a 'consumer insight' is and how to build insights, using the immersive learning gathered in Phase One as the foundation.

4 Explore ways to build on insights to identify possible strategic actions.

5 Illustrate with global case studies how to design and run an Activation Session.

CASE STUDY   Activating health trends insights

Consumers are increasingly frightened of becoming elderly and sick, a burden on their families (according to many studies I have conducted using research techniques to uncover non-conscious emotions). Life expectancy is increasing and so is the incidence of chronic diseases. Some reports indicate that half of all consumers – in the US and the UK – now have a chronic disease by the age of 60;

yet the threat of governments raising the retirement age also looms large. As a result, 'healthier living' is arguably the most important consumer macro-trend that exists today. For some consumers, healthier living has become the focus of their lives and they spend several hours each day practising, teaching and communicating about physical and spiritual approaches to wellness. In the social media age, self-publishing their healthy lifestyle practices on micro-blogs or in YouTube videos is highly influential with worried consumers looking for solutions.

Recognizing these consumer trends, the US strategy team for a UK-owned ready-to-drink (RTD) beverage corporation decided to curate a Strategic Learning Journey for its senior sales, marketing and R&D executives, in order to spearhead portfolio innovation strategy (ModelPeople, 2006). A week-long consumer immersion and insight activation process was planned, to develop deep insights into the health practices of leading-edge consumers and activate insights into brand and new product innovation. The 30-strong team headed to Southern California and, in six small groups, spent a day observing and interviewing 18 leading-edge consumers, of all ages and backgrounds, who were practising or teaching a range of 'healthier living' techniques including acupuncture, quantum touch, qigong holistic meditation, Pilates, yoga, aromatherapy, massage and ionic cleansing. The goal was to observe and derive consumer language around healthy lifestyle motivations, beliefs and behaviour as a basis for building insights in this space. 'It's all about balance, keeping mind and body in homeostasis', said Patrick. As he spoke, he was literally balancing on a slackline strung between two trees in a public park in San Diego, a practice to promote core strength and mental focus. Patrick, 33, also practised qigong seven times a week and mixed up green food smoothies for lunch. 'I was on depression meds before I took up meditation', said Kate, aged 51. 'I avoid sugar, it's the worst stimulant there is' (Katie made this comment some five years before the recent bad press around sugar). 'Meditation and yoga are what energize me now, and I only drink pure water, flavoured with lemon or lime.'

In their small groups, the strategy team took hundreds of consumer verbatim comments like this and, over the following three days, clustered the ideas and built them into over 40 insights. Reframing the consumer context with a healthy living perspective was critical to the team whose mindset had been oriented towards traditional products and consumer needs. They then ideated innovation platforms and brainstormed ideas for new products, ingredients, packaging, brand positioning and marketing communications. Combining the Immerse and Activate phases of the Strategic Empathy Process proved to be a highly efficient, fast-track method to produce a two-year roadmap and pipeline of ideas for developing healthier beverages. As importantly, the process opened the strategy team's eyes to the future world of their mainstream beverage consumers.

Introduction

Figure 7.1 Phase Two of the Strategic Empathy Process

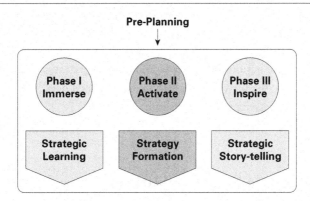

SOURCE: ModelPeople Inc

In the last two chapters, we explored methods and tools for deriving immersive, empathetic consumer learning. However, as we saw in Chapter 1, for this learning to be *strategic learning* it has to result in insights which are shared by the strategy team, and which can be activated into marketing strategy, ie action results from the learning. Building individual learning into the team-based *strategic learning* required for marketing strategy formation – what Crossan *et al* (1999) call 'integrating' learning – is a critical step in marketing strategy formation, and it's a difficult step, especially when so much consumer data and observations have been collected in Phase One. Therefore, Phase Two of the Strategic Empathy Process, called **Activate**, has been designed to help teams integrate learning and use it as the basis for collaborative marketing strategy formation. This process is implemented in strategy team Activation Sessions, held following completion of Phase One. In Chapter 7, we will explain the three steps of the insight activation process, applied to different marketing strategy areas.

Three steps to insight activation

In Phase Two, the strategy team first uses the empathetic understanding they developed in Phase One **to build the key consumer insights (actionable nuggets of learning) and then they build off these insights to identify potential**

strategic actions. We call this process **Activation** of insights into strategy. The Insight Activation Process has three major steps. The first step is to complete analysis of all the consumer data collected in Phase One, including any existing data or tacit knowledge which was reviewed prior to conducting immersive research. The second step is to use this data as a foundation for building fresh consumer or customer insights, which is done in one or more activation sessions: strategy team collaborative work sessions held soon after completion of immersive research. The third step is to identify possible strategic actions. Validating and selecting strategic actions is not a goal in this process; however, identifying what steps need to be taken to do so is a goal, as is assigning responsibilities.

Three steps to insight activation

Step 1: Analyse immersive research data.

Step 2: Build fresh consumer or customer insights (insights are not data!).

Step 3: Identify potential strategic actions.

Step 1: analyse immersive research data

Data analysis is as important as data collection. Analysing the observations and data points collected in immersive research *in depth* is essential, because this builds the foundation for developing fresh consumer or customer insights which might lead to breakthrough new ideas for marketing strategy. Ideally, two to three weeks should be allowed for analysis, depending on data quantity and resources available. A preliminary mini activation session, held immediately after immersive research is complete (held in-field if the strategy team has observed the research) can be very useful in capturing the team's impressions while they are still fresh and identifying questions and priorities for further analysis. However, it's important to avoid jumping to conclusions or allowing first impressions to become accepted wisdom, so make sure the strategy team is briefed to keep an open mind at this stage. It's common for an experienced researcher to have developed initial theories while conducting interviews. Observers from the strategy team will also have been struck by new ideas or common themes. However, we have a tendency to select data points that are consistent with and reinforce existing insights, rather than those which are dissonant and which may actually feed breakthrough insight. Therefore, it's essential not to skip thorough analysis of all the data.

The first step in analysis is organizing the data collected. Transcripts may be made of interview discussion, using audio or video recordings. Photographs should be organized into contact sheets, classified by participant or by theme (eg auto exterior, interior). Any visual material produced by participants, such as e-collages, should be organized together with explanatory text. All this raw material is an important resource for the strategy team when they come to the next step in the activation process: developing insights.

The next step in data analysis is to code data. Coding involves tagging source material as it is analysed. Tags are typically chosen relative to the learning objectives established at the outset of our learning journey, and are developed as analysis progresses to reflect themes that are emerging. Tags can also be identified as positive or negative comments, or may also identify characteristics of the participants such as gender, age or location, so that themes can be analysed by type of participant to identify similarities and differences between sub-samples (eg men vs women). Coding facilitates the aggregation of source material including text and images, for easier identification of common themes, what Glaser and Strauss (1967) call 'constant comparative analysis' (though they were writing in the late 1960s when coding was done via margin notation or even, as they note, based on memory). In practice, the experienced researcher finds memory very useful in coding and comparing qualitative data; indeed, some themes clearly emerge as data collection progresses. Glaser and Strauss argue that constant comparison enables the analyst to draw conclusions about the properties of what they call 'categories' ('themes'). For example, in the bottled water case study later in this chapter, we identified a 'success' theme in India related to consumption of bottled water. By comparing data points for participants who epitomized this theme, both text and image selects, we noticed that the properties of the 'success' theme were youthful appearance, body-con personal style, education and an ambitious mindset; and that the participants who held these views were aged under 25, single and more likely to be male.

There are many other approaches to analysing qualitative data of which I will mention a couple I use regularly in addition to constant comparative analysis. *Narrative analysis* is frequently used in qualitative consumer research analysis, reflecting the extent to which language shapes meaning and the importance of consumer language in marketing communications. Here it's important to analyse the context in which language is used (the consumer narrative relative to the research topic), as well as what type of language is used, to understand the full meaning. For example, in the fitness case study in Chapter 6, we analysed consumer stories about their walking practices and identified how different words were used to describe walking in different contexts, each walking context (eg going from A to B, going for a walk and 'fitness walking') having its own practices, beliefs, emotions and iconographies.

Since Strategic Empathy is grounded in deep understanding of how people *feel*, a *phenomenological* approach to data analysis is also commonly used. One such approach, based on the beliefs of the philosopher Edmund Husserl (1999), is directed towards discovering the essence of an experience and its essential properties, based on the intensive study of individual experiences, and is widely used in healthcare research (eg Thorne, 2000), including my own. For example, in the allergy study which opens Chapter 8, we used Deep Visualization to drill down to the experience of an allergy attack, physical and emotional, and the way in which the sufferer experienced a diminished sense of self-purpose.

Technology is daily creating new options for text and visual analytics and coding. At the time of writing there are many proprietary and off-the-shelf software packages that help with contextual text analytics and coding – Quirkos for example, which is low cost for students – though many are not optimized for use with qualitative data. Online platforms like ModelPeople's PeopleBlogSpot allow automatic aggregation and coding of text and images collected during online research. When it comes to audio and video analysis, voice recognition software is still not reliable (as Siri users will confirm!) and the quality of interview audio can result in transcripts with too many errors to be used for analysis and coding. However, this field is developing and a few commercial research platforms now claim to record and transcribe consumer mobile video.

Planning an activation session

As soon as data analysis is completed, an insight activation session should be held with the entire strategy team. This typically lasts one to three days and its purpose is threefold:

1 integrate consumer and customer learning within the strategy team;
2 build off learning to develop fresh consumer or customer insights;

3 generate potential strategic actions and allocate responsibility for validation.

Ideally the session is held away from strategy team members' office locations, in order to minimize possible disruption from phone calls or e-mails. For this reason also, limit smartphone and laptop use to breaks (or disconnect Wi-Fi!). Schedule plenty of breaks with nourishing snacks and refreshments.

It's usual for the insights specialists on the strategy team (along with any outside research specialists) to present the consumer data analysis at this activation session. If video has been taken during immersive research or prior mobile studies, individual clips or a rough-cut can also be shared to bring the analysis to life. When designing the data presentation, it's important to avoid the temptation to present data non-stop for several hours. It is also essential to help the strategy team listening to absorb and process the data themselves. For example:

- Ask them to review any field notes they took before the session and bring along some new observations they made: share these within the group.

- Instruct them to jot down on Post-it notes any 'Ahas' or new ideas that occur to them as they are listening. These Post-its can be used later when building insights.

- Break up the data presentation into sections of an hour or less and take a half-hour in between sections for the group, or pairs of individuals, to share what struck them as a fresh idea.

Another approach, which is effective if the strategic question is narrowly focused and data points are few, is to have the entire strategy team work on developing insights from raw data, such as transcripts, photographs and their own field notes as observers. I have also given client strategy teams edited transcripts which highlight the key themes I have already identified in my own analysis, so that the team can be hands-on with raw data analysis in a time-efficient manner.

Step 2: build fresh consumer or customer insights

Why is building insights so important? It's a common misconception that insights are the same thing as data. In fact, insights (while they are built out of consumer, customer and shopper data) must, like strategic learning, be expressly action-oriented; that is, they must provide direction and inspiration for strategy formation and implementation. Insights should provide the foundation of the key elements of marketing strategy (see Chapter 3) including:

- selection of target market segments;
- deep understanding of target consumer or customer needs;
- brand positioning architecture;
- product design, usability and innovation territories;
- communications strategy, including messaging and media;
- channel selection and shopper marketing strategies including promotion.

So, if insights are not the same as data, what are they? A well-crafted insight articulates – *in consumer language* – a consumer behaviour, belief, dilemma or desire which indicates an unmet consumer need. Critically, insights are written from the consumer or customer viewpoint and not from the corporate viewpoint: that is, an insight does not describe what the corporation's products or services will do for the consumer. An insight describes the consumer's unmet needs in the way that the consumer himself would. It should be evident that empathy with the consumer's viewpoint is the *sine qua non* of a good insight statement; one European corporation I have worked with even requires that insights should evoke a consumer reaction of 'you clearly understand me'.

Insights may have context. For example, they may be relative to a geographic culture or may be a contemporary articulation of consumer needs relative to a category of products at a point in time. This is common in rapidly evolving industries like technology or fashion, and these insights may be useful for short- or medium-term activation. Insights may also reflect important consumer shifts which have longevity (eg the impact of modern living/working patterns on meal consumption which we saw in the opening case study in Chapter 4). However, a true insight is more deeply situated in terms of a fundamental consumer need, meaning that the insight may not change much over time but the way that the business delivers against the insight might change. In his classic paper *Marketing Myopia*, Theodore Levitt (1960) emphasizes that the entire organization must view itself as a customer-creating and customer-satisfying organism and must not define this too narrowly in terms of existing products. For example, Detroit in the 1950s prioritized product insights (which drove development of existing large cars) over the deeper consumer need for affordable maintenance and running costs, which opened the door to the Japanese (small) car industry in the US. Equally, in the computing industry, IBM lost out to PC makers running Microsoft Windows by focusing on product (mainframe computers) instead of recognizing the consumer need for personal computing capabilities. In turn, of course, Microsoft lost momentum to Apple's iOS and Google's Android operating systems by being late to attract younger consumers with mobile capabilities. These examples should illustrate how tough it is for successful companies to break out of product orthodoxies which are wildly profitable and develop and activate fresh consumer insights in a changing marketing environment. Activating consumer insights cannot be regarded as a one-off event.

Many definitions of an insight are to be found in marketing literature and many corporations have their own definitions, but here's the one I use:

> An insight is a **deep truth**, grounded in **empathetic understanding** of **consumer behaviour, beliefs, experiences or needs**, which **unlocks breakthrough thinking** about the **business opportunity** to serve them better.

We can pull apart this definition, to highlight the important ideas:

- **Deep truth.** As we have discussed, an insight does not reflect merely a temporary blip in consumer behaviour or attitudes. We cannot take strategic action on this. However, insights may have short-term category context or reflect shifts in consumer behaviour which are important for strategic activation.

- **Empathetic understanding.** Insights must be grounded in the empathy developed for consumers and customers during the immersive research process. Not only this, but insights should honestly reflect the language and emotion expressed by the consumer.

- **Consumer behaviour, beliefs, experiences or needs.** An insight must define what the consumer is currently doing, thinking or experiencing that leads to an unmet need or desire. This is often expressed as a 'dilemma'.

- **Unlocks breakthrough thinking.** This is perhaps the most important element of an insight. In order to effectively inspire strategy, an insight must be a fresh idea, or must be reframed in a fresh way.

- **Business opportunity.** Insights are not just interesting pieces of information about the consumer or customer. Insights must be actionable and offer the organization an opportunity to serve consumers better. However, as we discussed, an insight does not relate to the organization's products but to what the consumer wants to achieve, and this must be clearly articulated.

Insight architecture

Insights should be written in a consistent way, so that they are clear to all stakeholders who may be responsible for forming or implementing strategy. Again, many corporations have their own insight architecture, but the following is what we use at ModelPeople:

1 **Target consumer/customer/shopper.** Who is he/she and what are the relevant facts about him/her?

> eg Working parents who believe that there are social and health benefits for the family in sitting down together on work nights to eat a meal prepared at home from healthy, natural ingredients.

2 **Consumer situation (dilemma).** What the consumer is currently doing or thinking that leads to an unmet need or desire and a potential business opportunity.

> eg 'I want to put a home-cooked meal on the table to nurture my family, but I don't have time when I get home from work.'

3 **Consumer end-state.** What end-state or benefits does the consumer want to enjoy?

> eg 'I wish I could produce a healthy home-cooked meal that everyone will love in under 10 minutes.'

How to build insights out of data

The process of deriving insights from data begins in the activation session, though it is typically completed following the session, in order to fully refine insight architecture. There are a number of creative and cognitive exercises which can help the strategy team focus in on the most important consumer data and build insights, which we explore below:

- **Theme clustering.** Clustering consumer data points into themes is an effective and commonly used technique for deriving insights, because it is an easy and visual means of thinking about the relationship between data points. Working individually, participants in the activation session will write down important or new ideas which arose from the immersive research conducted in Phase One. This can be done during the data analysis presentation (see Step 1) or using notes taken during Phase One fieldwork (team members should be instructed to bring these to the activation session). Ideas are written down on Post-it notes and then, working in small groups, the Post-its are stuck up on a large poster board or wall (see Figure 7.2).

Figure 7.2 Theme clustering

Once stuck up, the Post-it notes are then moved around into groups or clusters of ideas which are related within the cluster and are different from ideas in other clusters. Once each cluster is formed, the theme is named using another Post-it. Any photos or other material collected during immersive research can also be included. A cluster represents any ideas which can be developed into an insight. For example, in the opening case study, we identified a cluster called 'I need a guru', based on observing and listening to the consumers in the immersion talk about how hard it was to practise healthy living without trusted guidance. This was turned into an important insight which led to the development of new products and communications strategies.

- **Repetitive questioning.** Repeatedly asking '*why?*' of important themes (identified in a clustering exercise for example) can help the strategy team to construct an insight. This is a form of laddering consumer benefits: that is identifying what the consumer is trying to achieve at the deepest level. Asking '*why?*' stops when it appears that the most meaningful answer has been derived.

Repetitive questioning to derive insights: example

Observation:	'It's hard to stick to a healthy regime on my own.'
Why?	'There's no-one to advise and encourage me.'
Why?	'I need advice from someone I trust and respect to resolve questions and encouragement that I'm making progress.'
Why?	'When someone I trust and respect recognizes my progress and removes road-blocks to progress, it motivates me to carry on.'
Why?	'I can stick to a healthy regime that works for me.'
Why?	**...no more meaningful answers**
Theme:	**'I need a guru.'**
Insight:	**'I want to have a healthier regime but it's so hard to do it on my own. I wish I had a guru to advise and encourage me, which would motivate me to stick to my regime.'**

- **Consumer profiling.** Consumer profiling involves using detailed profiles of the actual consumers observed in immersive research to construct insights. This can be helpful because it brings the consumers dilemma, needs and goals to life in a very real way, and facilitates the use of consumer language in constructing insights. For example, in the opening case study, the groups reviewed transcripts and field notes for each character they had observed and used the consumer's own words to articulate health regimes, dilemmas, benefits sought, unmet needs and goals. Groups then presented their characters to the rest of the team, using drama and emotion! They wrote these up on Post-its and clustered them, which led to the identification of key themes including the example shown above. Groups reviewed each other's themes, and then added any inspiring ideas to their own theme clusters, before working on insights for a handful of the key themes.

- **Reframing the consumer context.** We saw in Chapter 1 how strategic learning can be inspired by going outside the organization to create new perspectives and bring in new voices (Hamel, 1998). This also holds true during the insight building process. Insights can be inspired by reframing consumer data in the context of another category, and exploring how successful companies delight consumers within that context. This can be done just before and during an activation session, by inspiring a different mindset among the strategy team. Expert presentations or immersions are a great way to do this; for example, in the mini case study below, we brought in a beauty expert to talk about the consumer's world from a beauty perspective, before building insights and innovation platforms. A strategy team responsible for shopper innovation at a global beverage corporation team visited a wide range of retail stores to explore new ideas in retail environments different from the grocery and mass outlets they were used to. When developing luxury automotive insights, we have explored other luxury categories such as high-end fashion, yachts, artwork or home furnishings.

MINI CASE STUDY
Reframing the consumer context in oral care

'Teeth are in vogue', Mona, a talented and creative make-up artist working on Hollywood photo shoots told the strategy team. She showed us magazine covers and ads featuring models like Georgia Jagger, whose teeth are part of their personality and overall look. 'When I style a model for a shoot, I can select certain shades of lipstick to make teeth look whiter.' Over the previous six months, the strategy team for a global leader in oral care products had conducted immersive consumer research in the teeth whitening category (ModelPeople, 2013), and now the team was taking part in a three-day activation session to build consumer insights and identify potential strategic actions in terms of new product ideas for a new whitening product.

Team members were used to ideating new products in the oral care category but realized that ideating in the whitening category would require a different mindset. Therefore, they did some homework before coming to the session, involving visiting beauty and cosmetics counters and boutiques in Santa Monica, a leading-edge US beauty market where they had decided to hold their session in a hotel meeting room, where they could not be disturbed. The goal of the homework was to immerse themselves in the mindset of an affluent and knowledgeable beauty consumer prior to building insights and identifying potential new product ideas to appeal to her or him. They also photographed or purchased products which seemed innovative and relevant as inspiration for the session. Mona's talk was designed to ground the team in beauty language and culture before they began building insights. Over the next three days, the team developed more than 20 potential innovation strategies. Ideas were illustrated during the session by an artist and a strategic architecture was developed for each one, outlining the advantage of the idea and what would be required to realize the idea. The best ideas were developed into product concepts for design exploration and consumer validation.

- **Reframing using other stakeholder perspectives.** An alternative way to reframe insights by creating new perspectives is to ask the wider stakeholder group to comment on developed insight architecture. This is often done by inviting other stakeholders into the activation session – either for the whole session, or as guest presenters to talk about their own tacit knowledge or strategic initiatives. This has a couple of added benefits:
  - gaining understanding and early buy-in to insight activation by involving a wider stakeholder group in the development process;
  - identifying emergent strategy in other areas of the organization which might spark ideas for new strategic actions.

Alternatively, developed insights can be shared via the company intranet, using a software platform which allows employees to comment or add their own ideas. Insights can even be shared with consumer champions via online communities.

MINI CASE STUDY
Bottled water: activating insights into brand positioning

He is head of the family, health conscious, very ambitious in life, up-to-date. He won't accept compromise.   *India brand persona*

She enjoys life to the fullest. She believes in the American dream. Loves nature, friends and laughter.   *US brand persona*

Bottled water is a surprisingly complex category for the ultimate 'basic necessity'. It holds many levels of cultural meaning, which differ by geographic market. In the US, bottled water is a healthy alternative to other (less healthy) beverages like soda or coffee. In some European countries, it's a regional specialty to be enjoyed as much as a regional beer. In India it can mean the difference between life and death, if (as one middle-class mum told us) your child's school water fountain is contaminated with typhoid; or it can be associated with a modern, youthful lifestyle which includes gym membership and wearing Western fashions.

The US-based marketing strategy team for a bottled water brand had embarked on a Strategic Learning Journey to develop 'global' brand positioning, starting with their two lead markets: the US and India (ModelPeople, 2012a). The team had observed ethnographic interviews and Creative Workshops in the US, and had run a two-day activation session to build insights and ideate positioning spaces, based on US learning. This included a first attempt at a brand positioning wheel. Positioning spaces were turned into written concepts, with the help of the Indian brand team, which were used as stimulus in Creative Workshops held in Mumbai and Delhi. Following analysis of the immersive research in both markets, potential positioning strategies were identified by analysing how consumers had laddered brand benefits and the language and imagery they used. Analysis identified several potential strategies that would not work in both markets, including 'safety' (which is not a relevant issue in the US) and 'success' (which is expressed very differently by Millennials in the US and India). However, some common areas were also identified which offered the opportunity for brand differentiation on a common positioning platform.

The strategy team along with the Indian marketing team then held a second activation session and invited a wider stakeholder team to attend, including representatives from advertising, PR and promotional agencies and R&D. The group of 25 attendees heard presentations from the insights and brand teams about the immersive research analysis, insights and the initial brand positioning wheel developed following US research. Five teams then worked with the research analysis to develop brand positioning architecture and target consumer personae, based on the personae developed by consumers in the Creative Workshops. After presenting their individual positioning architectures, the entire group revisited the brand positioning wheel and reached consensus on how it should be refined to take the Indian learning into account. The strategy team then worked to refine the brand positioning wheel and validated it in consumer concept research.

Step 3: identify potential strategic actions

Once insights have been developed, the strategy team must turn its attention to activating insights into potential strategic actions. This process may begin during the first one to two activation sessions, after insights have been built. More likely, however, the strategy team will need to reconvene further sessions in order to identify and prioritize the possible choices of strategic action.

A potential strategic action is a scenario that explains how the business will leverage the insight to serve consumers better. At this stage, the goal is not to validate strategic actions; validation will take place at a later stage by means of feasibility analysis and further consumer testing. For now, the goal is to generate ideas for new strategic scenarios. Scenarios address one or more elements within marketing strategy. For example, we may propose new product, pricing, channel or communications strategies which offer the business an opportunity to serve consumers better in the way our new insights dictate.

The strategy team should generate scenarios as a group, but the initial development of ideas should be done individually or in pairs. Research (Amabile *et al*, 2002) suggests that larger groups are not good at brainstorming new ideas under pressure, not least because of the social desirability bias we discussed in Chapter 6, but also because of the way the brain processes new information (as we discussed in Chapter 2). Neuro-economist Gregory Berns (2008) maintains that, to perceive things differently, strategists must bombard their brains with things never before encountered, because the brain has evolved for efficiency and routinely takes perceptual short cuts to save energy. It's almost impossible to completely get rid of the influence of past experience and other people's opinions. Only by forcing their brains to move beyond our habitual 'lazy', 'System 1' (see Chapter 2 for theory) thinking patterns and see things differently, can the strategy team begin to imagine truly novel alternatives. Therefore, to facilitate seeing things differently, the team attending the activation session should undertake some reframing activities, as we described above; bringing in experts from outside, or visiting a different consumer environment. At a minimum, the leader of the session might choose to suggest some thought-starter questions which include reframing questions, such as:

- How would Starbucks or Apple (or any relevant successful corporation) do this?

- Are there any strategy examples from other categories that we could adopt?

- How would our competitors deliver strategic action against this insight?
- What are the corporation's key competencies: the things we do well?

The goal of an activation session which is focused on identifying potential strategic actions is to generate many ideas, including those which are 'out of the box'. With this in mind, the session leader typically instructs the team not to be critical of scenarios or ideas generated too early in the process, which may result in good ideas being thrown away without due consideration. However, to avoid wasting time on ideas which would never fly, McKinsey (Coyne and Coyne, 2011) recommend defining any 'no-go' scenarios (such as changing IT infrastructure) which would not be approved. It's also essential not to be shy about ideas which are 'not invented here'. Truly new ideas are rare; many great ideas build on what's been tried before. As we discussed in Chapter 1, many effective strategies are the result of consistent patterns of behaviour which have proved successful. Such strategies should also be included in the scenarios developed by the team.

There are also strong arguments for building playtime into an activation session; or spreading activation over several sessions. Goleman (2012) suggests that the best ideas come when you have absorbed all the information you need to generate ideas, and then you 'Let it all go. Just relax'. Other approaches to generating ideas, such as synectics (Gordon, 1961), encourage idea generation through play; in this case, creating 'wishes' ('springboards') and exploring new contexts ('excursions') for consumer dilemmas.

Once potential strategic actions have been generated, they are shared with the whole strategy team for discussion and selection of the most promising ideas. One way of doing this is to give each team member (say) three votes to allocate to his or her 'favourite' idea. However, all the ideas should be captured and evaluated again during the process, to make sure nothing has been overlooked. The top ideas chosen by the team are then prioritized for further exploration. Some ideas may be relatively easy to implement and an immediate decision can be made about how to go about progressing them. Other potential strategic actions may be more complex in scope and require further investigation. The team may decide that these ideas should be explored within a smaller sub-group and allocate leadership responsibility for progressing them. Or they may decide to explore them further within the entire team. Lafley *et al* (2012) emphasize that potential strategic actions should not be explored merely at a high level. They recommend specifying the *advantage* the strategic action aims to achieve or leverage, the *scope* across which the advantage applies, and the *activities* throughout the value chain that would be required in order to deliver the advantage across this scope. Doing this has two benefits:

- It allows the strategic action to be pressure-tested by the team, by asking questions such as: 'What are the preconditions for success?'; 'What needs to change for this action to be realized?'; 'What resources will be required?'; 'How does this strategy improve the status quo?'.

- It identifies other stakeholders who may need to be brought into the team if this action is to be realized.

Agile insight activation

It may be necessary, for reasons of cost or timeline (perhaps there is an urgent competitive threat or market opportunity), to build and activate consumer insights very quickly, meaning there is limited time for immersive consumer research. In this situation, Immerse and Activate (Phases One and Two) can be conducted during a single activation session, held over one or more days. The first stage of the session involves reviewing existing consumer knowledge and developing a list of questions which need to be answered (knowledge gaps). A small consumer panel is recruited for discussion around the knowledge gaps, followed by an activation session to distil new learning into insights. At this stage further knowledge gaps are likely to be identified, so a second consumer panel is held to answer these questions and explore insights already developed. Finally, further activation sessions are held to confirm insights and begin identifying potential strategic actions.

MINI CASE STUDY   Agile insight activation in OTC healthcare

After a good night's sleep you greet the next day differently. But I don't want to take a pain med to fall asleep because it numbs my whole body. I want to enjoy restful, natural sleep and wake up feeling alive and ready to go.
Female natural sleep aid consumer

A small natural sleep aid brand had been off the market for some months following a product recall. The marketing team needed to relaunch the brand but lacked budget and timeline to undertake a lengthy Strategic Learning Journey, so they asked ModelPeople (2012b) to run a two-day activation session in a hotel meeting room. The objective of the two-day session was to refine brand positioning to better differentiate the brand within the company's portfolio of sleep products and activate new positioning in brand packaging and communications.

First, the insights team presented all available consumer research and, working in pairs, the strategy team developed a list of questions to explore with consumers, using the pyramid positioning framework (see Chapter 3) as a guide. Then through a moderated consumer panel, we explored needs, desired product benefits and brand perceptions for the portfolio brands. While the discussion was in progress, the observers were capturing 'Ahas' on Post-it notes, in the voice of the consumer. The consumer panel was followed by an insight generation session, during which the strategy team clustered their Post-its from the consumer discussion into benefit-based themes which might form the basis for positioning. Some of these themes were explored in another consumer panel which took place at the end of Day 1. On Day 2, working in small groups, the strategy team laddered benefit themes from functional to emotional benefits, developing some unique positioning ideas using exact consumer language. Then the groups completed positioning architecture for their brand and checked it against competitive and portfolio brand positioning to ensure it was both unique and differentiated. The final session of Day 2 was spent exploring ideas for activating developed brand positioning in communications and packaging.

Open innovation

Many companies now invite external collaboration in developing potential innovations. For example, Procter & Gamble have a programme called *Connect+Develop* which invites people outside the company to submit ideas for specified strategic initiatives such as online retail of disposable diapers (nappies). Similarly, commercial 'crowdsourcing' platforms have also been developed which help organizations develop ideas and concepts by running open competitions to provide ideas against a strategic brief.

Validating potential strategic actions

After identifying and scoping strategic actions with the most perceived potential, actions which cannot be immediately implemented are usually subject to further feasibility analysis, which may require consulting other stakeholders within or outside the organization; for example, retailers or manufacturing contractors may need to be sounded out. Further consumer testing may also be required to check consumer reactions to the proposed action. A detailed implementation plan will then be developed. Of course, as we discussed in Chapter 1, strategy development is rarely linear in the way that it may seem from this description! 'Strategy' can be emergent in the sense of an existing consistent pattern of behaviour. Validation in this case may involve deciding how a successful pattern of behaviour can be leveraged elsewhere. For example, a retail strategy developed by one key account team may be adapted for another key account.

Chapter 7 summary

1 In Phase Two of the Strategic Empathy Process, called **Activate**, the strategy team uses the empathetic understanding they developed in Phase One to build consumer insights and use them in collaborative strategy formation.

2 There are three steps to insight activation:

   – Step 1: Analyse immersive research data.

   – Step 2: Build fresh consumer or customer insights.

   – Step 3: Identify potential strategic actions.

3 Insights are derived from immersive research data analysis, and provide direction and inspiration for strategy formation and implementation.

4 The strategy team should hold an insight activation session following data analysis. This typically lasts one to three days and its purpose is threefold:

   – integrate consumer and customer learning within the strategy team;

   – build off learning to develop fresh consumer or customer insights;

   – generate potential strategic actions and allocate responsibility for validation.

5 There are various techniques to help with insight generation including theme clustering, repetitive questioning and reframing the consumer context.

6 Insights are used as a foundation for generating ideas about potential marketing strategic actions in the activation session. Potential strategic actions are prioritized and specified in the session, prior to seeking further validation and approval.

References

Amabile, T, Hadley, C and Kramer, S (2002) Creativity under the Gun, *Harvard Business Review*, August

Berns, G (2008) *Iconoclast*, Harvard Business School Publishing, Boston

Coyne, K and Coyne, S (2011) Speed is the key question, *McKinsey Quarterly*, March

Crossan, M, Lane, H and White, R (1999) An organizational learning framework: from intuition to institution, *Academy of Management Review*, **24**, 3, July

Glaser, B and Strauss, A (1967) *The Discovery of Grounded Theory*, Hawthorne, NY

Goleman, D (2012) New insights on the creative brain, *Psychology Today*, August 11

Gordon, W (1961) *Synectics: The development of creative capacity*, Harper & Bros, New York

Hamel, G (1998) Strategy innovation and the quest for value, *Sloan Management Review*, 39, **4**, pp 7–14, (Winter)

Husserl, E (1999) *The Idea of Phenomenology*, tr Lee Hardy, Kluwer Academic Publishers, Berlin

Lafley, A, Martin, R, Rivkin, J and Siggelkow, N (2012) Bringing science to the art of strategy, *Harvard Business Review*, September

Levitt, T (1960) Marketing Myopia, *Harvard Business Review*, July–August

ModelPeople Inc (2006) Activation of health trends insights into innovation strategy

ModelPeople Inc (2012a) Bottled water: activating insight into brand positioning

ModelPeople Inc (2012b) Agile insight activation in OTC healthcare

ModelPeople Inc (2013) Activation of beauty insights into oral healthcare innovation

Thorne, S (2000) Data analysis in qualitative research, *Evidence-based Nursing*, **3**

The Strategic Empathy Process Phase Three

08

Inspire: communicate strategic learning

CHAPTER 8 OBJECTIVES

1 Explore why strategic story-telling is important to communicate marketing strategy to the wider stakeholder group.

2 Discuss considerations for choosing story-telling media.

3 Explain the power of character-driven story-telling using consumer documentary film.

4 Give detailed preparation, shoot and editing guidelines for producing a consumer documentary video.

5 Illustrate with global case studies.

CASE STUDY
Inspiring creative strategy with emotional insights

'It almost makes me cry.' said the Creative Director of the ad agency, only half-joking; his voice really was breaking! We were reviewing the video footage from the depth interviews we'd just conducted (ModelPeople, 2014) with severe allergy sufferers, exploring the emotional impact of allergies. The ad agency had landed on a new creative strategy to differentiate a global OTC allergy brand based on emotional benefits, but the creative team had asked for the brief to be brought to life with some real-life consumer stories to inspire creative execution. In the video, Alice, a middle-aged lady from Texas, was describing how severe allergies had caused her to miss the Easter Egg Hunt which she organized for her nieces and nephews every year. It was her simple story of how she felt about being left out, which had moved the creative head. 'I guess arranging the hunt helps me bond with them', Alice explained. 'I love kids, and for whatever reason I was not blessed with any. Being with my nieces and nephews gives me the opportunity to be that nurturing figure. It fills the void of not having my own children. It hurts me when I can't join in with them.'

Our Strategic Learning Journey for this project had engaged a team of 15 brand and ad agency executives in listening to stories like these, bringing home to them first-hand rich narrative about how the allergies impact the sufferer. We kicked off the learning journey by asking 40 consumers to tell a story about their allergies on mobile video, and post it on our online platform. Consumer videos sometimes showed the height of an allergy attack, showing as well as telling us about the emotional impact of the condition. Using this consumer content as a casting tool, we selected the best 20 characters for in-home depth interviews. Pre-casting helped us weed out inarticulate research subjects and also allowed us to shorten the interview time, saving camera time and costs in-field. Film maker Jeff Myers shot wonderful footage of these highly emotional interviews. Using the kinds of non-conscious emotions and emotional memory elicitation techniques we described in Chapter 6, we uncovered how repeated allergy attacks undermine an individual physically, mentally and in social and work situations. The dislocation the sufferer feels is so extreme that they even feel unable to carry out what they see as the important roles in their lives: mother, father, loving aunt, head of department, pastor, team coach. Allergies make individuals unable to self-actualize (in Maslow's words); to integrate (in Jung's words) their personal psyche with their universal human psyche; to be the complete individual they are meant to be.

Members of the brand team and the ad agency team observed the interviews. After they were complete, we ran a short in-field Insights Activation Session to capture individual insights and instincts and begin to integrate group learning. Then the research and video production teams turned the insights into a graphic-rich presentation, built around individual consumer stories, which showed how the consumer stories enhanced understanding of the creative strategy. In addition, a video chapter was created to support each key strategic message, to bring consumer emotions even more powerfully to life. The presentation was used with a much wider stakeholder group of marketing staff and agency creative teams to develop empathy with the sufferings of their consumers as a basis for developing creative and marketing execution.

Introduction

Let's return to the premise in Chapter 1 of this book for a moment. If we want to nurture strategic learning within an organization, as a basis for marketing strategy formation and activation, then we have to create widespread, organizational empathy for how consumers think, feel and behave. This is where Phase Three of the Strategic Empathy Process comes in. Phase Three, which we call *Inspire*, involves communicating deep insights in a way that creates widespread empathy for consumers and customers as a basis for planned and emergent strategy formation.

Inspiring stakeholders: three strategic goals

Phase Three has three important strategic goals:

1 Inspiring strategic action among the wider stakeholder group. In Chapter 1 we saw how strategic learning starts with the individual and the work team but must become *institutionalized* in marketing strategy at the organizational level (Crossan *et al*, 1999). Therefore, the marketing strategy team must *inspire* deeper understanding of the consumer as a basis for strategic action – what we call Strategic Empathy – with the wider stakeholder group. This group includes the many 'marketing strategists' within the organization who will be responsible for implementing planned marketing strategy and forming emergent marketing strategy. It may also include external stakeholders such as advertising, shopper marketing or PR agencies, retail partners, investors or non-profit members or donors.

2 Promoting a culture of curiosity for continuous strategic learning. Over the long term, we want consumer empathy to grow and evolve with a changing environment. Just as a good personal relationship develops over time, the organization's intuition for its consumers and their relationship with the company's brands must strengthen over time, offering opportunities to meet their needs better and thereby build brand equity and value. Strategic Empathy is not static but evolves over time as the consumer and context evolves. Therefore, it's important to share team-based strategic learning with the wider stakeholder group, inside and outside the organization, as a foundation for future learning and to inspire curiosity to learn.

3 Engaging employees and other stakeholders with a sense of shared purpose. Nurturing Strategic Empathy on a widespread basis is not just about marketing strategy formation, but also about nurturing the very purpose of the organization. Nonaka (2007) makes the point that an organization is not a machine but a living organism which can have a collective sense of identity and purpose. Strategic Empathy, therefore, cannot be the sole property of the marketing or strategy departments. Empathy with consumers connects employees with the organization's wider purpose: it *inspires* a shared understanding of what the organization believes about its brands, products or services and how they offer superior value that genuinely meets important consumer and customer needs. Employees, volunteers, suppliers and customers want to work for and with organizations which have a clear sense of purpose. In this respect, widespread, *institutionalized* Strategic Empathy is crucial to many aspects of organizational strategy, including human resources and procurement.

Figure 8.1 Phase Three of the Strategic Empathy Process

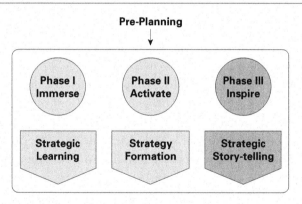

SOURCE: ModelPeople Inc

We call Phase Three in the Strategic Empathy Process *Inspire* because we want widespread communication of strategic learning to be powerful and memorable so as to inspire learning, engagement and strategic action. We approach this communication challenge with *Strategic Story-telling* (see Figure 8.1). Chapter 8 explains what strategic story-telling is, why it's effective, and how to implement it.

Story-telling, not presenting

The challenge for the marketing strategy team is not just to *present* the marketing strategy but to bring the objectives, strategies and foundational consumer or customer and brand insights to life in a way that connects with the audience and *builds empathy*. This is what we call *strategic story-telling*. There is growing enthusiasm for the power of story-telling in communicating marketing strategy, and a growing belief that strategists have to become story-tellers to inspire the transformational strategic action that is required to drive brand growth (Morgan, 2015). HR specialists predict that over the next few years, story-telling will become one of the top three skills required by the specialist insights and strategy executives who support marketing in the development of strategy (Cambiar, 2015).

Why is story-telling so powerful at communicating a strategic message? Neurobiology, psychology and anthropology all play their part in helping us to understand this. Telling a great story can be very effective in evoking empathy with consumers because a story causes the brain to mirror the thoughts and emotions expressed by the story-teller. Neuroscientists (Gowin, 2011) have demonstrated that story-telling causes the same area of the brain to light up simultaneously in both story-teller and audience. This suggests that the story-teller's audience does not just listen to the story but *connects emotionally with it* (and may even demonstrate this emotional connection by smiling, laughing, frowning; even crying). Other research evidence (Zak, 2014) suggests that character-driven stories consistently cause oxytocin synthesis. Oxytocin is the neurochemical that enhances human beings' sense of empathy. Presentation approaches which use character-driven stories with emotional content have been shown to make complex information persuasive and memorable.

Anthropology helps us understand the emotional impact of story-telling with reference to the earliest forms of stories: myths. For example, Claude Lévi-Strauss (1978) noted the astonishing fact that myths, despite seeming to be arbitrary and meaningless, are surprisingly similar across human cultures of different periods and geographies. Mythology attempts to fulfil a basic human need to create order in the mind. Myths are powerful because they help human beings understand who they are and where they come from. For example, Charles Long (2013) explores how many cultures have a version of a creation myth, which explains how the natural world was formed and how human beings came to exist and achieve a higher level of civilization than other animals.

Psychology is also helpful in giving us models which guide our understanding of the structure of story-telling. Beginning in the 1920s, Carl Jung (1929a) noted that mythological motifs appeared in individual dreams, often without any apparent external influence. Jung called these mythological images and patterns 'primordial images' or 'archetypes' and suggested that they made up the unconscious psyche; what he referred to as the 'collective unconscious', a second, 'inherited' psychic system (identical in all human beings). The collective unconscious, referred to as 'the psychic life of our ancestors right back to the earliest beginnings', is continually trying to influence conscious thought processes; therefore, while archetypes are themselves unconscious, they are given conscious expression by individuals in story-telling and art as well as in dreams.

Jung identified many archetypal events such as birth and death, archetypal figures such as the mother, the child and the wise old man and archetypal motifs such as the Flood. The inherited, universal nature of archetypes explains why they appear in myths and stories of all ages and across cultures. For example, most ancient cultures, dating back to the Sumerians (Epic of Gilgamesh) in the late 3rd century BC, had a version of the Biblical Flood, and Hollywood still exploits this motif today in the apocalyptic movie genre. The collective unconscious (what modern Jungian analysts call the objective psyche) underpins immediate consciousness, or the personal psyche. Jung believed that a person could achieve a state of individuation or wholeness of self by integrating the personal psyche with the objective psyche which connects human beings in a universal sense, giving them their deepest sense of identity and empathy with each other (Jung, 1929b). Using a Jungian framework, literature specialist Christopher Booker (2004) has suggested that stories tend to take shape around a limited number of archetypal patterns and characters which illustrate a universally meaningful message about the human journey, its obstacles and crises, and the endeavour to find balance and connection with other humans as a means of realizing personal identity and wholeness of self.

These theoretical frameworks will be helpful later on in this chapter when we consider how to construct a story. However, before we can do that, we need to consider for whom we're constructing the story; our target audience.

Defining the audience and media approach for strategic story-telling

In organizations with thousands of employees and stakeholders, bringing the marketing strategy to life and building empathy with consumers and customers through story-telling is a challenging proposition. Therefore, it's essential to consider the audience for institutionalizing strategic learning via story-telling **at the outset** of the Strategic Empathy Process, and also determine what communications media are most appropriate for each type of audience.

Firstly, consider the different types of people who make up the audience for strategic story-telling. How do they absorb information and what level of detail do they need? For example, senior management have many demands on their time and attention span. They need a high-level overview of marketing strategy. Product designers, by contrast, tend to thrive on nuance; they will gain inspiration from a high level of visual detail. Advertising creatives, as we saw from our allergy case study, often gain inspiration from day-to-day lifestyle scenarios. It's essential to take the time to think through – and consult with – the different types of people who need to activate marketing strategy and what inspiration they may need.

Next, it's important to consider what types of media would reach the target audience most effectively. For example, a three-minute video summary with text slide conclusions or a PowerPoint with short video clips may be right for time-sensitive senior management or retail buyer presentations, but lengthier audio podcasts or narrated video may be more insightful for sales teams who spend hours travelling by car or plane. Interactive online media or installations may reach office-based workers best.

When considering media for strategic story-telling, the goal should be to make communications as visually- and contextually-based as possible. Humans remember pictures much better than words because, as researchers (Grady *et al*, 1998) have shown, pictures more effectively engage the memory-related regions of the brain. Researchers (Isola *et al*, 2011) have also shown that pictures which show people, especially those that show them engaged in some sort of context, whether active or social, are the most memorable of all. This is hardly surprising. From the earliest cave paintings and Egyptian tomb frescoes, humans have depicted people in the context of their lives, social relationships and hierarchies. In the 21st century we follow reality TV characters like the Kardashians and tell stories about our own lives, minute by minute, on social media. Moving pictures are more impactful than static. While many possible visual media formats exist, video is currently the most powerful and effective medium for strategic story-telling, though it is also complex and expensive to produce.

Commonly-used media formats are:

- **Edited video,** which can be shot using hand-held camera or static camera, mounted on a tripod. GoPro-type action cameras can also be clipped onto a participant or mounted (eg in a vehicle) to give an in-motion, location perspective. There are many different approaches to editing which we discuss later in this chapter. I prefer to tell the story in a 20- to 30-minute consumer documentary, which can be enhanced with text slides to communicate key strategy points. A two- to four-minute executive edit can also be produced for senior management. However, clips can also be linked to a PowerPoint presentation to bring in the voice of the consumer.

- **PowerPoint presentations.** PowerPoint is a familiar medium for communicating strategy, especially to senior executives. PowerPoint is challenging for story-telling because it imposes an inflexible information architecture, but it is low cost. There are some simple approaches to bring the story to life and build empathy with listeners such as:

  - Creating archetypes which personify different consumer segments.

  - Using contextual photographs.

  - Highlighting consumer language in verbatim quotes.

  - Including 'look–feel' pages, made up of design or consumer lifestyle photographs and other imagery. Design and creative audiences use imagery extensively, both to inspire and to present their work. Consumer-derived imagery (eg from e-collages) gives them an idea of the topic-specific imagery and category semiotics which are top-of-mind for consumers.

  - Creating an animated PowerPoint with a narrated voice-over which can be played through from start to finish. This is not a lower-cost option than edited video but it does allow for greater text and graphics inclusion. For example, we did this to bring beer consumer segments to life in a key account sales presentation for a global beer marketing corporation (ModelPeople, 2012).

- **Open Source presentation tools** which allow more dynamic presentation of data and images, such as Prezi or Storymaps.

- **Printed media** such as books or laminated cards. Many on-demand services exist to produce these at reasonable prices. While more expensive to produce than some other media, they can look impressive enough to have staying power on a bookshelf or in a desk drawer. For example, we (ModelPeople, 2007) copy-wrote and produced a 20-page soft-cover booklet for a food brand manufacturer which told the story of the changing landscape of home cooking and food shopping. The booklet was sent out to the grocery trade in order to position the manufacturer as an expert in the field. It made reference to multiple information sources to weave the story, but critically it personified women we had interviewed in ethnographic research, to bring human empathy to a data-heavy story (ModelPeople, 2007). This case study opened Chapter 5.

- **Intranet.** Many organizations have a secure intranet offering access to company data such as sales figures and uploaded custom research reports. In theory this provides stakeholder access to accumulated learning, but in practice the amount of data available can make it hard to tell a streamlined and compelling story. Customizable dashboards, which integrate data points from multiple sources into a single presentation, are now in use in many major corporations.

- **Installations** on company premises:
  - For example, if space allows, a consumer 'room' which builds out the consumer archetypes and lifestyle using photos, video, posters or artefacts such as clothing can tell the consumer story in an experiential way. Some organizations (eg apparel designers) allocate a room to do this; others take advantage of corridors or lobby spaces.
  - Designers and architects also frequently use conceptual installations as 'design inspiration', an integral and essential part of framing their design process. This type of installation does not begin life with a (marketing) strategic story-telling purpose, but imagery collected during immersive research may subsequently become part of a design inspiration imagery installation.

- **Social media** can also be used to publish consumer content, though some companies have run into trouble for publishing such content without permission. However, this is a public forum which has limitations for candid consumer learning.

- **Live internal conferences** are a common way to socialize consumer learning. For example, we (ModelPeople, 2010) produced a graphic-rich presentation to synthesize key learning from restaurant ethnographies for a franchisee conference. We also created a video edit of ethnographic interviews with gaming enthusiasts (ModelPeople, 2005). This was shown at a sales conference for a game developer and we then introduced the participants on-stage in a live talk-show format, opening it up to questions from the floor.

We have stressed the importance of visualizing consumers and context in strategic story-telling, to create an empathetic connection. Therefore, in addition to thinking about the audience and medium for strategic story-telling we must also plan what kind of consumer content can be collected *at the outset* of a learning journey. Consumer content is defined as any media produced by consumers themselves (such as social media, e-collages, photos and written stories) or any media recorded by researchers, which features consumers or customers (such as video, audio or photography).

Collecting consumer content for strategic story-telling

Strategic story-tellers have a little less literary licence than fictional story-tellers. We must build empathy by authentically communicating the consumer story, using real characters; the consumers and customers whom we met on our learning journey. Marketers may be tempted to create presentations using generic clip art, stock video and fictional characters or script to communicate the message. After all, that's what happens in TV advertising. However, in strategic story-telling, authenticity is critical, for several reasons.

First, research protocol requires that we are respectful of the individuals whom we talk to and don't misrepresent them or their stories. But there's an equally important reason to be true to the voice of the consumer, from a strategic perspective. Over-editing, interpreting what consumers say, and overuse of stock video footage risks distorting the message, and its strategic implications. A story constructed this way misses the nuance that can spark new insights. It can also feel like marketing propaganda. By contrast, real stories from real consumers seem to inspire genuine empathy as well as new insight into what matters: the consumer and his or her life context relative to the company's brands. This may be because the human brain is good at spotting the difference between genuine emotion and a well-scripted fake. Or it may be that the cultural dominance of social media and reality TV means that real stories (or at any rate the careful representation of reality) has become more important to 21st-century audiences. Whatever the rationale, we should *use original consumer content only and edit it honestly*. Generic clip art, stock video or made-up consumer quotes should be used only where unavoidable in strategic story-telling.

The immersive learning journey approach which we described in Chapter 5 lends itself to creating people- and context-driven, picture-based presentations of the marketing strategy because it offers the opportunity to record people and context in many formats including video, audio, photography (including online photos and video) and other graphic formats like sketches made by the participant (eg representations of 'what menopause feels like to me'). Consumer-generated pictures such as selfies, diaries, photographs, mobile video, collages and drawings can also be included if permission has been given, and the consumer's identity is protected.

Protecting consumer confidentiality is of paramount importance. The US Market Research Association Code of Standards requires researchers to protect the privacy of research subjects and keep confidential any data which might identify them to third parties without their consent. It also requires that any data which is collected may only be used for the purpose to which the subject has agreed. Therefore, it is important to let the subject know that photographs will be shared internally with the research team and with the client who has sponsored the study, but will not be used for public promotional purposes. It is a good idea to ask for agreement to this in writing. Facilities who recruit research respondents typically do this but it is worth reviewing their protocol and perhaps developing your own custom version.

It is important to consider the quality of consumer content as well as the type. The most common mistake marketers make is in not collecting high enough quality content (especially video) to use in high-level presentations; for example, with senior executives or retail customers or in large employee presentations such as sales conferences or town-hall type meetings. Home-made video can have a charming, authentic quality to it. It can also be difficult to watch and can distract audience attention from the message! By contrast, a well-made video edit can have a shelf-life of several years and pay for itself over and over in terms of marketing effectiveness. If professional hand-held camera is truly not affordable, consider high-quality photography and audio instead.

Tool box

Phase Three planning checklist

At the outset of a Strategic Learning Journey it's important to decide:

- What are the target audiences for communicating the marketing strategy?
- What types of media would tell the strategic story most effectively to these audiences?
- What type and quality of content can we collect while in-field with consumers?
- What implications does budget have for content choice?

CASE STUDY   Multi-media story-telling: video gaming

There were around 60 in the audience in Paris, mostly marketing and creative people responsible for EMEA (Europe, Middle East and Africa) markets. Giant posters were up all around the room, each one showing a consumer segment archetype with a description in the consumer's own words of how and why he or she liked video gaming, and everyone in the audience had a spiral-bound booklet containing all eight consumer archetypes, portrayed in consumer language. The PowerPoint presentation was structured around bringing these archetypes to life by showing, in pictures and words, the lifestyle of the segment consumer, how and why gaming fitted into that and what emotional needs it met. A separate chapter for each segment kicked off with a five-minute video profile of the gamers we had interviewed who best exemplified the segment.

This was the second presentation that the strategy team had made; the first one had been in San Francisco a couple of weeks earlier, to the US team (ModelPeople, 2007). A global video game company had conducted a ground-breaking segmentation study to better understand gaming motivations and needs among different types of gamer. Historically, the company had focused on developing popular console game franchises, targeted at 'hard-core' male gamers. However, the consumer environment had changed with the launch of the Wii which made gaming easy and acceptable for family and casual gamer use, with titles like *Just Dance* and *Monopoly*. At the same time, more women had started to play puzzle games like *Tetris* on Nintendo DS or mobile, finding them easy and quick enough to fit into a coffee break between work or family commitments. And titles for tween girls which helped them play and learn about the world were also doing well, boosted by parental approval. The company realized that opportunities for future growth lay in broadening its portfolio for casual gamers, to complement their blockbuster titles, which appealed to hard-core gamers. The purpose of the segmentation study was to identify discrete segments of gamers which could be targeted when developing or acquiring new titles. The study had been designed by the director of consumer research, a psychologist, and was comprehensive and imaginative in scope. Each segment was defined in terms of the core demographic (eg tween girls, women aged 30–55), their attitudes and behaviours in terms of gaming involvement and shopping for games, the emotional benefits sought (eg 'blow off steam', 'feel intelligent'), and the key game play elements sought (eg 'allow me to compete', 'make me feel immersed in a historical setting').

ModelPeople's project assignment was to bring each segment to life, which we did in a complex combined methodology designed to explore personal and social gaming motivations and behaviour. Research methods included one-on-one depth interviews, parent/child dyads and friendship triads which were held in-home and included observations of social gaming behaviour. These were all filmed by Jeff Myers. Over 40 hours of footage was edited into eight five-minute video chapters, one for each segment. The video, along with the booklets, posters and PowerPoint summary was shaped into a multi-media presentation designed to inspire the employees responsible for designing, programming and marketing the games to innovate new games and existing titles to better meet the needs of these new gamer segments. Over the following two years, company sales passed the €1 billion mark for the first time.

Character-driven story-telling

As we have seen, research (Zak, 2014) tells us that the most powerful and persuasive stories create empathy with the human characters. They become real to us. Therefore, we care about what happens to them. Realistic, character-driven story-telling is a long-established way of bringing important and meaningful messages to life for an audience. Almost three thousand years ago, Homer's epic narratives of human-like gods and god-like heroes were some of the earliest forms of character-driven story-telling. We don't know whether Homer's characters and context were historical, as opposed to mythological, but in story-telling terms, it hardly matters. As Lévi-Strauss (1978) notes, for societies without writing, mythology pre-dates history, and fulfils the same function: to ensure that the future remains faithful to the present and the past. These thrilling stories had a 'strategic' message about the present and the future: they inspired pride in a heroic Greek national ancestry. Some four centuries later, the classical tragedies of Aeschylus, Sophocles and Euripides offered similarly meaningful messages; by dramatizing the tragic struggles of human beings against fate in the form of the gods, they gave audiences new emotional insights into their own human existence and purpose. Shakespeare built on this classical tradition, bringing heroes like Hamlet and Brutus more subtly and fully to life, by highlighting the impact of individual character, motivation and choice on 'real' history.

Irrespective of when it was created, literature critics have demonstrated that successful character-driven story-telling shows characters whom we care about, on a journey in which reversals, crises and happy (or tragic) endings take due course. Like Cinderella, our hero or heroine may start out in a dark place of fear or confusion before experiencing a surprise happy ending, resonant with hope for the future. Or they may, like Oedipus, Don Draper or Sleeping Beauty move from having it all to suffering a tragic mishap of fate or misjudgement and suffer reversals and crises before a final happy awakening or tragic denouement. The story-teller must evoke dramatic tension in the audience. It has been demonstrated (Zak, 2014) that *if a story can create dramatic tension* so as to grab our attention then *we will feel empathy with the characters.* Christopher Booker (2004) explains in detail how stories across the ages have used mechanisms such as fear, suspense, confusion and disruption, surprise, mystery, excitement, wonder and hope for the future, to create tension and build empathy. Academic researchers have also attempted to measure the elements of a good story and have drawn similar conclusions (Escalas, 2008).

Tool box

A well-crafted story can be said to:

- show the protagonist taking action to achieve a goal;
- tell the listener how the protagonist and other characters are thinking and feeling;
- give insight into how personal evolution or changes in the life of the protagonist occur;
- involve the protagonist in a crisis or turning point;
- have a clear beginning, middle (crisis or turning point) and end.

Consumer documentary video

Consumer documentary video is my preferred medium for strategic story-telling because it is character- and context-driven. It shows consumer action related to the marketing context, as well as human thoughts, feelings and motivations. Dramatic tension can easily be built using narrative, dramatic pacing and music.

Consumer documentary film has its roots in early ethnographic film which visualized context as well as an experience of social reality or 'being there'. The researcher spent long periods of time with the subject, recording the experience as if the camera were an extension of eye and arm. The narrative is not scripted or reconstructed by editing and it seeks to record behaviour and context, rather than develop character or motivation. The classic early ethnographic film is Robert Flaherty's *Nanook of the North* released in 1922. It records social reality so faithfully and slowly, that one critic described this film as 'taxidermic'! Nevertheless, these early videos were important in establishing truthful video communication that inspires understanding of the subject.

Consumer documentary film is different from other types of documentary, in that it has marketing strategic purpose and context. It merges approaches from ethnographic and documentary film. We immerse with the subject like the early ethnographic film makers, but for half a day rather than six months. We are independent observers of social reality but we do loosely script the experience through an interview guide. And we do reconstruct the experience through editing which visualizes the consumer through the lens of our marketing strategic purpose. ModelPeople's consumer documentary is produced by an experienced documentary film maker, Jeff Myers, and as such it also borrows from documentary film which dramatically documents the characters' experiences from the director's viewpoint.

Director's notes by Jeff Myers

Ethnographic and documentary film making have merged somewhat. Coming from the documentary film end of things, I approach each of these projects as though we're making miniature documentaries. Great documentaries are in the details; in this case, the house they live in, the

▶

clothes they wear and the food they eat. These variables can and do tell us a lot about who the subject is and where they come from. Just like in a documentary, each person on screen needs to be a three-dimensional character. The information they're giving us means nothing if we don't care about the character. We remain as neutral as possible while we are shooting so we can gather all of the information we can. If this is done well, we are able to stay open to the truth of the footage and the material will guide us to the final cut through careful and thoughtful editing. Once we understand the consumer story, we have to hook into the emotional connection of the idea. We formulate the vision and look of the documentary and determine our overall goal of how we want the audience to feel. To me, the research that we did should tell a story that views like a miniature movie. We need character arcs and an emotional connection to draw the viewer in. Our intent is to provide deep consumer insight. The client needs to receive a consumer documentary that helps them determine how to improve their ability to meet the needs of the consumer.

Video production guidelines

Preparation

Producing consumer documentary film requires careful preparation before the research fieldwork begins. In particular, the shooting conditions need to be discussed with the director:

- Will the video be shot indoors or out? If the shoot is in a consumer's home, assume that lighting conditions may not be ideal and that secondary lighting may be required.

- What time of day will the shoot begin and end? Lighting conditions may change over the course of the interview, for example, if it's held in the later afternoon.

- Will the interviewee be seated throughout or will he or she be moving around? A camera stick mount (monopod) may be required as well as a static tripod.

- How many people are to be interviewed? This may influence choice of sound recording technology.

- Do we want the interviewee to undertake an exercise requiring a 'body camera': for example, so we can observe what the interviewee is doing, without the camera being present, such as shopping in a store? Or perhaps we want the interviewee to do something in a tight corner, such as explore their bathroom cabinet, when a tight-in body camera angle might be useful.

- Do we need more than one camera to have a different camera angle? For example, if we have more than one person being interviewed this may be helpful. Movies always use more than one camera but we typically can't afford to do this for consumer documentary films.

Director's notes by Jeff Myers

The majority of our consumer documentary work has been shot on the Sony EX3 camera. The downside is that it's a big camera, but I like it because it does well in low light, has a fixed lens with a long range, can shoot 60 fps, and has XLR audio inputs. You can dial in the look you want and then save the setting in your picture profile. I prefer a rich, slightly saturated image with crunchy blacks. We shoot our interviews at 24 frames per second, to keep that cinematic look. Interviews are shot on a tripod with a fluid head to keep the camera 'alive'. We're usually in a family room, a kitchen or a dining room. There's always a window in one of these rooms and if it's day time then I want to take advantage of that natural light. If it's evening then I'm looking for a chair with a lamp next to it. I also bring a 1X1 LED light with me as a fill if necessary.

Remember we're doing this interview to hear what the respondent has to say, so audio is pretty important! We use Sennheiser wireless lavalier microphones (known as 'lavs' or lapel mics), which are clipped onto the interviewee. I like them because they're small and produce good sound. The downside to wireless lavs is you're going to get 'hits' on the audio now and then. You have to scan the different frequencies to find the channel with the least amount of noise and you might have to make adjustments during the interview. As a back-up I also bring a Sennheiser shot gun mic, to attach to the camera. It's not the best, but you'll get decent audio that you might have to spend some time cleaning up in post. It's more important to get something than nothing. The wireless lavs are great because the

▶

subject is free to move around. It's also important to get separate audio tracks for the moderator and the respondent. Most of the time we want to cut the interviewer's question out of the video, but sometimes it's important to hear the question. With separate channels I can easily turn either one up or down in post.

In the editing room I'm always wishing we had used a second camera. But I can't drag around and set up two big cameras in the time I have available before each interview. There's been a huge advancement in small cameras. GoPro's have come a long way and allow us to get a second angle. At times a GoPro might be a better solution when you need to be discreet. Even though we may have permission to shoot somewhere, some places frown on seeing a big camera and crew of people walking through their store. However, what you gain with discretion in the GoPro you lose in audio. While the size of the camera and picture is amazing, the built in mic leaves much to be desired. But sometimes you just have to do the best you can do and make the best of it.

At ModelPeople we strive to use the latest technology to gain the maximum connection. As we look to the future, technologically there are a lot of great options out there. The Canon XC10 is a camera I like. It shoots 4K, looks fantastic, has a fixed lens with decent parameters, it's small and it's lightweight. The downside is there are no XLR audio inputs. The on-board mic is decent and you could supplement it with a zoom recorder with XLR inputs and use the wireless lavs that we talked about earlier. This is a decent solution, but you will have to sync everything in the editing room. Not a big deal if you just shot one interview, but if you shot 17 interviews and each one is three hours long... that adds up. Find the equipment that works for you.

It's also essential that we have secured permission ahead of time to film the subject. There's no point in turning up ready for a three-hour interview and shoot if the subject doesn't want to be filmed! We ask for signed 'video release' forms ahead of time, which state that the rights to use the video belong to ModelPeople, for everything except consumer advertising use. However, obtaining the video rights does not release us from our obligations, as researchers, to protect the confidentiality of our research subjects. We never film anything that may give away the identity of the interviewee, such as anything (like a letter) with their full name or address on it or anything that identifies the location (such as a house name or street name). We may not film minors without parental permission, so we tend to avoid doing so unless it's essential to the video. Similarly, we don't film other family members without written permission. If we are filming in public, we don't capture other people in the background; and if this happens inadvertently we will avoid using the footage or will blank out faces in post-production.

Filming

When we first meet the consumer or customer who is to be the subject of the video we want to shoot, we have to work very quickly to put them at their ease and establish rapport, while setting up the camera and sound equipment. We discussed the importance of establishing rapport with a research subject (especially in ethnographic research), and the concerns and limitations, in Chapter 6. Even though we have secured written permission to film, the presence of a camera often gives a consumer second thoughts and it's the researcher's objective at the outset of a filmed interview to minimize this natural nervousness so that the camera does not introduce a significant research artefact (by changing the behaviour of the subject). The researcher will engage the subject in conversation about a topic that's easy and pleasant for them, to relax nerves, establish rapport and give Jeff time to set up.

Ethnographic film maker Bruno Moynié (2014) describes himself (presumably tongue-in-cheek) as engaging in a form of 'seduction' of interview participants; that is, his goal is to establish more than superficial rapport, but a level of comfort, even affection, that will make the interviewee forget all about the camera. Let's remember that the end purpose of Phase Three of the Strategic Empathy Process is to inspire empathy for consumers or customers. It follows that the end purpose of consumer documentary film is to help the strategy team to communicate how consumers are thinking, feeling and behaving. If the researcher and film maker don't themselves create an empathetic connection with the research subject, then it will be tough to ensure that emotion and reality come across on camera. I once observed a highly qualified ethnographic research professional take a very neutral, detached approach in some automotive in-home interviews. Her approach was undoubtedly calculated to reduce the subjectivity of the research process by controlling her responses to the participant. Unfortunately, for the observers, it was like watching the poor research subject being slowly turned on a spit under a high-powered microscope. The result was camera footage of people who looked and sounded uncomfortable and stilted, like frightened rabbits in car headlights! To create inspiring ethnographic film, the researcher must regard interaction with the participant not as a formal Q&A, but as an informal exchange, a conversation between equals. Judith Okely (1996) suggests that, rather than trying to control the subjectivity of the social research process, one can accept that 'the specificity and individuality of the observer are ever present and must therefore be acknowledged, explored and put to creative use'. This is particularly true when trying to shoot video that will inspire Strategic Empathy.

Moynié describes creating a level of comfort with his film subjects as having an instinctive element and I have found this to be the case too. He cites the example of retail workers who instinctively mirror their customers' body language or accent to establish rapport. Being an English woman working extensively in North America, accent is hard for me to mirror! However, I do find myself mirroring (and amplifying, for encouragement) the participant's positive body language, especially their smiles and eye contact. I take care not to wear expensive or distinctive clothes or jewellery, and to try to respect local customs regarding female dress. In many cultures, accepting refreshments or talking about kin also establishes a bond, and I do this too. Moynié also emphasizes the importance of finding an angle to relate to the participants that is genuine. Doing this and also remaining a neutral observer is tough. However, I have found that if you are well briefed on the topic and cultural context which you are exploring and genuinely curious about what the participant tells you, then the conversation will flow. Participants often tell me that no one has ever listened to them like I do, and for me that's a measure of success, however poignant.

Filmed interviews are often attended by observers, members of the learning journey team. While it's essential for them to be part of the conversation, they can also inhibit the development of personal rapport between researcher and subject which is necessary to get really deep emotional insight. At worst they can distract the interview and sustain it on a level of polite superficiality. It's essential to brief observers ahead of time on how to be silent, invisible *observers*. We have a one-page observer protocol, which we go through carefully with learning journey team members, before we go into field. This includes waiting to be invited to ask their questions and not just jumping in at what might be a disruptive juncture, not wearing clothing which identifies their organization or brands, and being respectful of the subject's time, personal space and culture. It's particularly important to have pre-briefed observers on what to do at the set-up stage of the interview, so they don't interfere with the researcher's efforts to quickly build rapport. Ask observers to wait until we have agreed with the participant where the interview is to be conducted, and where the camera needs to be positioned relative to where I am sitting. Only then can seats be found for observers. The researcher should remind observers to turn their mobile phones off too, and refrain from texting and checking e-mail during the interview, which can be distracting, and even insulting.

Researcher and camera person must agree on a way to communicate or provide direction during the interview. We need to ensure we capture the high-quality footage we need to tell the consumer story later on. The researcher may need to direct the camera to take specific shots (eg of products or room set-ups) which he or she wants to capture for strategic reasons. The camera person may need to direct the researcher to ask the subject to repeat specific statements of actions (perhaps more than once) so these can be re-captured on film. The goal is always to allow the researcher and the subject to unfold the story between them in a natural way, without intervention. Therefore, the camera person should always take direction from the researcher and should never seek to influence the subject, because it introduces a new element of subjectivity into the interview, and may also be disruptive to the unfolding of the emotional story. However, if researcher and camera person are used to working together, the camera person may sense when he or she can direct the subject without interrupting interview flow or rapport. For this reason, researchers should try to develop a long-term working relationship with one camera person.

As the practice of ethnography in consumer research has expanded, the issue of reflexivity – self-examination of the way in which the researcher has conducted ethnographic research and the impact of this on what happens – has gained added importance. It can certainly be argued that 'directing' the filming of ethnographic research is diametrically opposed to the intent of true ethnographic film, which aims to record whatever happened faithfully, as it happened. However, it's important to emphasize that we are not asking the research participant to do something unusual or that we have scripted ahead of time. *We are asking them to reconstruct something that we have observed them do or say so that we can capture it effectively for use in communicating strategy.* Charlotte Aull Davies (2008) puts this in perspective by noting that Flaherty himself had a deconstructed igloo specially formed, so that he could easily film the inside. She also cites the early example of James Mooney, who studied Native Americans over the period 1887–1907, and who arranged for the Ghost Dance to be performed not at night as customary, but during daylight so he could photograph it. The photos still have ethnographic relevance because they were taken during naturally occurring events. Aull Davies compares this approach with that of Edward S Curtis, whose widely admired photographs of Native Americans were staged, so as to remove any hint of Western dress or technology.

For the interviewer, there are some special techniques for ensuring the camera footage can easily be edited. First, it's important not to make any noise while the interviewee is speaking, which may be picked up by the mic. When I first started interviewing on camera, I was surprised at how much audible encouragement I gave the interviewee, frequently saying 'uhuh' or 'I understand', and laughing and commiserating out loud. This all appears on the soundtrack and may seriously compromise the final edit. Equally, if external noise (traffic, phone ringing, dog barking) occurs during the interview, stop, wait and if necessary, repeat the question. Secondly, it may be necessary to direct the interviewee to restate an important soundbite, and if necessary to play their comment back to them and ask them to repeat it again, to ensure that the point comes across clearly without 'ums' and 'ers'. If the interviewee is doing something that needs to be captured on film, then it may also be necessary to ask them to do it more than once. I prefer to step back and let Jeff take the lead at this point, as he has a professional 'eye' for what will work well on screen.

Tool box
Researcher checklist: filming consumer interviews

- Brief observers ahead of time, and consider using a formal observer protocol sheet.

- Establish rapport with the interviewee immediately, by asking some easy questions, while the camera is set up.

- Be well briefed on the research topic and cultural context; think about your own personal approach to creating a genuine emotional connection with the participant.

- Agree with the camera person how to communicate instructions during filming.

Director's notes by Jeff Myers

A stranger has invited you into their home and is about to share intimate details of their life with you — never take that lightly and always be respectful. When we get to a respondent's house, we don't have a lot of time to waste setting up. The first thing I'm looking at is the light. And don't be afraid to push the gain on the camera. A grainy image is better than a dark image. Don't forget, it's about what they're saying first and foremost and then we try to make it as interesting as possible through photography. Just make sure you get the shot.

I always put the respondent slightly left or right of frame and have the interviewer on the opposite side, but off camera. I feel it's best to have the interviewer as close to the camera as possible so that the respondent's eyes are looking just a little to the right or left of the lens. I feel it creates a better sense of connection for the viewer to be able to look into the respondent's eyes when they are talking. And always make sure the respondent is speaking toward the microphone. If they're looking left then put the lav on their left side. It doesn't do any good to have a fancy mic that's pointing away from the person speaking.

The next thing I'm looking for is depth and background. Always try to avoid putting the respondent against a wall. The image always looks flat and compressed, you get no additional information about the person from a white wall and it's just an ugly shot. Try to pick a background that tells you something about who the person is as it pertains to the topic at hand. For instance, if we're talking about food I want to put the respondent in the foreground so that we can see their kitchen in the background. While I'm getting information from them about the meals they prepare I can also see in the background the kitchen where they prepare those meals. Another important trick to remember is change the frame with each new answer and I like to zoom in or out to add dramatic effect at different parts of the answer.

At some point we get up and look into their kitchen, open the cabinets and the refrigerator; or look in their closet or bathroom cabinet. It's important to remember all of the details they've been talking about and get the b-roll shots that will be needed for inserts in post-production. The mementoes they have on the outside of the refrigerator can be as important as what's inside. Frozen dinners along with family pictures and soccer practice schedules might be just the shots you need to colour the

▶

story that they've told. I can't say this enough – shoot all of the details that you can find. For example, if we're doing a project on pain management and they've been talking about this spot on their neck, and how it nags at them, I'll ask them to sit on their bed and rub the spot that hurts. 'Show me where it hurts and if there's anything you do to get relief (a stretch or a self-massage) then I want to see that too.' If used correctly, slow motion can make the mundane more impactful. I like to shoot moments like this in slow motion, from far away. In the pain management example, the distance between the camera and the subject helped expresses the loneliness the sufferer felt in these moments. Each shot should move the story along.

When we're up and on the move, I use a combination of monopod and hand-held camera techniques. I want that hand-held feeling because it adds that sense of realism to the moment. I feel that the camera is most 'alive' when it's in my hands. But sometimes you just can't hold the camera forever and if you're zoomed in all the way it can get shaky. That's why I have the monopod. It stabilizes the camera just enough but maintains some of that hand-held spirit.

Editing

Editing consumer footage typically takes about two weeks and has three stages which are essential to produce the desired outcome: a video which communicates the key insights; is entertaining to watch; and inspires strategic action. The four stages are script writing, rough-cut, final cut and output.

1. Script writing

Editing a consumer documentary video starts with writing a script, and this should be done by a researcher or marketer who is part of the strategy team, with the input of the specialist video producer. This is because the script should primarily support the marketing strategy and highlight key insights and strategic priorities. But equally importantly, it should, as we have seen, evoke dramatic tension to engage the audience's attention and create empathy with the characters and their experiences. The director's input to this aspect of script development is critical. For example, in the infant product recall case study below, we built up empathy with the characters by showing the weight of responsibility they felt in keeping their babies safe. We evoked mothers' fear and confusion about the recall before showing the 'happy ending' (brand trust was not compromised) and 'hope' for their continuing close relationship with the brand. Good field notes or transcripts of consumer interviews are essential to identify the best consumer footage to tell the story. It is helpful for the researcher to make notes of good soundbites or specific shots as he or she is actually conducting the consumer interviews; and also to make note of the time-code at which the soundbite occurred. This helps when trying to fashion a short script out of hours of video footage.

Time-length must be considered when developing the script. Two minutes may be right for senior executives but other audiences may appreciate a longer, more nuanced story. I have found that a 20- to 30-minute edit is ideal to tell a story in detail without losing the listener's interest. Finally, always share the script with the strategy team to make sure the best soundbites have been selected and the narrative supports the strategy.

Tool box
Video script checklist

- What are the key strategic insights and how can you best communicate them in the voice of the consumer captured in your video footage?
- How can you develop the story and the character of the consumers in your video so that the audience cares about them and empathizes with their emotions?
- How can you pace the narrative so that it creates and maintains dramatic tension by evoking emotions such as fear, suspense, confusion, surprise, mystery, excitement, wonder and hope for the future?
- Time-length: what is best for the audience you are trying to reach?

CASE STUDY
Rebuilding confidence with stakeholders after an infant product recall

Infant brand relationships are built on a solid foundation of parents' trust, often built up over generations. The question for our client's executive team was whether a high-profile infant product recall had undermined this valuable brand equity. While no child had been harmed, there was still concern about whether parents' emotional trust in the brand had been irreparably compromised. They had asked me (ModelPeople, 2008) to conduct a Strategic Learning Journey for senior executives and develop a video which could inspire reassurance and rebuild confidence within their organization and partner marketing agencies.

We began by doing a Semiotic Scan for trust, using this exercise to produce visual imagery to explore with the research participants. We ran four-hour ethnographic interviews with mothers of infants, held in-home and including a visit to the store where they usually buy the brand. Members of the brand and senior executives observed the sessions, which were filmed by Jeff and his colleagues. We also ran a debrief session immediately after the last interviews, to discuss our observations and the strategic learning which needed to be communicated to the organization and agency partners.

'I honestly had tears in my eyes when I saw this', said the Insights Director when he reviewed the first cut of the video. The script started out demonstrating the tremendous weight of responsibility which new mothers felt, to protect their child from harm. 'This life is yours, so it's scary', said Vicki. 'It's more than a responsibility', said Kate. 'I'm in charge of his life.' The script demonstrated how a strong nexus of implicit trust in the brand had been built up over time across several dimensions: experiential, authoritative (based on a paediatrician's recommendation) and familial (based on family tradition). The script then took us to a dark place before showing us a happy ending with some important lessons for the future. Parents had been baffled and scared by the recall of a product they relied on to help care for their babies, but brand trust proved powerful enough to be resilient.

However, important lessons were learned about the need to more transparently communicate the reasons for the recall through trusted agents like paediatricians, pharmacists and family-oriented social media. The Global Insights Director and the production team worked on seven subsequent edits together, adding text slides to communicate the key strategic points that had been learned about how to improve communications in a crisis like this. A two-minute cut-down was produced for board use and the longer, 10-minute version was shown to over 2,000 employees in town-hall meetings to communicate the learnings about how to handle a crisis better but also to inspire confidence in the enduring strength of the brand's trust with US moms.

2. Rough-cut

Expect several rough-cuts as the footage is refined to tell the story. Sometimes the soundbites that I have chosen from notes or transcripts don't look as good in the actual footage, or the camera person or editor may have suggestions from their perspective behind the lens. The editor and I work back and forth, to get the best clips from a strategic and a film perspective.

There may be additional footage which can be incorporated into the edit, for example:

- consumer mobile video of the type taken in the opening case study to this chapter;
- 'spy' glasses video footage taken by subjects when shopping or undertaking some other task where we were unable to film;
- body camera footage.

These types of footage are of lower quality so should be used sparingly but it can give additional perspective to the consumer story.

Finally, it's important to share the last rough-cut with the strategy team to gain agreement that it communicates the strategy. It's also really helpful to show it to a fresh pair of eyes: someone who is the audience for the video to see whether it does, in fact, communicate the strategy and inspire empathy.

3. Final cut

Once the last rough-cut is approved by everyone, Jeff works his magic with secondary footage or b-roll, music and sub-titles:

- The footage from Jeff's camera is of the consumer talking to the researcher. Secondary footage (called b-roll) is taken on a second static or body camera, or is what the camera person takes to give a broader perspective of the consumer's context: for example, shots of the home, important artefacts such as possessions or brands they use, or activities they've shown us to give us insight, such as changing an infant's clothes, driving a car or trying to install a new router!
- Different types of music are selected (eg upbeat, darker, quiet and tender) to help the pacing of the edit. Jeff adjusts the sound levels so music evokes emotion but never covers up what the consumer is saying. Music is essential to building empathy in video and conveying the tonality of the consumer experience.

- Finally, we might decide to help the audience take out a specific message from the video by using black text slides or sub-titles to communicate key points. We might use slides to break the video up into themes or chapters. Sub-titles are always used to translate foreign language footage into English or if the speaker is difficult to understand. Sub-titles can also be used to pull out key words which we want the audience to remember, perhaps themes that have been repeated by several consumers.

Director's notes by Jeff Myers

Once we get to the editing room, that's where the magic happens. All of the little pieces finally start fitting together. Claire takes great notes in the field and also works with a transcriber to shape the story into a script. We might have 40–50 hours of footage. That's a lot! Make sure you have enough computer storage space. I use external hard drives to store and back up footage. The first thing you want to do is lay down the story. Get all of the soundbites in order so that you can make your point. Then we layer in b-roll to help colour the story. This is where all of those detail shots we collected in the field come in, to help dramatize what the respondent is saying.

The final piece of the puzzle is the music. I use a combination of classical, movie soundtracks, hip hop and pop music. The first few seconds of the piece you really want to grab the viewer's attention. Make sure it's visually and sonically stimulating. And make sure you change music tracks to help accentuate the shifts in story. Peaks and valleys are important. I might start out high, then shift to a slower, darker type music when they start talking about the pain they experience or the struggle to cook a meal with their busy schedule. Then the music might climb to a peak when the brand saves the day. Just make sure that all aspects are symbiotic: story, visuals and music.

---

4. Output

Typically a video is burned to DVD because of the large file size, but clips or chapters can also be linked to an electronic document for seamless presentation.

Virtual reality consumer video?

3-D films have been around for several years and, as we have seen, are finding their way into virtual shopper research. Cameras and viewing technology already exist to allow us to make consumer video that gives stakeholders a more visceral experience of what it might be like to share a family dinner or care for a newborn baby. US news organizations are experimenting with the technology in online news reporting: in November 2015, a leading US news site ran an 11-minute VR documentary of three children who had been displaced by political turmoil, which immersed viewers in their world and enabled them to truly hear their voice. The printed news vehicle distributed 1.7 million Google Cardboard viewers, and in so doing became, overnight, probably the biggest publisher of VR content to date. Their VR app also offered ambient footage of some of the memorials which sprang up in Paris after the terrorist attacks there (*New York Times,* 2015).

Tool box

Checklist: editing consumer documentary film

- Has the final rough-cut been shared with the strategy team and a couple of representatives from the target audience, to ensure it communicates the strategy *and* inspires consumer empathy?

- Has b-roll been used to communicate consumer context and show items or artefacts (possessions, brand choices) or activities that are important to the story?

- Have music, text slides and chapters been included, to make the consumer story easier for the audience to understand?

- Is a stand-alone video enough or is there also a need for individual video clips embedded into a presentation to help bring facts to life?

Chapter 8 summary

1 Phase Three of the Strategic Empathy Process, *Inspire*, has three important strategic goals:

- inspiring strategic action among the wider stakeholder group;
- promoting a culture of curiosity for continuous strategic learning, to ensure Strategic Empathy is nurtured over time;
- engaging employees and other stakeholders with a sense of shared purpose.

2 Marketing strategy must be communicated through strategic story-telling, to bring objectives, strategies and foundational insights to life and build empathy with stakeholders. Presentation approaches which use character-driven stories with emotional content have been shown to make complex information persuasive and memorable.

3 It is essential to plan for strategic story-telling before the immersive learning journey (Chapter 5) is implemented:

- define the audience, media approach and budget for strategic story-telling;
- decide what type and form of consumer content can be collected during the immersive learning journey.

4 Consumer documentary video can be highly effective for strategic story-telling because it is character-driven and lends itself to building dramatic tension, which is essential to capture audience attention. There are several watch-points:

- Careful preparation is essential for filming consumer interviews, including:
  - planning shoot location and equipment needed; for example, camera, tripod, lighting, covert camera (eg recording spy glasses);
  - securing written permission from the interviewee to film and use the footage for internal strategic purposes.
- A script should be developed by the marketing strategy team with input from the director on optimizing character development and dramatic tension.
- Use only high-quality, authentic consumer content, which protects consumer confidentiality.
- Several cuts will be reviewed by the strategy team before music and text is added.

References

Aull Davies, C (2008) *Reflexive Ethnography: A guide to research selves and others*, p 132, Routledge, London

Booker, C (2004) *Seven Basic Plots*, Continuum, London

Cambiar (2015) *4th Annual Future of Research report*, Cambiar Consulting

Crossan, M, Lane, H and White, R (1999) An organizational learning framework: from intuition to institution, *Academy of Management Review*, vol 24, **3**, July

Epic of Gilgamesh, believed to date back to 2100 *BC* – the hero, Gilgamesh, meets the immortal man Utnapishtim, who describes how the god Ea tells him to build a huge vessel, in anticipation of a great flood that would destroy the world, to save Utnapishtim, his family, friends and the animals

Escalas, J (2008) Advertising narratives: What are they and how do they work? Referenced in Woodside, A. When consumers and brands talk: story-telling theory and research in psychology and marketing, *Psychology and Marketing*, February, pp 102–03

Gowin, J (2011) Why Sharing Stories Brings People Together, *Psychology Today*, 2 June

Grady, C, McIntosh, A, Rajah, M and Craik, F (1998) Neural correlates of the episodic encoding of pictures and words, *Proceedings of the National Academy of Sciences of the United States of America*, **95**, no 5

Homer (edn 1991) *The Iliad*, Penguin Classics, London

Isola, P, Xiao, J, Torralba, A and Aude, O (2011) What makes an image memorable?, *Computer Vision and Pattern Recognition Conference*

Jung, C (1929a) The significance of constitution and heredity in psychology in *Collected Works*, 8, p 112, Routledge & Kegan Paul, New York (1960)

Jung, C (1929b) The concept of the collective unconscious in *Collected Works*, 9, p 42, Routledge & Kegan Paul, New York (1959)

Lévi-Strauss, C (1978) *Myth and Meaning*, pp 11, 13, 43, University of Toronto Press, Toronto

Long, C (2013) Myth and Mythology, *The World and I Online*, December

ModelPeople Inc (2005) Live Q&A with video gaming segments at developer sales conference

ModelPeople Inc (2007) Printed booklet produced for grocery trade based on ethnographic research and syndicated data analysis

ModelPeople Inc (2008) Stakeholder video edit for infant healthcare product recall

ModelPeople Inc (2010) Animated conference presentation for family dining restaurant franchisee conference

ModelPeople Inc (2012) Narrated, animated PowerPoint sales presentation for a global beer marketing company

ModelPeople Inc (2014) Ethnographic research for advertising strategy activation in OTC healthcare

Morgan, B (2015) Stan Sthanunathan on why insight is a broad organizational function, *Research online magazine*, 6 January – quote used: 'How do you add value to the data so that it inspires and provokes transformational action?'

Moynié, B (2014) Seduction in the Field, in *Handbook of Anthropology in Business*, ed R Denny and P Sunderland, Left Coast Press, San Francisco, CA

Myers, J, Perch 13, Los Angeles, CA

New York Times online (2015) November 20 [last reviewed February 2016]

Nonaka, I (2007) The Knowledge Creating Company, *Harvard Business Review*, July–August

Okely, J (1996) *Own or Other Culture*, p 28, Routledge, London

Zak, P (2014) Why your brain loves good story-telling, *Harvard Business Review*, 28 October

The Strategic Empathy Process in a non-profit organization

09

CASE STUDY Strategic Empathy and mental health

The first time I was sectioned, I was locked in a room with cement to sleep on. The second time I was given a bed with linens and people to talk to. I made friends.   *Mental health patient, Uganda*

I've never met a doctor that I could talk to... but my new doctor really listened to how I felt... I always felt like I was in control.   Mental health patient, UK

A global mental health charity wanted to raise awareness and drive change in the area of dignity for patients. Before launching any fund-raising or awareness initiatives, they wanted to conduct deep insights research to understand how mental health patients, caregivers and professionals viewed the idea of dignity, based on their experiences. Using our online platform, PeopleBlogSpot, we set them two tasks:

- Write a story which illustrates what 'dignity in mental health' means to you.

- Using pictures and words, create an e-collage to represent 'dignity in mental health'.

The exercise went out to 180 people in 22 countries, who were nominated by local offices. A team of professional researchers working pro bono translated the questions into local languages and helped with supporting participants and translating stories. The information was so rich that we were able to develop a new taxonomy of dignity in mental health (ModelPeople, 2015) which illustrated different dimensions of the concept. This in turn inspired a powerful video communicating the experiences of vulnerable mental health patients and the design of a new symbol for fund-raising. Both were unveiled at a global conference to launch the initiative. The highlight of the conference was a young woman who had taken part in the online research. She described her struggle to get help with anorexia. 'When you break your arm, everyone can see you're wounded and they say *sorry* and wish you *get well soon*', she said; 'but, when you're suffering inside, it's much harder to notice.' She brought the audience of clinical professionals to their feet in empathy with her experiences and her courage in talking about them.

Introduction

In preceding chapters, we have proposed the idea that strategy formation is often an emergent process, involving many people within the organization, rather than a 'black box' approach to formal planning, conducted by specialists. We explored the Strategic Empathy Process, a team-based approach to strategy with three steps: developing empathy with customers and stakeholders through immersive learning; activating tacit knowledge and learning into strategy implementation; and inspiring empathy and strategic understanding with a broader stakeholder group. We also explored methods and tools for implementing this process within the *commercial* context of consumers, customers and brands. Yet the idea of Strategic

Empathy is especially powerful in many *non-commercial* organizations, especially those for whom empathy with vulnerable people is at the heart of their purpose. Strategic Empathy processes and methods have been used in non-profit contexts with diverse groups of stakeholders to achieve organizational goals. In this chapter, we will look at the application of the Strategic Empathy Process in non-profit organizations.

'Customer-focus' in the non-profit organization

Andreasen and Kotler (2007) note that many non-profit organizations are not truly customer-focused, even though (they state) managers in these organizations 'make it abundantly clear that they wish to be'. They also identify that marketing strategy is regarded primarily as communication and promotion, with little customer or competitor research done, and no attempts at market segmentation. However, my experience suggests that there may be a more complex series of factors at play. While the management of a non-profit may be business-oriented and familiar with developing marketing strategy, other stakeholders in the organization may have very different perspectives. Strategy formation may be unfamiliar or may be regarded as a suspect, 'commercial' activity which absorbs precious resources with little benefit to vulnerable populations (unfortunately, recent scandals involving the social enterprise activities of a few major charities may have reinforced this suspicion). 'Customers' may be equated with donors, who (though essential) may be judged to be less important than a vulnerable population served by a charity, for example. Or 'customers' may be regarded as too ignorant or unmotivated to understand 'what's good for them': for example, in the case of a health non-profit or public health institution trying to effect behaviour change; or an arts non-profit staging drama with niche appeal. Aside from differing goals among staff, non-profits engage large numbers of volunteers – often with highly individual motivations and goals – who can be tough to mobilize around shared goals and actions, and easily disenfranchised (at high cost to the organization). As we saw in Chapter 1, strategy is often not planned but emergent; that is, it evolves based on patterns of behaviour across an organization. Nowhere can this be more true than in a non-profit!

I'd like to suggest that 'customer-focus' is an unhelpful way to frame the marketing strategy process in a non-profit organization. Even the term 'marketing strategy process' is probably alienating to many staff and volunteers. And yet organizations need to agree on their core stakeholder groups, vision, purpose, goals, financial objectives and action plans: in other words, they need to define the components of a marketing strategy, even if they don't name it as such. Non-profit organizations also need to direct – committed and energetic, but possibly chaotic – emergent strategy formation towards a shared purpose and goals, to motivate staff, volunteers and (crucially) donors. For, as we saw in Chapter 3, people want to be associated with a brand that has meaning, purpose and values. In this chapter, I will propose that 'empathy' is a more helpful way to frame the non-profit strategy process, because it speaks powerfully to shared purpose and values: the reasons why staff, volunteers and donors are engaged with the organization in the first place.

CASE STUDY   Empathy in patient care

What would an epidemic of empathy in healthcare look like, asks Thomas Lee, MD (2014)? Patient experience is a dynamic issue for healthcare executives, clinical staff, governments and industry leaders. Patients now judge healthcare providers not only on clinical outcomes, but also on their ability to be compassionate and deliver excellent, patient-centred care. Lee notes that, to date, healthcare organizations have 'used carpet bombing strategies, in which all personnel are instructed to be more sensitive to patients' needs'. For example, the published business plan of the (government-funded) National Health Service in the UK is titled *Putting Patients First*, and the stated business objectives for patient experience are to '... place patients at the heart of what we do... and listen to staff'. The document talks about 'patient rights' and 'patient feedback', which seems to suggest demarcation lines between politicians, managers, staff and patients. Yet Lee (2014) recommends not highlighting negative behaviour but focusing on spreading empathetic behaviour, using the best doctor–patient relationships as exemplars in communications, to spread learning about empathy benefits and techniques.

This is an appreciative inquiry (AI) approach (Cooperrider and Srivastva, 1987), which emphasizes discovering (via story-telling) what works best and dreaming about what the organization could be like (Seel, 2008). The Cleveland Clinic in Ohio, where AI was conceived, now runs an annual 'Empathy + Innovation Summit', which claims to bring together healthcare professionals 'who are committed to not just the patient or caregiver experience, but also to the human experience'. Cleveland Clinic has also launched a (now famous) ad campaign which unites the perspectives of patients and healthcare professionals around empathy for one another (Cleveland Clinic, 2013). The ad shows patients, relatives and staff going about their business with thought bubbles over their heads: 'Son is on life-support', 'Can't take in treatment options', 'Nearing the end of a 12-hour shift'. The ad concludes with a challenge: 'If you could stand in someone's shoes, hear what they hear, see what they see, feel what they feel, would you treat them differently?'

How the Strategic Empathy Process works in a non-profit

The three phases of the Strategic Empathy Process (Immerse, Activate, Inspire) are consistent in a non-profit context. However, there may be differences in emphasis and much less consistency in process implementation, driven by disparities in resources and organizational culture. Furthermore, the diversity in size and membership of non-profit organizations requires the process to be adapted to meet the specific skills and needs of stakeholders in each case. Perhaps the biggest difference in emphasis is that, in a commercial organization, the strategy team perceives itself as distinct from the consumers whom their organization serves. In a non-profit context, this may not be the case. The membership of a charity, for example, very likely includes many representatives from the population whom the charity serves. For example, the membership of mental health charity the World Federation for Mental Health includes mental health professionals, but also patients, their caregivers and families. The entire membership group should be represented within the strategy team, making it much less homogeneous than is the case for a commercial strategy team. Therefore, when conducting experiential research during the Immerse phase of the process, we must remember that some of the individuals on the strategy team are participating in shaping understanding of *their own* needs; in fact, their tacit knowledge and first-hand experience of issues facing service users is essential to the research, and a primary source of information. This has implications in many areas, including choice of research methods and team-working approach. Methodologies developed in the field of participatory action research may be helpful in addressing this (see tool box below).

Tool box

Participatory action research (PAR) approaches

- PAR is collaborative, democratic research and action for social change (Kindon *et al*, 2007), which involves people who are affected by an issue, taking part in generating and using knowledge about it. PAR consciously integrates the values of the participants and uses their diverse experiences as an opportunity to enrich the research process.

- PAR is a process of recurrent stages of **action** and **reflection** on goals, plans and outcomes; however, it has no blueprint and is flexible in use.

- The steering group leading the PAR process will be made up of a wide range of interested parties and is flexible in composition: for example, a small group may pull in the wider community as required; or the whole group may follow the process through with members dropping in and out.

- Some key questions to determine are concerned with the effective composition and work process of the steering group leading the research on behalf of the wider stakeholder population (Pain *et al*, 2012):

  1 Who will be involved and are the people on the steering group representative of the wider group affected by the issue?

  2 How will the steering group work? How often will meetings be held?

  3 What are the goals and desired outcomes? Time frame?

  4 How are roles decided: who will facilitate the meetings?

  5 How will meetings be conducted and disagreements resolved?

  6 How will findings be shared with others affected by the issue, and what media are most effective for this?

We will use a case study to illustrate how the Strategic Empathy Process was used to create a strategic plan for one non-profit organization. For the purpose of completeness, this case study illustrates how a strategic plan was created from start to finish: using the template in Chapter 3 and building on collaborative strategic learning, but using a PAR-type model for teamworking. However, as we have noted, some non-profits might not undertake this type of planned approach to strategy formation. They may choose to use individual elements of the Strategic Empathy Process, or specific methods, to address emergent strategy questions or adapt the process to the resources available. The case study (Brooks, 2012) is for an Episcopal parish church, which may not, at first glance, seem particularly useful in a broader context! However, a church is highly representative of a non-profit in that its members have diverse needs and perspectives, are both donors to and recipients of the organization's services, are passionately engaged in the purpose and values of the organization, and face real challenges (in a very VUCA environment!) in determining how to target resources to recruit and motivate new members.

Case study: strategy formation in an Episcopal parish church in California

1. Introduction

The parish church in question was a lovely, historic building in an affluent seaside town in sunny coastal California. Membership was about 800 people, of whom about 400 attended services weekly. The parish community was long-established and skewed middle-aged and older. However, it also attracted new members moving into the area, especially families with young children who wanted a religious education for their children, which is not offered in US public schools, by constitutional law requiring the separation of church and state. The initiative to develop a strategic plan came from the rector who had been called some three years earlier. At that time, the parish had developed strategic goals but these were now five years old and no longer fully reflected the needs and dreams of the parish. Therefore, the vestry (the democratically elected church 'executive management') appointed two members of the parish congregation to co-chair a new planning process.

2. Pre-Planning

The goals of the Pre-Planning phase of the Strategic Empathy Process are:

- **Identify the strategic issue, agenda and time frame.** The parish faced some issues including campus space and diversity; but principally saw opportunities to expand its community and live out its ministries more fully, especially in providing outreach services for vulnerable people. The goal was to take no longer than a year to create a five-year plan, which would be broadly structured like a business strategic plan (see Chapter 3 for details on this), including:

- parish mission;

- parish vision and values;

- current situation and goals for the future;

- tactical objectives for each goal;

- strategic actions for each objective;

- milestones for vestry approval.

While this may have felt ambitious, it was seen as important to create detailed objectives and action plans which would form a foundation for coordinated staff, vestry and ministry planning (mitigating the effect of budgetary and planning fiefdoms which can be characteristic of how a non-profit functions day-to-day). The time frame was much longer than would have been the case in a for-profit organization, reflecting the difficulties of a participatory team process. It is practically challenging to bring together a large group, many of them volunteers, on a regular basis.

- **Put together the strategy team to represent the wider stakeholder group.** The critical first step was to identify the stakeholder team to be involved. The rector wanted a large team to include representatives from all the parish stakeholder groups (eg seniors, families with children, teens, ministry leaders, clergy and staff). She felt this was important to ensure that the needs and perspectives of the entire parish were represented and also to ensure positive word-of-mouth among these different stakeholder communities. In practice, this large group of about 25 was rarely completely in attendance at meetings; people dropped in and out as their interests and commitments dictated, and other 'outside experts' (such as members with special expertise in areas like children's ministries) were invited to join meetings. However, everyone was included in e-mail communications about progress and encouraged to take part.

- **Agree on team process.** The first meeting was a full-day workshop spent in agreeing the strategy process, but also how the process was to be managed. The team agreed three principles: *parish-wide, listening-based, consensus driven.* The team also agreed that meetings would be a combination of small group activity, evening meetings for feedback/consensus and full-day workshops to develop specific elements of the strategic plan such as vision, mission and goals. The team also spent time building team relationships over breakfast, lunch and conversation. As time went on, the value of *reflecting* (Kindon *et al*, 2007) became clear, as the diverse group sometimes struggled to reach consensus. It was important to allow time to debate contentious issues so that the whole team moved through the process as one. Many times the power of prayer as a reflective tool was proven – in a non-religious context, taking a break for personal reflection, or asking small groups to reframe issues by consciously taking the opposing perspective, may be helpful.

3. Phase One: Immerse

Figure 9.1 Phase One of the Strategic Empathy Process in a non-profit

SOURCE: ModelPeople Inc

The goal of Phase One (Immerse) of the Strategic Empathy Process is to gain shared knowledge and experiential learning as a foundation for strategy formation (see Figure 9.1). The parish undertook several research exercises and also consulted on key elements of the plan such as the vision. However, they did not conduct experiential research, rather relying on the tacit knowledge and individual experiences of strategy team members and ministry leads who were widely consulted. The potential risk of this approach is that existing beliefs are reinforced rather than challenged. While the research completed did uncover areas where the strategy team's view differed from that of others in the parish, these differences were perhaps not as viscerally understood and acknowledged as they might have been with the benefit of true experiential research: observing and talking in depth with a wider range of parishioners and external stakeholders, such as users of outreach services like homeless programmes and residents of the town.

The following types of research were undertaken:

- **Qualitative research.** Recognizing that much of the day-to-day functioning of the church (and also member passion) rested on the lay ministries (eg 'teens and young adults' or 'outreach'), the first research exercise was organized around them. The strategy team divided into eight groups who were tasked with consulting with ministry leads and active parishioners, using a semi-structured list of questions (shown in the tool box below). The goal of consultation was to engage with the experiences of people running church activities on the ground (who did not want to be part of the strategy team) and to capture their dreams for the future.

Tool box
Qualitative parish feedback

A semi-structured questionnaire was designed to get initial parish input to key elements of the strategic plan before the strategy team began discerning them. Small groups within the strategy team got feedback from parishioners involved with each ministry, and round-table discussions were conducted at the party, held to kick off the process with the wider parish. The groups completed the questionnaire in the three weeks after the first meeting and gave feedback at the second meeting. The questions were:

1 Who are the key members of the parish most closely involved (who need to be consulted)?

2 Describe this ministry in five years' time: what's your dream/vision?

3 What is the purpose *(mission)* of this ministry at St P's today?

4 Whom does the ministry serve and what are their needs?

5 What does St P's do well in this area? What do we want to do better? Are there any constraints? *(SWOT)*

6 What could St P's do better over the next five years to achieve the dream/vision? *(goals)*

- **Data analysis.** Analysis of existing data is important to develop a picture of the non-profit as a baseline for establishing future direction and goals: what is called the 'current situation'. The parish database proved to be out of date but the treasurer provided accurate and up-to-date analysis of donations, which showed some important information about core stakeholders. For example, while families with children under 16 comprised only 20 per cent of all families in the parish, they comprised over 40 per cent of all donors. However, in terms of size of donation, seniors (long-established members of the congregation) were also an important segment of donors. This data helped the team to prioritize goals and budget allocation for specific programmes.

- **Quantitative research** provided substantive feedback from non-profit members on the current situation and priorities for the future. The strategy team developed a simple survey using the low-cost online research platform, Survey Monkey, which was e-mailed out to all parishioners. About 40 per cent of the active members responded – a very high response rate for this type of survey which was attributed to parish-wide communications and word-of-mouth. The survey asked respondents to rate strengths, weaknesses, opportunities and threats to the parish, based on a list of attributes developed by the strategy team, with space given for other issues to be identified. It also asked for the respondent's age, socio-economic, family and ethnic status, service attended and length of membership so responses could be compared for sub-groups. Feedback indicated strengths in clergy, liturgy and programmes for different age groups but weaknesses in campus facilities and ethnic/LGBT diversity. Opportunities were seen as a growing local population. Interestingly, the main threats were seen as external: earthquakes and schism in the worldwide Anglican Church. When the results of the SWOT survey had been analysed, they were presented to the parish in a lunch forum and round-table discussions were facilitated by strategy team members facilitating. A worksheet was used as a guide (see tool box below).

Tool box

Parish consultation worksheet: parish goals

When the results of the SWOT survey had been analysed, they were presented to the parish in a lunch forum and round-table discussions were facilitated by strategy team members facilitating. A worksheet was used as a guide:

Based on the results of the SWOT survey just presented, please list up to five priorities or goals for the parish over the next five years. These priorities should address one or more strengths, weaknesses, opportunities or threats. Please say in each case which SWOT finding you are addressing.

Role of facilitators:

- ensure that everyone speaks, is listened to, and their opinion valued and understood;
- document the results of your table's discussion on the worksheet;
- give a verbal, one-minute summary of your table's conclusions;
- meet with other facilitators and co-chairs for a 30-minute debrief immediately following the forum.

4. Phase Two: Activate

Figure 9.2 Phase Two of the Strategic Empathy Process in a non-profit

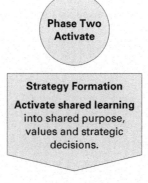

SOURCE: ModelPeople Inc

The goal of Phase Two (Activate) of the Strategic Empathy Process is to activate shared knowledge and learning from Phase One into shared purpose and values, and strategic decisions. Several full- and half-day workshops were run to do important tasks such as discerning parish vision and goals in collaboration with the entire strategy team. Other tasks such as quantitative research and setting detailed objectives were delegated to the co-chairs or team members with relevant experience. It is realistic to expect that over a long process like this one, energy and commitment will decline, requiring some details to be worked out at the executive and staff level.

The workshops had two purposes: reviewing and refining the work done in the prior workshop; and team activation of the next element in the strategic plan. Hence there was a regular cycle of *reflecting* on work that had been done in prior sessions (and inviting new perspectives from team members who had missed the session) and *action*. It can be difficult to encourage everyone in a large, mixed group like this to feel comfortable sharing their experiences and thoughts. Creative exercises are helpful in encouraging all team members to articulate their ideas. Working in small teams is less intimidating than working alone; however, team composition should be planned. Mixing up different perspectives encourages debate of issues; if a topic is sensitive, then putting people in friendship pairs is helpful.

Tool box
Sample creative exercise for non-profit activation workshop

The first workshop kicked off the strategy process with a task that was deeply engaging and motivating for everyone in the group: discerning parish vision and values: their hopes and dreams for the future. This exercise is an excellent choice for non-profits which are restructuring, downsizing or merging, as it is future-oriented rather than backward-looking, focuses discussion around beliefs and values held in common and builds empathy between team members.

1 **Creative visioning.** The team divided into four small groups and used images torn from magazines to create their vision of the parish on poster boards. The small groups then presented their ideas, and as they were presenting, the facilitator wrote down, on Post-it notes, 'value' words which came up (such as diversity, tradition, love, serve).

▶

2 **Values clustering**. The Post-its were put up on the wall and reviewed. All the poster boards were put up on easels and teams then wrote their own value Post-its, adding them to the wall. The group then helped the facilitator cluster the Post-its into groups, each of which represented a value. The session ended with agreement on a list of potential values, which were discussed and agreed at the next meeting.

3 **Follow-up.** At the following workshop, teams worked on a draft Vision statement and values. An example of a Vision statement produced in the workshop is:

> *St P's is an accepting church community that celebrates tradition and diversity in our spiritual formation. We live out Christ's word as we connect to and serve our neighbours around us. Embracing tradition for tomorrow!*

5. Phase Three: Inspire

Figure 9.3 Phase Three of the Strategic Empathy Process in a non-profit

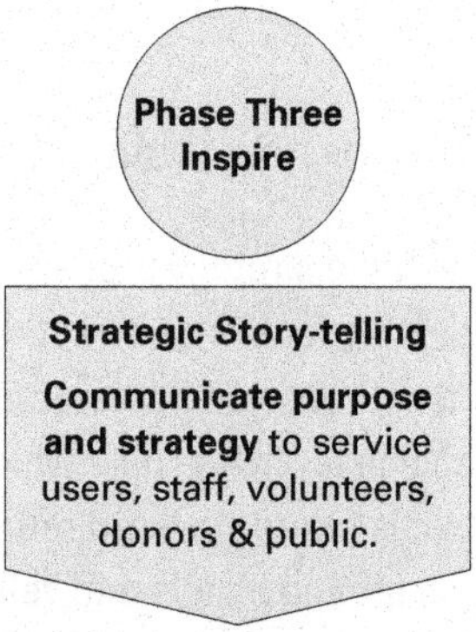

SOURCE: ModelPeople Inc

The goal of the Inspire phase of the Strategic Empathy Process is to inspire shared understanding of the organization's purpose and strategic decisions among stakeholders. This has the benefit of shaping emergent strategy formation, as well as communicating the formal strategic decisions that have been made, and the rationale for making them. Story-telling can be an engaging way to do this, because it's easily understood by different audiences (especially in a church environment where members are used to Bible parables). Additionally, as we saw in Chapter 8, audiences connect directly with the emotions expressed in story-telling, and the members of the parish strategy team were passionately engaged in visioning the future of their church.

Communication was emphasized from the outset, to engage the parish and local community in the process, using many different communication channels. A kick-off party was held to introduce the process and the team and to consult the wider stakeholder group. A web page was established to report on planning milestones: for example, a video was made of team members presenting parish vision collages and speaking to their hopes and dreams. Another video described the process and milestones achieved after four months, which was played at parish meetings. Monthly reports were published in the church magazine and team members volunteered to give verbal reports at services. Perhaps most effective, the Mission statement was set to music and sung regularly at services! Several formal consultations were built into the plan, at which the team presented strategy outcomes (like the vision, mission and values) and invited the parish (in small groups) to discuss and feedback on outcomes. Informal consultations were also held with city neighbours.

6. Outcomes

The Strategic Empathy Process in this non-profit organization had several important outcomes, not least of which was strengthening shared understanding and excitement in the organization's purpose, values and vision for its future: what it profoundly stood for and how that might be nurtured, grow and bear fruit. New directions were chosen as goals, objectives and action plans were debated in ministry and vestry meetings. Weaknesses were identified in the SWOT, which led to new initiatives: to build diversity, including discerning the celebration of same-sex marriage; and to set up an Advocacy ministry to empower social justice efforts. Identifying constraints on future development in the SWOT also resulted in a campus planning effort which led to a major capital campaign to raise substantial funds for buildings and other resources.

Effective immersive research methods and tools

As we saw in the case study, there can be a tendency for non-profit organizations not to undertake experiential research, in the belief that the tacit knowledge and experience of members of the organization allows them to understand the needs of those whom they serve. Research cost may also be a significant issue. Not doing experiential research may be justified if the team represents all members and the process emphasizes listening, reflection and consensus so that all stakeholder experiences can be heard and reflected on. However, it should not be assumed that experiential research is unnecessary. It's also essential to make sure that research tasks are accessible to all members of the organization and those whom it serves, including vulnerable people. For example, in the opening case study, we had been nervous about using an online research methodology with vulnerable mental health patients, and indeed, some may not have participated as a result of the methodology chosen. The combination of budget and time constraints prevented us organizing in-person interviews which would have been ideal. However, we invested significant time in encouraging and supporting participants to do the online tasks.

Chapters 5–6 detail research methods, tools and ideas which can be easily adapted for a non-profit context. A brief summary is given in the tool box below, to help the reader find the relevant sections in Chapters 5–6, where more information can be found on implementing these methods.

Tool box

Summary of low-cost immersive research methods and tools for non-profits

- **Tacit knowledge** is the sum of the profoundly lived experiences of organizational members. However, this is not always easily articulated, so that the team can share learning. Some of the tools in Chapter 6 such as story-telling or Deep Visualization may help with this; for example, one workshop was kicked off by asking team members to relate an experience that embodied the essence of the non-profit to them personally. This was the first workshop I have ever run which started in tears, though they sometimes end that way!

- **Ethnographic** research involves observing a situation first-hand: for example, observing a patient's hospice experience and talking with the patient, staff and family members. Such encounters can be a rich source of story-telling for internal strategy communication, particularly if video-recording (with the participant's written permission) is appropriate and confidentiality is respected. Volunteer stories can also be a rich source of inspiration for the organization and also for donors (see next section and Chapter 8).

- **Qualitative** research includes focus groups (eg with volunteers) or individual interviews (eg with major donors). These can be tricky to run well, and an outsider point of view is often helpful. Many professional researchers are willing to do pro bono work, but participants may need to be incentivized.

- **Online.** Online research can be free if you DIY with a platform like Survey Monkey which offers good templates for a range of tasks such as donor or volunteer feedback. These surveys help track the journey individuals follow when deciding to support a non-profit, and their experiences. Other online platforms allow you to do deep insights research online which is essential if your organization or population is global (see opening case study for how to do this).

Supporting fund-raising

Of course, one of the biggest challenges facing non-profit organizations is fund-raising. Here, the Strategic Empathy Process supports three main goals:

- **Understanding what donors are looking for** (benefits) in exchange for their support. In Chapter 2, we discussed the importance of understanding 'customer' needs and values: what benefits they seek and what 'brand' values resonate with them. Benefits may be tangible: tickets to an enjoyable event, for example. More likely, however, benefits sought are likely to address a complex mix of functional, emotional and socio-cultural needs. For example: self-actualizing personal values and purpose;

building self-esteem from feeling good about giving; 'belonging' to a societal group which values charitable giving. Or all three at once. Andreasen and Kotler (2007) note that 'non-profit organizations need a good understanding of the motives for giving to be effective at fundraising'. Deep, shared understanding of motives for giving can be built across a non-profit organization via experiential learning, the focus of Phase One. This understanding can be used to prioritize donor segments (as the church did when it identified families with children and seniors) and organize programmes and design communications with them in mind. Chapters 5–6 explain how to do this.

- **Articulating a purpose which speaks powerfully to donor needs and values.** In Chapter 3, we saw how powerful brands engage people (and differentiate from competitors) by weaving an authentic story about their functional, emotional and cultural meaning. Non-profits need to do this in order to stand out from other organizations competing for donors. Purpose also motivates volunteers, who are themselves donors of time or money – or both. Phase Two of the Strategic Empathy Process focuses on how to articulate purpose in a differentiated way. Chapter 7 explains how to do this, building on the 'brand positioning' framework in Chapter 3.

- **Developing more powerful and persuasive donor communications.** Researchers have proved that developing empathy with individuals can lead to more positive attitudes towards a stigmatized group (Batson *et al*, 1997) and that empathy with individuals provokes altruism: a desire to offer help, including money (Batson, 2011). For example, the Gothenburg (Sweden) street newspaper has a communications platform called *Faktum Hotels* (2016), which invites donors to 'book a room' in areas of the city where the homeless community sleeps. Their website shows graphic photos with a grimly realistic soundtrack to create empathy. Urban Ministries of Durham (North Carolina) raise funds with the help of an online game, *Spent* (2016), which puts potential donors in the decision-making seat of a single parent on the brink of homelessness. Through playing the game, donors start to feel the emotional impact of living on the poverty line and how hard it can be to escape the vicious cycle of debt. In Chapter 8, we explain how to use individual stories to create powerful communications which inspire donors and volunteer empathy with service users.

Chapter 9 summary

In a non-profit organization, the Strategic Empathy Process can minimize many barriers which face conventional strategy planning processes because:

1 It recognizes that strategy is emergent and that strategists exist all over the organization.

2 It requires all organizational stakeholders to be engaged in the process (including those who are not typically involved in a non-profit context, such as volunteers).

3 It is rooted in team-based experiential learning to create empathy with the needs, goals and experiences of those whom the organization serves. In the case of a non-profit, beneficiaries, volunteers and donors.

4 It emphasizes empathy-driven communication of learning and action steps to all stakeholders to inspire shared purpose and shape emergent strategy formation.

5 Empathy is a core value in many non-profit organizations, and aligns with staff and volunteer values, contrasting with the commercial framework of customers and strategy.

6 The outcome of the process is the articulation and communication of organizational purpose and values which emphasize emotional and cultural meaning. This creates a consistent and compelling story to help drive fund-raising and social enterprise opportunities.

References

Andreasen, AR and Kotler, PT (2007) *Strategic Marketing for Non-profit Organizations*, pp 46 and 282, Prentice Hall, New Jersey

Batson, D, Polycarpou, M, Harmon-Jones, E *et al* (1997) Empathy and attitudes; can feelings for a member of a stigmatized group affect feelings towards a group? *Journal of Personality and Social Psychology*, vol 72, 1, pp 105–15

Batson, D (2011) *Altruism in Humans*, pp 57–58, Oxford University Press, New York

Brooks, C (2012) The Strategic Empathy Process in an Episcopal Church Parish

Cleveland Clinic (2013) https://www.youtube.com/watch?v=cDDWvj_q-o8 [last viewed February 2016]

Cooperrider, DL and Srivastva, S (1987) Appreciative inquiry in organizational life, *Organizational Change and Development*, 1, JAI Press, Stamford, CT, pp 129–169

Faktum Hotels (2016) http://en.faktumhotels.com/about [last viewed February 2016]

Kindon, S, Pain, R and Kesby, M (2007) *Origins, Approaches and Methods in Participatory Action Research: Connecting people, participation and place*, pp 36–45, Routledge, Abingdon

Lee, T (2014) How to spread empathy in healthcare, *Harvard Business Review*, 17 July

ModelPeople (2015) Immersive online research with mental health patients, carers and professionals and *Taxonomy of Dignity in Mental Health*, paper given at the 2015 International Mental Health Congress, Lille, France

Pain, R, Whitman, G and Milledge, D (2012) *Participatory Research Action Toolkit*, https://www.dur.ac.uk/beacon/socialjustice/publications/participatory [last viewed February 2016]

Seel, R (2008) http://www.new-paradigm.co.uk/introduction_to_ai.htm [last viewed February 2016]

Spent (2016) http://playspent.org/ [last viewed February 2016]

GLOSSARY

Activate insights into marketing strategy: to articulate the key consumer insights (actionable nuggets of learning from immersive consumer research) and to use them in collaborative strategy formation.

Agile research: using technology or iterative in-person qualitative research to reduce in-field timeline and get faster learning.

Category: in this book, used to mean a product category, eg 'beer'.

Channel: in this book, used to mean a mode of sales distribution, eg 'grocery' (stores).

Co-creation: a marketing approach or phenomenon of consumer-centred brand value generation, in which consumers play a part in creating elements in the brand value proposition, for example by creating and virally spreading brand messages online. Also a research and brand innovation approach, which invites consumers to suggest new brand elements such as new beverage flavours.

Creative Workshops: extended group research sessions which use a wide range of creative and indirect techniques to explore non-conscious attitudes and co-create strategic solutions.

Customer Journey Mapping: a visual representation of the route customers take as they interact with the company's products and services. It combines quantitative data with qualitative, experiential and emotional insights.

Deep Visualization: an immersive research tool which allows the researcher to access the consumer's deep-seated emotional memories and non-conscious emotional brand associations through relaxation and repetition.

Digital ethnography: 'digital' ethnography is focused on emergent culture found on the internet and comprises both quantitative (eg network analysis) and qualitative (eg sentiment analysis) techniques. Compares with: 'online' and 'mobile' ethnography, which are methods to gather 'offline' ethnographic data online or via mobile devices; and 'netnography' in which a researcher immerses him- or herself in online conversations in an empathetic way.

Dyad: an in-depth interview with a pair of participants who are strangers.

Emergent marketing strategy: a pattern of responses by employees and managers which creates an adaptive approach to marketing strategy formation, as opposed to a pre-planned approach.

Emic: approach to ethnography looks at socio-cultural systems and meaning making with a specific culture *from the first-hand perspective* of participants in the culture.

Ethnographic interview: in ethnography in a business context: a semi-structured protocol which asks different kinds of ethnographic questions and allows time for observation and unstructured conversations.

Four Ps: Product, Place, Price and Promotion; the 'marketing mix', defined as the set of variables which can be used to influence consumer response and achieve marketing objectives.

Friendship pair: an in-depth interview with two people who know each other's attitudes and behaviours in relation to the study topic.

Grounded theory: a qualitative research methodology which emphasizes the emergence of a theory from the field data as opposed to using the data to support or falsify hypotheses.

Laddering: in a marketing context, linking consumer perceived benefits in a hierarchy from bottom to top. A technique of the means-ends chain model theory (Gutman, 1982) (see page 70 of this text for Gutman, 1982 reference).

Metaphor elicitation: an immersive research tool which allows the researcher to access the consumer's deep-seated emotional memories and non-conscious emotional brand associations through visual or spoken expression of the unfamiliar, unspoken or non-conscious in terms of the familiar.

Methodology: research approach, location and number of interviews.

Mission statement: the Mission statement is an overarching, timeless expression of the company's purpose and aspiration *relative to its consumers, customers and other stakeholders*, addressing what the company seeks to accomplish and how it seeks to accomplish it.

Mobile ethnography: see Digital ethnography.

Netnography: see Digital ethnography.

Protocol: the form which the consumer research interaction will take, described in a moderator guide or discussion guide.

Quantitative research: numerical data derived from a sample population using structured and coded questions.

Recruiting criteria: the variables chosen to define the different types of consumers whom we wish to include. This decision is based on the research objectives.

Recruiting screener: the tool which recruiters use to screen a population of potential research participants and select those whom we have chosen to include.

Salience: positive top-of-mind awareness.

Sample size: the number of participants to be included in our research project, based on project scope (how many different sub-groups are there?) and budget.

Screening criteria: the variables chosen to define the different sub-samples to be included in research. This decision is based on the Strategic Learning objectives.

Screening questions: an ordered list of questions encompassing selected screening criteria, used by a recruiter to qualify research participants.

Segment typing tool: an interactive tool which automatically places a respondent in a target consumer segment based on responses to a list of questions derived from a statistical algorithm.

Semiotics: the study of signs (in a marketing context, signs in culture). Signs point to the underlying codes or systems of meaning which structure consumer attitudes and behaviour. Brand symbols are forms of signs.

Social desirability bias: tendency of research participants to report behaviour or attitudes in a more socially acceptable direction in a group setting.

Somatic marker: as proposed by Damasio, an emotion-related bodily response (based on past learning) which can drive automatic, gut-level decision-making.

Strategic Empathy®: empathy-based learning and insight which is shared across the organization and activated into marketing strategy, both planned and emergent.

Tacit knowledge: subjective insights, intuitions and hunches, which may be rooted in experience formed on the job or in personal beliefs and mental models, and which may form the basis for completely new approaches to creating value for customers.

Usability (UX) research: a specialized field which involves applying user observation, experience-based feedback and prototype or site interface usability testing to website design.

Values statement: values are enduring core beliefs. They are distinctive guiding principles for the operations of the organization that never change.

Vision statement: a Vision statement is forward-looking and represents a viable dream about how the organization will look in five or more years. Vision defines what the organization aspires to be and to do for its stakeholders.

INDEX

Note: *Italics* indicate a Figure or Table in the text.